THE POLITICAL ECONOMY OF
JAPAN'S LOW FERTILITY

The Political Economy of
Japan's Low Fertility

Edited by FRANCES MCCALL ROSENBLUTH

STANFORD UNIVERSITY PRESS

STANFORD, CALIFORNIA

2007

Stanford University Press
Stanford, California

Printed in the United States of America on acid-free, archival-quality paper

Library of Congress Cataloging-in-Publication Data

The political economy of Japan's low fertility / edited by Frances McCall
Rosenbluth.
    p. cm.
  Includes bibliographical references and index.
  ISBN-13: 978-0-8047-5486-6 (cloth : alk. paper)
    1. Fertility, Human—Japan. 2. Women—Japan—Social conditions.
3. Women—Japan—Economic conditions. I. Rosenbluth, Frances McCall.
HB1061.P65 2007
331.4
                                                          2006007573

Typeset by Newgen in 10/12.5 Palatino

Contents

Tables

Figures

Acknowledgments

Writing a book is always something of a communal process, given the many people who provide inspiration and input. This book, being an edited one, is explicitly so, and I first thank the authors, who participated in multiple workshops and grappled collectively to generate the ideas we present here. The chapter authors represent several social science disciplines—political science, economics, and sociology—and it speaks to their engagement with the topic and to their intellectual generosity that we were able to cohere as a productive group. It was stimulating and challenging for all of us to try to think from someone else's disciplinary vantage point. As an astute reader may quickly grasp, we did not necessarily drop our own biases, but our chapters in combination undoubtedly provide a richer view than any one of us could have produced alone. I like to think that the volume has multifaceted "fly vision" of the kind that Carol Gluck advises historians to adopt. Along the way, we also benefited enormously from the comments and suggestions of discussants from several disciplines: Linda Edwards (economics), Nancy Folbre (economics), Siv Gustafsson (economics), Kimberly Morgan (political science), Kenneth Scheve (political science), Daniel Seldon (anthropology), Karen Shire (sociology), and David Weinstein (economics).

Without financial support, this intellectual process would not have been possible, and I wish to thank the Georg W. Leitner Program in International and Comparative Political Economy, the Yale Council of East Asian Studies, the Kempf Fund of the Yale Center for International and Area Studies, and the Yale Institute of Social and Policy Studies for their part in funding several conferences. The Abe Foundation supported my field work on the family-work balance in Japan, Sweden, Germany, and the United States in 2001–2002. The Georg W. Leitner Program in International and Comparative Political Economy, the Yale Council on East Asian Studies, and the Yale Provost's Office provided me with additional research funds. For all of this, I am deeply grateful.

My part of this book would not have been possible without outstanding research assistance. Thomas Angus Casey, who died tragically in a kayaking accident while this book was in process, contributed invaluably to the collection of comparative statistics on fertility and female labor force participation. Jun Saito skillfully gathered and processed data on Japanese labor markets and fertility for me, and save for his successful gambit to become a Diet member in Japan in October 2002, would have been coauthor of one of these chapters. Rafaela Dancygier, Stephen Kosack, Natsu Matsuda, Jung Kim, and Erica Franklin also provided able assistance at various stages of data gathering and analysis. Abbie Erler and Theocharis Grigoriadis edited and formatted the entire manuscript with skill and good humor. Matthew Light and Claudia Schrag started out as research assistants and ended up as coauthors on a paper on the politics of low fertility, from which I draw in the introduction to this book. The paper was awarded the Sage Award for the best paper in comparative politics presented at the 2002 annual meetings of the American Political Science Association, which inspired me to keep this book project in motion. We thank Michael Wallerstein (committee chair), Sophia Perez, and Matthew Shugart for the award and for their helpful suggestions. Abbie Erler did a wonderful job helping to edit the book in the final stages.

I also thank the daycare workers, mothers, politicians, and civil servants in Japan and Sweden who took the time from their busy schedules to respond to many questions. My research assistant Erica Franklin was a superb surrogate for me in Sweden, managing to elicit thoughtful responses from Swedish politicians and public sector workers on a range of questions. I am particularly grateful to Jun Saito's family who made fieldwork in Yamagata a great deal more fun than it might have been: Jun's father drove a bus for our entourage from one childcare facility to another, and Jun's mother interspersed our interview stops with picnics in scenic places. Jun's wife Naomi helped my children play with the children in the Japanese childcare centers we visited, playing the role of babysitter and cross-cultural facilitator. The boat ride down the Mogami River was one of the most memorable ways I have ever combined family and work.

This book would have been much weaker without the comments from many other colleagues who have heard or read various versions of the Low Fertility project: Kathy Bawn, Carles Boix, Jose Cheibub, Gary Cox, John Ferejohn, Rob Franzese, Geoff Garrett, Joyce Gelb, Peter Gourevitch, Anna Grzymala-Busse, John Huber, Torben Iversen, Junko Kato, Bob Keohane, Masaru Kohno, Ikuo Kume, Mathew McCubbins, Fiona McGillivray, Fiona Scott Morton, Vicky Murrilo, Helena Olofsdotter, Hideo Otake, Hugh Patrick, Jonas Pontusson, Mark Ramseyer, Susan Rose-Ackerman, Alastair Smith, David Soskice, Gillian Steele, Michael Thies, Yu Uchiyama, Jim Vreeland, and Karen Wynn. I am grateful to the Yale Women's Faculty Forum, the Japan Legal Seminar at the Harvard Law School, the Policy Studies Group of former Dietmember Motoo Shiina, the Japan Political Science Association, and the East Asian Studies Center at Wesleyan University for inviting me to present the ideas of this book. We also benefited greatly from exceptionally insightful and helpful comments of two outside reviewers for Stanford University Press, who, I have learned, were John Campbell and Joyce Gelb. They saved us from numerous embarrassments and put us onto some additional materials.

Finally, I thank my family, who prompted my interest in women's issues in the first place. People who know me laugh when I tell them I'm writing about low fertility, because having three children puts me in the high fertility range in any rich democracy. If you believe the argument of the book—a woman-friendly labor market, government subsidies for childcare, and spousal support can help women to combine a career and caring in the way that men have always taken for granted— you might guess that my husband has been a wonderful partner. You would be right. Among other things—many other things—Jim moved *twice* from one coast to the other to accommodate my career moves. As for my kids, they haven't made my life easier in any way, but they have made it richer.

We dedicate this book to our families.

Contributors

Patricia Boling   Political Science, Purdue University
Mary C. Brinton   Sociology, Harvard University
Margarita Estévez-Abe   Government, Harvard University
Keiko Hirao   Sociology, Sophia University
Eiko Kenjoh   Economics, University of Amsterdam
Frances McCall Rosenbluth   Political Science, Yale University
Sawako Shirahase   Sociology, University of Tokyo
Junichiro Wada   Economics, Yokohama City University

PART ONE

Introduction and Overview

CHAPTER 1

The Political Economy of Low Fertility

FRANCES MCCALL ROSENBLUTH

Introduction

Japan's fertility rate is at a historic low, at 1.25 children per woman on average in 2005 (Organization for Economic Cooperation and Development 2006). This is considerably lower than the population replacement rate of about 2.1, meaning that Japan's population is shrinking. Japan is not alone among industrialized countries in trending downward in population size: Italy, Spain, and Korea rival Japan for the lowest fertility rates on earth, and Europe south of Scandinavia comes close.

Why should we care about low fertility? One oft-cited reason is fiscal health. Governments of low-fertility countries are in a near panic about who is going to pay taxes and social security premia when the demographic crunch produces more retirees than workers. They also worry about what will happen to the economy as the number of consumers shrinks, and about the geopolitical implications of smaller absolute size as a nation. On the other hand, lower population density can, with strong productivity gains, increase per capita income and quality of life and environmental health, and population size has never had a very close connection to national peace and security. The economic problems associated with low fertility can be overstated.

In this book, we are interested in fertility for a different reason: it may be a fairly good indirect measure of female welfare. Peter McDonald and Shigemi Kono, two demographers working on separate continents, each find a connection between "gender-friendly policies" and higher fertility in comparative data (Kono 1996; McDonald 1999, 2000). Alicia Adsera, an economist, notes that fertility rates and female employment have become positively correlated across developed countries since the 1980s (Adsera 2003).

This will strike some readers as an appalling idea. After all, feminists in the United States have struggled for women's equality in the public sphere by downplaying their reproductive role, and celebrate the ability of women to reduce the number of children they bear in order to advance in other realms. What we argue here, however, is that low levels of fertility in Japan and in much of the developed world may not be freely chosen, but rather reflect how hard it is for women to work in the labor market and care for their families at the same time. Rather than give up on the labor market in the face of childcare burdens or an inhospitable workplace, many women seem to be striving all the harder, even when it means delaying, curtailing, or forgoing having children. If, as we argue in this book, gender-friendly policies can boost fertility by relieving women of choices they would rather not make, we can use variation in fertility as a useful comparative measure of the constraints on women's ability to balance family and career.

We are not interested in touting fertility as a normative good, nor do we have any "target" fertility that we expect to see when women and men share more equally in productive and reproductive work. Once men internalize more of the costs of childrearing, they are likely to favor fewer children than before, even as women feel freed up to balance family and career a little more easily. These are empirical questions, in answer to which the countries with the most gender-friendly policies provide some clues, as we will discuss below.

To put our thesis in simplest terms, fertility tends to be depressed where vested interests impede female access to the workforce, and higher where easy labor market accessibility and childcare support make it easier for women to balance family and career. Contrary to the possibility that women discouraged from the labor market will go home and have babies, women may instead expend more effort—forgoing children in the process—to get in the door, climb the promotion ladders, and struggle against glass ceilings.

Embedded in this explanation is the notion that women actually want to work outside of the home in addition to taking care of their families at home. Few people question that the average man wants to both work and have a family, but some readers may counter that men as well as women would prefer to stay at home if social norms permitted.

As I discuss more fully below, the argument is less that women like working outside the home (although many undoubtedly do) than that the labor market provides them with a source of economic independence. Without a potential source of livelihood outside of the home, women risk poverty in a world where divorce rates are relatively high, and risk misery should their husbands take advantage of their inability to strike out on their own. If we assume that women, as well as men, benefit from the household bargaining leverage and exit options that come with an outside source of income, specialization in childrearing and housework may serve women poorly. Knowing this, women may seek a place in the labor market even if it means having fewer children. All else equal, the harder it is for them to secure a foothold in the labor market, the fewer children they will bear.[1]

In the remaining sections of this introductory chapter, I lay out some alternative hypotheses to the idea that low fertility reflects constraints on female labor market participation. I then present some evidence for the argument offered here, comparing Japan with other countries and comparing different regions of Japan that have different labor market properties. I conclude by providing a layout for the remainder of the book.

Alternative Hypotheses

Here I recount two explanations of low fertility that many readers will find more familiar: culture and economic efficiency. They are not so much wrong as inadequate. I will then begin to build the case for why these conventional explanations do not fully account for the facts that we observe. The chapters in the rest of the book pick up some of these threads and examine them in greater detail.

Culture: Japan and Elsewhere

Most scholars of Japan well know the special claims made for the power of Japanese culture. The strongest—and least defensible—versions imply that there is something immutable, or at least very ancient, about the core values of Japanese society, and that these values mold young Japanese minds in much the way that they have from time immemorial, through many layers of reinforcing socialization. The flaw in this position, of course, is that Japanese social norms have changed a great deal over the past two millennia of "Yamato" civilization.[2] The ideal of the devoted stay-at-home wife and mother (*ryosai kenbo*) probably emerged sometime during the thirteenth to seventeenth centuries in the small, elite samurai class that lived free of an economically productive role in society. The vast majority of the Japanese were farmers, artisans, and merchants who were rarely in a position to spare the wife from an economically productive role, and children were cared for by grandparents, older siblings, or—when income permitted—servants from poorer families. Women are, it seems, in a weaker economic position in agricultural societies than in hunter-gatherer or postindustrial societies, given the greater importance of brawn in much agricultural work than in gathering. In hunter-gatherer societies, women typically provide the bulk of caloric needs for themselves and their families (Hrdy 1981, 6). But the woman's role was also important in much of Japanese agricultural history, and women were allowed to own property until the fourteenth century (Amino 1999, 59). What Goode cleverly calls the "samurai-ization" of the Japanese populace—where the at-home mother that in one era only samurai could afford became a generalized cultural ideal—seems to have emerged only in the last 150 years with the emergence of the large firm sector where "the lord" of each family had to commute to a factory or corporate office and earn money for his family (Goode 1993).

I have no intention of trying to discredit the power of cultural norms, but wish rather to show how these norms are subject to the reinforcing or corrosive pressures from the economic and political systems that intertwine with the social. I take culture to include the composite and cumulative effects of mental shortcuts that people use to simplify life decisions. There is at least a weak efficiency bias inherent in many of these rules of thumb: the norms that "work" are reinforced naturally. To the extent that political systems distribute power unevenly, however, norms may also be manufactured and reinforced deliberately. Some norms, such as deference to authority or the importance of female submissiveness, for example, are more of an admission of what is tolerated by the powerful than what would be preferred by a majority if a genuine choice were available. Given the costs of fighting the powerful at every turn, it is not surprising that there is a strong human tendency to internalize constraints or even oppression and to self-interpret them as preferences (Sen 1990; Folbre 2005).

It is true that many Japanese today—including many young women— believe that a virtuous mother stays at home until her child is at least three years old, and that pursuing career ambitions is as selfish and disgraceful for a woman as it is self-sacrificing and noble for a man. But it is also true that many young Japanese mothers feel trapped and isolated.[3] To infer from that widespread belief that there is a unique Japanese position on motherhood ignores the labor market constraints that render these norms tenable. We can see from a comparison of the present with Japan's own past, and a comparison of Japan with other countries, that the idea of mothers as exclusive nurturers of children is an idea that gains power from a particular configuration of incentives. When a woman's labor outside the home becomes more remunerative, these norms tend to become destabilized (Badgett, Davidson, Folbre, and Lim 2000; Geddes and Lueck 2002; Rindfuss, Brewster, and Kavee 1996).

Neoclassical Economics: Opportunity Costs

Another lens with which to view fertility comes from economics. Economic assumptions about human behavior, in particular the notion of optimization (maximizing welfare, subject to constraints), provide a useful way to get around the problem of constraint-conditioned preferences that sometimes goes unattended in cultural approaches. Constraints are typically more visible than the preference-formation process, making the examination of constraints a useful way to help us understand the choices people make.

Gary Becker won a Nobel Prize for his work applying economic reasoning to social behavior, including the household division of labor, fertility, and divorce (Becker 1962, 1981, 1985). In his model of household specialization, couples maximize family welfare by an extensive division of labor in which one spouse specializes in market work and the other specializes in household work. He makes no presumption that the man or the woman will stay at home, other than to say that a woman's career interruption on account of childbirth may give her the comparative advantage of producing family-specific "goods" such as higher-quality children. The gains from trade, where each spouse contributes where he or she is most productive, produce an efficient household economy in the sense that welfare is maximized.

An underlying premise in Becker's specialization model is increasing returns to human capital, by which he means that people get better and better at what they do with experience, and are remunerated accordingly. Some have also taken him to mean that the investment in the "quality" of children—meaning how well nurtured children are emotionally and intellectually—is best made at home. But nowhere does he write that.

Following the work of labor economists such as Jacob Mincer (1958), Becker argued that declining fertility reflected higher opportunity costs of staying at home in industrial countries with diverse economies. As the value of children as farm labor declined and as women found more opportunities for remunerative work outside the home, the calculation of household welfare tipped in favor of female labor market participation and fewer children and/or subcontracted childcare.

These economic models are elegant and provide the best available explanation for the universal relationship between industrialization and lower fertility. What they do not explain, however, is the variation in fertility in rich countries, and why fertility is higher for some countries at the upper ends of female labor force participation. By treating the household division of labor and fertility as family decisions, these models miss the distributional consequences of these choices and the power structures that may underlie them.

Household Bargaining

By looking at spouses as individuals rather than as fragments of a fused family unit, bargaining models reveal an important dimension of potential inequality within the family (Folbre 1994; Gustafsson 1993; Iversen and Rosenbluth 2003; Lundberg and Pollak 1996). A division of labor in which the man works outside of the home may load him down with the stress of the workplace, but it also confers on him assets that are more mobile than the woman's. In the event of marital dissolution, he has the ability to take his work experience more or less seamlessly with him and maintain his economic standard of living. The woman in this scenario has not built up work experience and, absent stringent alimony laws and enforcement, could find herself in relative poverty. Nature adds another liability of its own, because the male attraction to youth and beauty makes it harder for the woman to find another marriage partner as she ages.[4]

Given the potentially large costs to a woman of not maintaining some level of economic independence, the efficiency explanation for why women are more likely to stay at home misses something crucial. Even if, for the sake of argument, household welfare would be higher with these gains from trade, the fact that the man has greater bargaining leverage on account of his superior exit options affects, at least potentially, how those gains are distributed. It is even possible, as Braunstein and Folbre (2001) have argued, that a man might prefer a smaller overall (welfare) pie if he has sufficient family bargaining power to give him a big enough slice to compensate. By keeping his wife at home, he can use her fear of marital breakdown to transfer more housework and other tasks onto her shoulders.

I do not wish to argue that men explicitly think this way, nor that men have collectively organized society in such a way as to subordinate women. Self-interested behavior is subtle, pervasive, and often invisible to ourselves when we are the protagonists. Because much of this behavior is unconscious, I put little stock in the possibility that men as an entire group have managed to act collectively to promote selfish ends. The long-standing nature and near universality of gender inequality requires a different kind of answer than male conspiracy.

An explanation that looks at labor markets for insights into the relative exit options of spouses seems closer to the mark.[5] To oversimplify, hunter-gatherer societies gave both sexes important, if different, access to food self-sufficiency, leading to relative equality between the sexes. With the adoption of sedentary cultivation, particularly heavy-tool- and animal-based farming that favored the use of brawn, women became less central to the production of food and specialized in tasks that could not by themselves ensure a woman's survival on her own. Industrialization probably deepened, at least for a time, the specialization of family labor, given the commutes and work away from home that factory work entails. Women were even less able to care for their children while working, and retreated into the home upon childbearing.[6]

In the pages that follow, I consider the usefulness of this line of argument by evaluating evidence from Japan and other developed countries. If we find that fertility is unrelated to work opportunities for women, or if we find that better work opportunities for women lead invariably to lower fertility—the opposite of what our argument predicts—we would appear to be wrong. If, on the other hand, we find that fertility correlates positively with favorable labor market conditions for women, it is time to reevaluate the simplest cultural or opportunity-cost arguments.

Explaining Japan's Low Fertility

In this section I lay heavy blame for Japan's low fertility on the relative inaccessibility of Japan's labor market to women. Given how hard it is for women to make it in corporate Japan, even the government's increased support of childcare over the years has been inadequate in motivating women to mix working life with motherhood.[7]

At least until the asset bubble burst in the early 1990s, a large literature in institutional economics was devoted to detailing how the particular institutions of Japanese capitalism improved on unconstrained markets. Cross shareholding among *keiretsu* firms and ties to main banks allowed firms to stabilize their cost of capital, which in turn allowed them to guarantee lifetime employment to their core workforce.[8] At least in the rapid-growth years, when the demand for labor exceeded the supply, Japanese firms had an incentive to woo workers with this kind of guarantee.

This "isomorphism between financial markets and labor markets," as Aoki called it, was believed to be a linchpin of Japan's superior productive capacity. Big corporations did not have to worry about fluctuating stock prices affecting their cost of capital and could therefore focus on longer-run objectives. Core workers of large firms were not afraid of being laid off, so they invested in firm-specific capital. Firms, in turn, could invest heavily in the training of these workers without fear that they would take that investment out the door with them (Aoki and Patrick 1994; Aoki 1984, 1990; Hoshi, Kashyap, and Scharfstein 1990; Koshiro 1994).

As Margarita Estévez-Abe, in this volume, insightfully points out, the implications for women of low interfirm labor mobility are ominous. The costs to an employer of hiring and promoting women are higher when workers are expected to build up firm-specific investments over the course of their careers. If a woman interrupts her career to care for children, the firm's investment in that woman is reduced, and lost altogether if she doesn't come back. Moreover, if firms make lifetime commitments to their core workers in order to elicit investments in firm-specific skills, they need an expendable part of the labor force to accommodate business-cycle ups and downs. Either a woman gets herself into the core workforce, or finds herself in the buffer zone of part-time employment where jobs are not secure. Getting in is hard for a woman because firms want a cheaper category, and it easier for them to have such a category if women are socially labeled as housewives.

Even if a woman succeeds in getting hired or promoted into the core workforce, if her husband is also in the core workforce, they *both* have to make a success of their careers in their respective firms or they are out of luck because there is little interfirm labor market in case they need to look elsewhere. If they are competing with other employees who share this all-or-nothing attitude, they are not likely to say no when their bosses ask them to stay late, or when their bosses take a group of (almost always) guys out for drinks when the day is done. Working days for the core workforce are long. Who takes care of the kids? to paraphrase the memorable phrase of Nancy Folbre (1994).

A weakness of this new institutional analysis of the Japanese economy is that it doesn't explain where these institutions came from. A functionalist explanation that points to the efficiency-enhancing features of these institutions fails to explain why these institutions did not emerge elsewhere. More damning still, some economists have pointed to the darker side of Japanese economic institutions. Weinstein and Yafeh (1995) argue that industrial policy led by the Ministry of International Trade and Industry (MITI) was cartel management at the expense of economic efficiency rather than the construction of market-improving mechanisms. In another paper (1998), they present empirical evidence for the case that main banks misallocated capital more than they helped firms solve management problems. If they are right, the inaccessibility of the labor market to women was not the inevitable if unfortunate result of a more efficient form of economic organization. There were noneconomic reasons for the particular form that Japanese economic institutions took.

Politics and Public Policy

Economic organization is shaped in part by government regulation, and economic efficiency is rarely the only thing government cares about. To grasp how the Japanese labor market has disadvantaged women, it is important to think about why the Japanese government created a regulatory environment that produced interfirm labor market immobility in the first place.

A single majority party, the Liberal Democratic Party (LDP), dominated postwar Japanese politics beginning in 1955 and continues in power in diminished form to the present day. The party has maintained strong bases of support in big business, agriculture, and small business and has used funds and voter mobilization capacity from these groups to appeal to voters. The electoral system that remained in place until 1994 pitted multiple LDP members against each other in most districts, so instead of running on a party platform, LDP members had to cultivate groups of voters who would be loyal to them personally. This generated strong political pressure for regulatory, budgetary, and tax favors for businesses, in exchange for campaign contributions to pay for expensive electoral machines (McCubbins and Rosenbluth 1995; Ramseyer and Rosenbluth 1993).

The effects of this political system on economic policy are not hard to find. The LDP coddled many producer groups with cartel-like legislation and other policy favors. One of the strongest cartels was in the banking industry, which, along with suppression of nonbanking forms of capital formation, led to the main bank form of financing that new institutional economists write about. It is straightforward to see how the rest of the labor-immobility story follows. But its origins are not in efficiency-maximizing institutions. They reside at least in part in the motivations of politicians seeking to secure their electoral fates.

If backbenchers' political motives interfered with microeconomic management, macroeconomic policy is harder to target to special interests. To be sure, the budget itself was carved into small, politically strategic pieces. But the *size* of the government budget was typically kept low with an eye toward protecting a favorable business climate.

We have seen that the government's probusiness policies underpinned low labor mobility by managing the bank cartel that made this possible. The LDP was also on the side of business when it came to keeping women out of the core workforce. Early party platforms of the LDP stated explicitly that women should stay at home to help their husbands be good workers (Jiyu minshuto 1979). The alternative—making it possible for women to join the labor force on an equal standing with men—was politically disagreeable. First, it would have required the government to pay potentially huge amounts of money for childcare support, which violated the party's pledge to its business supporters of keeping government expenditures to a minimum. Second, it would have increased the cost to firms of making lifetime employment guarantees. As we have seen, this guarantee works only when there is some buffer zone in the labor market that can expand and shrink with the business cycle. Third, it is quite possible that the LDP understood that working women would favor government expenditures to socialize some of the costs of family work. Either the LDP would have to spend more money, making its business constituency unhappy, or face the possibility that working women would vote systematically for the left. Given that trade-off, keeping mothers at home seems an entirely sensible political strategy.

It would be a serious exaggeration to characterize the entire Japanese economy as a large firm environment. To be sure, the big companies are at the top of the food chain, so to speak, and many of the most talented and ambitious young Japanese seek the status and job security of the large firm sector. But if medium to large firms produce three-quarters of the country's output, they account for only about 30 percent of the labor force. To the extent that large firms are more likely than small and medium-sized firms to have internal labor markets and therefore to place a premium on firm-specific skills, we might expect that women in the small firm sector do better in career terms. In fact, we do find stronger labor market attachment for women employed in small firms in Japan (Shirahase, this volume, Chapter 2). Although fertility data broken down in this way are unavailable, our line of argument would lead us to expect that women employed in the small and medium-sized firm sector might have somewhat higher fertility as well. On the other hand, employment in the small firm sector is less stable (there are far more bankruptcies and these firms typically don't have the luxury of making lifetime labor commitments), which explains why women are not flocking there.

The same is true when we consider women in the agricultural sector. Female labor force participation rates and fertility are both positively correlated with residence in relatively rural areas, even beyond the positive effect that comes from having grandparents available to provide some childcare. Fertility varies in Japan from Tokyo's rate near 1, to relatively rural areas with fertility closer to 1.8. Fertility and female labor force participation rates are positively correlated: working mothers are not having fewer children. Rather, it is the working women for whom combining work and family is made difficult by the labor market structure who are choosing not to have children. Of course, Japan has become heavily urbanized, so higher rural fertility does little to boost overall fertility rates.

The graph of Japanese women's labor force attachment over the course of their life cycle forms an M shape. M-curves show the dip in employment for women with small children, which, as Brinton (1989, 2001) and others have shown, is notoriously steep in Japan's case. Moreover, the second "hump" is not only lower, but also qualitatively inferior to the first, because many of the women reentering the job market after a break of some years take part-time work with lower wages, benefits, and job security than for full-time jobs.

More rural prefectures in Japan have flatter M's, suggesting that women are more likely to continue working during their childbearing years. The economic requirements of the household farm never permitted the idea of working mothers to disappear in rural Japan, despite a certain degree of "samurai-ization" of Japanese social norms with industrialization. Far be it from us to say that rural women "have it made"; they have struggles all their own. But compared with women trying to carve out careers in the big firm sector, women in the agricultural sector seem to be less squeezed in their choices.

The Topography of Constraints for Japanese Working Mothers

Both fertility and female labor participation were higher in prewar Japan than they are today. Prior to industrialization, it was taken as natural and unavoidable that mothers, as long as they were able-bodied, would help in the fields while in-laws or siblings took care of younger children. As we have just seen, the pattern still holds in relatively rural regions in today's Japan. With industrialization, fertility dropped without increasing female labor participation.

Industrialization brought with it urbanization, and a flocking of the population into cities. This new environment discouraged mothers from working in several ways. The previous section already recounted the labor practices of large firms that kept working mothers out, and these large firms are disproportionately in big cities. Second, many urban families lived as nuclear families, so the working mother could no longer rely on her mother-in-law to help with the children. Third, commuting times lengthened with urban congestion. On top of a long working day, a long commute can mean having someone else keep the child(ren) for twelve to fourteen hours a day, five and a half or six days a week.[9]

Clearly, the labor market situation was grim for a mother who aspired to a career. As we saw in the previous section, the LDP's pro-business orientation disinclined the government to step in aggressively with childcare support to make the balancing act manageable. Instead, the LDP government consistently reinforced the incentives for women to stay at home.

- In the early years, the government made childcare support available only to low-income families who needed income from both spouses, and put up high entry barriers to families with the means to live off of the husband's income. Expansion of availability, as well as in hours of operation, has come grudgingly and slowly.
- Tax policy favors spouses with a small amount of outside income.
- The government adopted Equal Opportunity Employment legislation in 1986, but was slow to enforce violations vigorously.[10]

- Japan is in good company in having no mandatory paternity leave policy, which would even out the cost to a firm of hiring a man or a woman for a career track position. Only a few Scandinavian countries have such a policy in place, but even theirs is of short duration.

All else equal, the market discounts a woman's wages by the cost of replacing her when she interrupts her career path for childbearing and family work (Katz 1997).[11] Margarita Estévez-Abe (this volume, Chapter 3) draws on the "varieties of capitalism" literature to argue that this is even more true for economies or sectors that reward employees on the basis of firm-specific or industry-specific skills. Although Japan's large firm labor market can be characterized as a firm-specific-skills market, the coordinated markets of Western Europe are more likely to encourage investment in industry-specific skills. Corporatist wage bargaining and industrial job security increase returns to skills that an employee can take to another job in the same industry. In the English-speaking countries, by contrast, labor markets tend to be a more fluid part of a liberal market economy.

In summary, government policy has done relatively little to compensate for a working environment that is inhospitable to working mothers. Given the party's political incentives, particularly under the old electoral rules, this is not hard to understand.

Fertility Elsewhere

The plight of Japan's working mothers—or of Japanese women who have to choose between work and motherhood—is shared by women everywhere to some extent. But the severity of the plight seems to vary across and within countries quite substantially. An examination of this variation gives us a useful way to check our analysis of the Japanese case. The overall pattern we observe is that fertility tends to have a nonlinear relationship to the strength of labor: fertility is relatively high in countries with weak left/labor power, declines with the power of unions, and then rises again as the strength of the left passes some threshold. This section lays out the logic behind this pattern and then compares Japan to Germany, Sweden, and the United States in some detail to check the links in the argument.

Variation in the strength of labor does not rest solely on different cultural milieus. Electoral rules seem also to have a discernible effect. Proportional representation electoral systems that operate in European countries are more likely to adopt coordinated market economies (CMEs), because coalition bargaining produces logrolls among the intense preferences of coalition parties and the organized groups they represent. By contrast, single-member district systems tend to have lower levels of public services, less generous social insurance schemes, and lower taxes for two reasons: first, parties are forced to appeal to a broader swath of interests before formulating party platforms; and second, voter turnout is systematically lower on the left than on the right, producing weaker demands for redistribution (Bartels 2002; Bawn and Rosenbluth 2006; Iversen and Soskice 2002; Rogowski and Kayser 2001; Rosenbluth and Schaap 2002).[12]

The Japanese electoral rules that prevailed until 1993 were not entirely proportional, though they were centrifugal in that intraparty competition produced a factionalized dominant party. A switch to more genuinely proportional rules such as a closed list system would have empowered a left party as proportional rules do elsewhere—because proportionality would have made a group such as labor, which is never a majority by itself, a strong and enduring niche for a national political party. A strong labor party and strong unions tend to reinforce each other. But as we will see in the German case, greater proportionality and labor power would not necessarily have increased female employment opportunities and fertility. Moving in the majoritarian direction—which Japan did in 1994 and which I will assess in the conclusion of this book—will likely push Japan's labor market institutions toward greater fluidity. We can expect the eventual demise of lifetime employment contracts for core male employees and, as a result, easier access for women into the labor market. Japanese fertility rates may be in for some recovery, but we have to wait first for the old institutions to gasp their last breath. They are still gasping.

Liberal Market Economies

More or less synonymous with liberal market economies (LMEs), majoritarian countries typically have weak unions and fluid labor markets and, as a result, build in less incentive for workers to invest in immobile firm- or industry-specific skills.[13] The costs of career interruption tend to be lower, both for the employer and for the employee, when workers bring with them portable skills. Ironically, women are advantaged by men's job insecurity, at least in the sense that a woman's career interruptions for childbearing are relatively less disadvantageous in the general-skills economies. Her job insecurity becomes less of a liability when everyone is insecure.

Female labor participation rates tend to be quite high in the LMEs of the United States, United Kingdom, Australia, and Canada. Employers have less reason to discourage women from work. Employers are not investing in a woman's firm-specific skills, so her career interruptions on account of childrearing represent less of a cost to the firm.[14] In 2000, 74.1 percent of American women aged twenty-five to fifty-four participated in the labor force, including 56.6 percent of women with a child under three years of age (Organization for Economic Cooperation and Development 2005). Moreover, women are more likely to work full-time than part-time, and are quite likely to continue working after marriage and childbirth. The gender wage ratio, which is the ratio of male to female wage medians for all hourly wage and salary figures, was in the 75–80 percent range in these countries in 2003 (Institute for Women's Policy Research 2004). This puts them in the middle tier for the CMEs, which exhibit more variance.

If we accept our proposition that fertility should be higher when women find it easier to combine a career with motherhood, we might expect LMEs to have relatively high fertility, compared to CMEs. This is, in fact, the case. To be sure, the high aggregate fertility masks substantial differences by income. As Figure 1.1 shows, women at the lowest income quartile are the most fertile, largely because they occupy

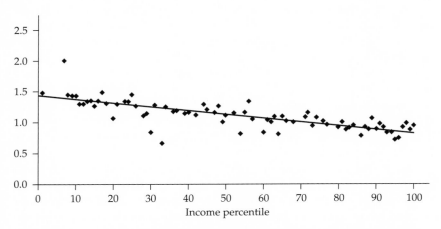

FIGURE 1.1 Average Number of Children of U.S. Working Women Ages 18–45, 1997

low-wage, low-skill jobs that apply smaller penalties for temporary absence from the labor market (Anderson, Binder, and Krause 2002). By contrast, women in the middle of the income curve may be unable to afford not to work, but may not make enough to subcontract much of their childcare. For them, the need to work seems to put a low bound on the number of children they bear. At higher income levels, women face higher opportunity costs in having children, but that is partially offset by large intragender wage inequality in liberal market economies that allows high-income women to pay others to help take care of their children. As a result, fertility relative to the woman's income does in fact decline in the United States but perhaps not by as much as one might expect.

Coordinated Market Economies

Consider, by contrast, the countries of Western Europe, which tend to have proportional electoral rules and coordinated market economies. Strong labor unions negotiate for a compressed wage distribution, employment guarantees to the extent possible, and generous unemployment insurance. An unintended byproduct is that workers are encouraged to invest in industry-specific skills because the likelihood of losing that investment is relatively small (Estévez-Abe, Iversen, and Soskice 1999; Estévez-Abe, this volume). Women are disadvantaged in the skills-investment game, unless left/labor is beyond some threshold of strength that frees the government to employ women in the public sector in sufficient numbers to offset the relative exclusion of women from the private sector. In Scandinavia, where women are disproportionately hired in secure government jobs that are unhinged from strictly productivity-based wages, both female labor force participation and fertility are considerably higher. Liberal market economies, such as those in the United States and the United Kingdom, have female labor force participation and fertility rates that are comparable to Scandinavia's, but by way of general-skills jobs in the private sector rather than public sector service jobs.

Note that Japan is anomalous here. Japan's strong internal labor markets, as we noted above, put downward pressure on fertility *despite* the weakness of the left and resulted instead from the competition for skilled labor among large firms in a growing economy. Long-term, secure loans from banks (and the financial cartels that underpinned them) made it possible for firms to make similarly long-term commitments to a core group of lifetime employees, with the result that other workers, including women, were needed as a flexible, expendable workforce.

Coordinated market economies exhibit wide cross-national (as opposed to intracountry) variation in fertility, which suggests by our framework that not all is equal in the nature of constraints that women face in entering the labor market. For women to enter the labor market on an equal footing with men in a specific-skills economy, the government makes up for the advantage men enjoy in the private sector either by disproportionately hiring women in secure public jobs or by heavily subsidizing the costs of childcare, or both. A comparison of Sweden and Germany bears out the importance of these differences in government roles.

The Sweden-Germany Comparison

Despite the many obvious similarities in their culture, their political and economic systems, and their overall level of development, Sweden and Germany pursued strikingly different policies in the decades after 1960 with respect to women's employment. The difference seems to have been on account of the relative strength of the political left in Sweden compared to Germany. Policies that help women gain access to the labor market are a nonlinear function of the strength of labor, where moderately strong labor—such as in Germany and most of non-Scandinavian Europe—keeps jobs secure for core male union workers by relegating women (and immigrants) to less secure jobs. In Sweden and the other Scandinavian countries, left governments were sufficiently strong and long lasting that they expanded the public sector without checks from the right, absorbing large percentages of women into public sector service jobs.

Women responded to the opportunities by moving into those jobs. Public provision of childcare, which is generous and nearly universal in Sweden, appears to have been more of a response to the need of working mothers by a spending-inclined government than a cause of their initial foray into the market. Now that Swedish women are well represented in public sector unions, and because public sector unions tend to be more militant than their private sector counterparts, women have gained a strong voice in left-leaning governments (Curtin and Higgins 1998, 77; Garrett and Way 2000).

It should by now come as no surprise to the reader that Swedish fertility levels are high by European, CME standards.[15] Public sector jobs

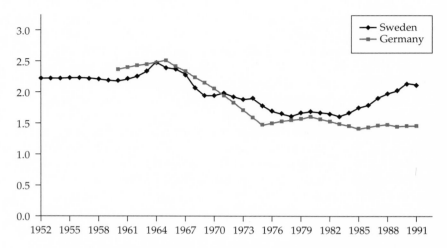

FIGURE 1.2 A Comparison of Swedish and German Total Fertility Rates
SOURCE: Data from Luxembourg Income Study Micro Database

that do not penalize women for career interruptions appear to allow Swedish women to be working mothers with as little struggle and conflict as any place in the world. Many Swedish women are single mothers, but both the gender wage gap and child poverty levels in Sweden, after taxes and transfers, are among the lowest in the world.

It is also worth noting that, although Swedish fertility is relatively high, it fluctuates *positively* with female employment levels (Adsera 2003; Ahn and Mira 1999; Hoem 2000). This is the most direct challenge to a simple opportunity-cost explanation for female fertility that we find anywhere. When government spending increases and public sector employment rises, women move at the margin into the labor force and fertility rises. When the government has to cut budgets, as it did in the 1990s, fertility declines in only slightly lagged response.

Germany's low female labor force participation of about 60 percent and low fertility of around 1.4 contrasts unfavorably with the Swedish case (Figure 1.2). What accounts for this difference, just a few hundred miles away? The German left, though not particularly weak, faced a strong and consolidated party on the right with which it alternated in government and with which it shared oversight of the Bundesbank. Because the Bundesbank does not face a monolithic party in power, it enjoys greater independence and freedom to react against wage settlements that it feels are inflationary (Franzese and Hall 2000). Even when the social democrats are in power in Germany, they cannot expand the public sector with as much abandon as the left party in Sweden. The percentage of women working in the private sector does not differ by all that much between Sweden and Germany. The stark contrast is in the percentage of women working in the public sector: nearly half of all working women in Sweden are government employees, whereas only about 5 percent are in Germany.

The German government is also less generous than the Swedish in subsidizing the costs of childcare. Although Germany, like most European countries, has a system of family allowances, the amounts paid out do not even approach the cash costs of rearing a child. Modest subsidies for parents, combined with structural constraints on women's employment, have predictably led to a stagnant birth rate (Dorbritz and Hohn 1999; Kreyenfeld 2004; Walby 2001; Wendt and Maucher 2000; Witte and Wagner 1995). German women who have career ambitions seem to know they must not interrupt their careers too much or too often.

Conclusions and Plan of the Book

This chapter has made the case for thinking about fertility as an indirect indicator of constraints on women deciding how to allocate effort and time between home and career. It is important to look for indirect indicators such as this, because more direct measures, such as preferences expressed in opinion polls, can often deceive. Women who understand how their choices are limited will not necessarily challenge them, even in an anonymous survey. As Amartya Sen (1984, 1987, 1990, 1992) and others have recognized, people with curtailed options often incorporate environmental constraints into their own mental terrain, where the constraints can become invisible and a part of the "common sense" or "normality" that is passed on from generation to generation.

It is certainly possible that unconstrained women will still choose to have fewer than the replacement number of children, and that is not our concern. Rather, we want to draw attention to the uneven burden that women bear in reproduction, and the consequences for their welfare that comes of a family-specific distribution of labor. When a woman does not have the possibility of economic independence from her spouse, she risks poverty in the event of divorce, and by extension, a weak bargaining position within the family on account of having poor exit options.

By comparing patterns of female labor force participation and fertility in Japan and elsewhere, we find strong evidence for the proposition that low fertility is at least in part a response to women's perceived need to try harder to make a go of it in the labor market. Some Japanese men suggest that "Japanese women are too selfish now to sacrifice on behalf of their children and families."[16] The next generation is a worthy cause, and there are undoubtedly biological as well as social reasons for the sacrifices parents have and will continue to make. But the notion that women should disproportionately bear the burden of investing in child welfare—sometimes defended by reference to a woman's larger physical investment in her children—ignores the substantial costs she pays in doing so. The partial embargo on childbirth that we observe in Japan and some other countries is, we believe, the inevitable result of not recognizing these costs.

The chapters that follow explore the various ways Japan's labor markets make it difficult for mothers to achieve career success, what the government has done about it, and what it must still do if it worries about low fertility. Our conclusion is that, to increase Japanese fertility—and indeed, this applies to the problem of low fertility in other developed countries—women have to be convinced that having children will not block their chances of keeping their jobs.

We do not go deeply into the question of whether women work because they have to or because they want to, but we note that women are disadvantaged in household bargaining in the traditional family where only the husband works. A woman who stays at home faces the possibility of a substantial loss of welfare in the event that her marriage breaks up, and therefore has a large stake in maintaining the marriage. Young Japanese women have watched their mothers make all sorts of sacrifices to keep their marriages going and seem to recognize that a woman who has the possibility of economic independence can relate to her marriage partner on more equal terms.

The following chapter by Sawako Shirahase provides a close statistical look at the relationship between a woman's economic status and fertility. She finds that in Japan, a woman's fertility declines with her income, suggesting that the more ambitious a woman is to be a financial success, the more she has to forgo having children. This parallels the situation of German women, who face challenges similar to those of Japanese women, on account of the high cost of career interruption in a specific-skills economy. As we have shown, women's income is less closely connected to fertility in the United States and Sweden because of the general-skills nature of the U.S. labor market and because of secure public sector jobs and generous childcare subsidies in Sweden. Reducing women's obstacles to career success is likely to be the most direct way for the Japanese government to stop the decline in fertility.

Part Two of the book contains three chapters on precisely how and why demand for female labor in Japan is limited. Margarita Estévez-Abe draws on the "varieties of capitalism" literature to argue that the cost of career interruption varies by how much economies or sectors reward employees on the basis of firm-specific or industry-specific skills. Given the high returns to firm-specific skills in Japan's large firm sector, she argues, it would take substantially more government subsidization of childcare to counteract the dampening effect on demand for female labor. Mary Brinton takes a look at the clerical sector, where women in the United States first made serious inroads into the man's working world, and asks why Japanese women have not met with much success there.

The chapter by Eiko Kenjoh undertakes an explicitly comparative statistical analysis comparing a woman's likelihood of dropping out of the labor market with childbirth in Japan, Britain, Germany, the Netherlands, and Sweden. She argues that government policies make a substantial difference in boosting labor market attachment in Sweden, and that the low quality of part-time work in Japan compared to, for example, the Netherlands, discourages more women from reentering the labor market. By implication, the Japanese government might boost fertility by either increasing public sector employment as in Sweden, or by regulating the part-time labor market to require better wages, job security, and benefits, as in the Netherlands.

In these three chapters, the conclusion is largely the same—the need of employers to make long-term commitments to core male workers makes them reluctant to incorporate women into the core category. The social classification of women as homebodies makes it easier for employers to treat women differently, but this is not just a cultural rut. As long as women disproportionately bear the responsibilities of childcare and other family work, the cost to an employer of hiring any given female is higher in probabilistic terms than that of hiring a male, who is more likely to stay in his job acquiring firm-specific skills all the while. The increased likelihood of a woman interrupting her career on account of her family responsibilities gives firms an incentive to discriminate against women. This is especially true in countries such as Japan, where the widespread use of long-term employment contracts accentuates the difference to employers of men, who can expect to work without interruption, and women who cannot.

Part Three of the book turns to constraints on a woman's supply of labor, holding constant the demand for her labor. The main constraint, as we have been discussing all along, is her role as the family's primary caregiver. The overarching point of this section is that government policy dealing only with childcare provision is likely to be insufficient to boost fertility, without dealing also with the problems that Estévez-Abe, Brinton, and Kenjoh discuss on the demand side. Patricia Boling recounts the history of public subsidization of childcare in Japan, and finds it wanting. Even if the levels of support are higher than in the United States, the subsidies would need to be even larger to have a positive effect, given the limited demand for female labor to start with.

Junichiro Wada looks at the politics of government funding for daycare and finds that, although the overall levels are inadequate to meet the demand for childcare, there are distributional consequences in how the money is allocated. Wada finds that there has been a substantial rural bias to funding and operational guidelines of childcare facilities. He argues that bias was in part due to electoral malapportionment that gave rural voters more clout, and in part due to the strength of the child minders' unions in rural districts. With electoral reapportionment in 1994, we should see—and he does—some evening out of rural and urban childcare subsidization. But again, because the labor market is so inhospitable to women, current subsidies are not nearly enough to induce more women to have children.

Keiko Hirao looks at another constraint on a mother's ability to work: the time demands placed on her by the Japanese market for education. This, too, is related to internal labor markets: because graduating from a good school is such an important signal to firms seeking skilled labor, and because workers cannot expect to move easily from one firm to another once they are placed, there is a large premium on getting into the best possible school. Mothers face an insurmountable collective dilemma—as long as some women are boosting, or at least perceived to be boosting, their child's chance of lifetime success, everyone else feels tremendous pressure to do the same. Runaway competition for childhood education in cram schools and homework is the result.

Part Four turns to policy prescriptions in my concluding chapter, which discusses implications of our analysis for policy choices. Japan's political economy is in transition, with major changes under way in both its party system and its labor markets. Japan is not likely to look the same in twenty or even ten years as it looks today. But it seems certain that Japan's fertility will languish as long as women fail to achieve more equal standing with men in the labor market. I discuss the tradeoffs involved in various policy choices the Japanese government might consider to increase gender equality, and assess the political feasibility and likelihood of these policies. But don't take my word for it. Read on for a deeper understanding of Japan's labor markets, their effects on female employment opportunities, and why government policies so far have failed to solve the problem.

Notes

1. Robert Goodin suggests instead a "feminist withdrawal rule" whereby, in the event of divorce, each partner takes "an equal share of all that has been invested in the household when they leave. By that standard, it is exploitative for the man to be able to withdraw a larger portion of his investments than the woman, simply because there are more 'caring' investments in her portfolio" (Goodin 2005, 24, cited in Folbre 2005, 15). Until divorce courts formulate and enforce a more even distribution of family assets upon divorce, it is safe to bet that women will continue to seek to secure their own economic resources.

2. On the basis of archeological and osteological evidence, scholars now believe that the modern Japanese people are a mixture of the hunter-gatherer Jomon people who probably migrated from north central Asia during the Ice Age some 15,000 or so years ago, and the more recent comers from the Asian mainland via the Korean peninsula, perhaps in several waves, between 500 B.C. and A.D. 300. This latter group established sedentary agriculture over much of the islands, known as the Yayoi culture. They called their country "Yamato," and today "Yamato damashi" or "Yamato spirit" is used to mean "Japaneseness." What this actually means is another matter, given how much Japanese society has changed in the intervening years.

3. Departing from the derisive characterization of motherhood as a cushy job that "comes with three meals and a nap" (*sanshoku hirune tsuki*), municipal governments in Japan have come to recognize that young mothers are vulnerable to depression and that child battery is not a rare and isolated phenomenon. An official in Yamagata told me that the typical at-risk child had a stay-at-home mother rather than a mother overstressed by trying to manage work and family (Interview, June 2001). For heart-rending tales of frustration collected from a hotline for mothers, see Joliet (1977). These anecdotes comport with evidence from the United States and United Kingdom that at-home mothers are at greater risk of depression than working mothers.

4. Although there is probably a cultural element to the premium on youth and beauty in a female partner, there also seems to be some hard-core universality to this male preference that is asymmetric with female preferences. Evolutionary biologists and psychologists explain this as a sort of hardwiring that evolved under a specific division of labor and the resulting sexually differentiated duration of fertility (the female's is much shorter).

5. This is not meant to be a complete or exclusive explanation, but one that nevertheless accurately captures some of the big patterns of human life. Another factor in the emergence of gender inequality, which I do not discuss here, is warfare. To the extent that community life is threatened by aggressors, we can expect preference to be given to features that can help protect the community, such as male solidarity, male aggressiveness, and male heirs.

6. The broad contours of this argument have support from a wide range of scholarly traditions, including Marxism, broadly construed (Engels 1884), economic history (Kuznets 1955), development economics (Boserup 1970), and evolutionary psychology (Hrdy 1991).

7. For a similar conclusion, see Leonard Schoppa (2006).

8. *Keiretsu* are Japanese corporate groups.

9. Not to mention, of course, the sick days and evenings she spends caring for her children, and her loss of productivity in the event that she is tired from the work she does at home.

10. Moreover, as economists point out, equal opportunity legislation can lead corporations to pay women less, unless something is also done about the cost to employers of hiring and promoting women. Perhaps the best to hope for from such legislation is in combating the corporate tendency to think of women primarily as part of the part-time buffer force.

11. This includes, of course, the sick days and evenings she spends caring for her children even upon returning to work, and her loss of productivity in the event that she is tired from the work she does at home.

12. Of course, as Carles Boix (1999) has pointed out, the configuration of interests at the time the electoral rules were adopted probably has much to do with which rules were chosen in the first place.

13. An important caveat here is that economies can only in the most abstract sense be characterized by an overarching type of labor market. Labor markets can vary substantially across sectors, as we saw in the Japan case. We use the CME-LME distinction here to draw broad brushstrokes, but expect to see considerable variation at the sectoral level.

14. The cost does not go away entirely because the employer still has to cover for her in her absence. But since the employer does not invest heavily in either men or women, her departure, even if it is permanent, does not represent as great a loss as it would for an employer who invests in employees in the expectation of a long-term return on that investment.

15. Though Swedish fertility had fallen to 1.5 in 1999, projections were for a stabilized fertility rate of 1.8 by 2010, based on the expectation that women are more likely to give birth when job prospects for women improve (Bernhardt 2000).

16. An unfortunate comment from a close academic friend.

References

Adler, Marina A. 1997. "Social Change and Declines in Marriage and Fertility in Eastern Germany." *Journal of Marriage and the Family* 59: 37–49.

Adsera, Alicia. 2003. "Changing Fertility Rates in Developed Countries: The Impact of Labor Market Institutions." Manuscript, Department of Economics, University of Illinois at Chicago.

Ahn, Namkee, and Pedro Mira. 1999. "A Note on the Changing Relationship Between Fertility and Female Employment Rates in Developed Countries." *Fundación de Estudios de Economia Aplicada, Documento de Trabajo 99–109*. http://www.fedea.es/hojas/publicaciones.html.

Amino Yoshihiko. 1999. "Sekai ni hirakareta Nihon rettô: Nihonshi no naka no nihonjin [The Japan that Opened to the World: The Japanese People within Japanese History]," in Ishii Yoneo; M. Yamauchi, eds.: *Nihonjin to tabunkashugi* [*The Japanese People and Multiculturalism*]. Tokyo: Kokusai bunka koryu suishin kyokai.

Anderson, Deborah, Melissa Binder, and Kate Krause. 2002. "Women, Children, and the Labor Market." *AEA Papers and Proceedings* 92(2): 354–358.

Andersson, Gunnar. 2002. "Fertility Developments in Norway and Sweden since the Early 1960s." *Demographic Research* 6. http://www.demographic-research.org/volumes/vol6/4.

Aoki, Masahiko. 1984. *The Cooperative Game Theory of the Firm*. New York: Oxford University Press.

Aoki, Masahiko. 1990. "Toward an Economic Model of the Japanese Firm." *Journal of Economic Literature*, 28 (March), 1–27.

Aoki, Masahiko, and Hugh Patrick, eds. 1994. *The Japanese Main Bank System: Its Relevance for Developing and Transforming Economies*. New York: Oxford University Press.

Badgett, M.V. Lee, Pamela Davidson, Nancy Folbre, and Jeannette Lim. 2000. "Breadwinner Dad, Homemaker Mom: An Interdisciplinary Analysis of Changing Gender Norms in the United States, 1977–1998." Manuscript, Departments of Economics and Sociology, University of Massachusetts, Amherst.

Bartels, Larry M. 2002. "Partisan Politics and the U.S. Income Distribution, 1948–2000." Unpublished paper, Woodrow Wilson School of Public and International Affairs, Princeton University.

Bawn, Kathleen, and Frances Rosenbluth. 2003. "Coalition Parties versus Coalitions of Parties: How Electoral Agency Shapes the Political Logic of Costs and Benefits." Paper presented at the annual meeting of the American Political Science Association, Philadelphia, August 28–September 1.

Bawn, Kathleen, and Frances Rosenbluth. 2006. "Short Versus Long Coalitions: Electoral Accountability and the Size of the Public Sector." *American Journal of Political Science* 50(2): 251–265.

Becker, Gary. 1962. "Investment in Human Capital: A Theoretical Analysis." *Journal of Political Economy* 70(5): 9–49.

Becker, Gary. 1981. *A Treatise on the Family.* Harvard University Press.

Becker, Gary. 1985. "Human Capital, Effort, and the Sexual Division of Labor." *Journal of Labor Economics* 3(1), pt. 2: S33–S58.

Bernhardt, Eva. 2000. "Sweden." *Europa—The European Union Online.*

Blau, Francine, and Ronald Ehrenberg. 1997. *Gender and Family Issues in the Workplace.* New York: Russell Sage Foundation.

Blau, Francine, and Lawrence Kahn. 1996. "Where Are We in the Economics of Gender? The Gender Pay Gap." *NBER Working Paper 5564.*

Boix, Carles. 1999. "Setting the Rules of the Game: The Choice of Electoral Systems in Advanced Democracies." *American Political Science Review* 93(3): 609–624.

Boserup, Esther. 1970. *Women's Role in Economic Development.* New York: St. Martin's Press.

Braunstein, Elissa, and Nancy Folbre. 2001. "To Honor and Obey: Efficiency, Inequality and Patriarchal Property Rights." *Feminist Economics* 7(1): 25–44.

Brinton, Mary. 1989. "Gender Stratification in Contemporary Urban Japan." *American Sociological Review* 54: 549–564.

Brinton, Mary. 1993. *Women and the Economic Miracle: Gender and Work in Postwar Japan.* Berkeley: University of California Press.

Brinton, Mary, ed. 2001. *Women's Working Lives in East Asia.* Stanford: Stanford University Press.

Bundesministerium fuer Bildung und Forschung [Federal Ministry for Education and Research]. 2001. Strukturdaten 2000/2001 [Structural Data 2000/2001]. Bonn.

Clerkx, Lily E., and Marinus H. van Ijzendoorn. "Child Care in a Dutch Context: On the History, Current Status, and Evaluation of Nonmaternal Child Care in the Netherlands," in Michael Lamb et al., eds., *Child Care in Context: Cross-Cultural Perspective.* Hillsdale, NJ: Lawrence Erlbaum. 55–79.

Conrad, Christoph, et al. 1996. "East German Fertility After Unification: Crisis or Adaptation?" *Population and Development Review* 22(2): 331–358.

Conrad, Christoph, Michael Lechner, and Welf Werner. 1996. *Population and Development Review* 22(2): 331–358.

Cowhey, Peter, and Mathew McCubbins, eds. 1995. *Structure and Policy in Japan and the United States.* Cambridge: Cambridge University Press.

Curtin, Jennifer, and Winton Higgins. 1998. "Feminism and Unionism in Sweden." *Politics and Society* 26(1): 69–93.

Dorbritz, Jurgen, and Charlotte Hohn. 1999. "The Future of the Family and Future of Fertility Trends in Germany." *Population Bulletin of the United Nations*, Nos. 40/41: 218–234.

Eduards, Maud, et al. 1985. "Equality: How Equal?" in Elina Haavio-Mannila et al., *Unfinished Democracy: Women in Nordic Politics*. Oxford: Pergamon Press. 134–159.

Engelbrech, Gerhard, and Alexander Reinberg. 1997. Frauen und Maenner in der Beschaeftigungskrise der 90er Jahre [Women and Men in the Employment Crisis of the 90s]. Werkstattbericht No. 11/8.9.1997. Nuernberg Bundesanstalt fuer Arfeit, Institut fuer Arbeitsmarkt und Berufsforschung.

Engels, Friedrich. 1884. "The Origin of the Family, Private Property, and the State," reprinted in Robert Tucker, ed., *The Marx-Engels Reader*. 1978. New York: Norton.

Esping-Andersen, Gosta. 1990. *The Three Worlds of Welfare Capitalism*. Cambridge: Polity.

Esping-Andersen, Gosta. 1999. *Social Foundations of Postindustrial Economies*. Oxford: Oxford University Press.

Estévez-Abe, Margarita, Torben Iversen, and David Soskice. 1999. "Production Regimes and Welfare States." Paper prepared for meeting of the American Political Science Association, Atlanta.

Estévez-Abe, Margarita, Torben Iversen, and David Soskice. 2001. "Social Protection and the Formation of Skills: A Reinterpretation of the Welfare State," in Peter Hall and David Soskice, eds., *Varieties of Capitalism: The Institutional Foundations of Comparative Advantage*. Oxford: Oxford University Press.

Fisher, Helen. 1999. *The First Sex: The Natural Talents of Women and How They Are Changing the World*. New York: Ballantine.

Folbre, Nancy. 1994. *Who Pays for the Kids? Gender and the Structures of Constraint*. New York: Routledge.

Folbre, Nancy. 2005. "Add Gender and Spin: Rethinking Political Coalitions in the U.S." Manuscript, Department of Economics, University of Massachusetts, Amherst.

Franzese, Robert, Jr., and Peter Hall. 2000. "Institutional Dimensions of Coordinating Wage Bargaining and Monetary Policy," in Iversen, Pontusson, and Soskice, eds., *Unions, Employers, and Central Banks*. New York: Cambridge University Press. 173–204.

Garrett, Geoffrey, and Christopher Way. 2000. "Public Sector Unions, Corporatism, and Wage Determination," in Iversen, Pontusson, and Soskice, eds. *Unions, Employers, and Central Banks*. New York: Cambridge University Press. 267–291.

Geddes, Rick, and Dean Lueck. 2002. "The Gains from Self-Ownership and the Expansion of Women's Rights." *American Economic Review* 92(4): 1079–1092.

Goldin, Claudia. 1997. "Career and Family: College Women Look to the Past," in Francine Blau and Ronald Ehrenberg, eds., *Gender and Family Issues in the Workplace*. New York: Russell Sage Foundation. 20–60.

Goode, William. 1993. *World Changes in Divorce Patterns*. Yale University Press.

Goodin, Robert. 2005. "Women's Work: Its Irreplaceability and Exploitability," paper prepared for Festschrift for Carole Pateman, in Iris Marion Young, Mary Shanley, and Daniel O'Neill, eds., Research School of Social Sciences, Australian National University.

Gornick, Janet C. 1999. "Gender Equality in the Labor Market," in Diane Sainsbury, ed., *Gender Policy Regimes and Welfare States*. Oxford: Oxford University Press, 210–242.

Gornick, Janet C., and Jerry A. Jacobs. 1998. "Gender, the Welfare State, and Public Employment: A Comparative Study of Seven Industrialized Countries." *American Sociological Review* 63(5): 688–710.

Gottfried, Heidi. 2000. "Compromising Positions: Emergent Neo-Fordisms and Embedded Gender Contracts." *British Journal of Sociology* 51(2): 234–259.

Gustafsson, Bjorn, and Urban Kjulin. 1995. "Public Expenditures on Child Care and the Distribution of Economic Well-being: The Case of Sweden." Occasional paper, Goetborg University.

Gustafsson, Siv. 1997. "Feminist Neo-Classical Economics: Some Examples," in Geske Dijkstra and Janneke Plantenga, eds., *Gender and Economics: A European Perspective*. London: Routledge.

Hall, Peter, and David Soskice, eds. 2001. *Varieties of Capitalism: The Institutional Foundations of Comparative Advantage*. Oxford: Oxford University Press.

Hammar, Tomas. 1985. "Sweden," in Tomas Hammar, ed., *European Immigration Policy: A Comparative Study*. Cambridge: Cambridge University Press. 17–49.

Hoem, Britta. 1995. "The Gender-Segregated Swedish Labour Market." In F. V. Oppenheimer and A. Jensen, eds., *Gender and Family Change in Industrialized Countries*. Oxford: Clarendon. 279–296.

Hoem, Britta. 2000. "Entry into Motherhood in Sweden: The Influence of Economic Factors on the Rise and Fall in Fertility, 1986–1997." *Demographic Research* 2. Available at http://www.demographic-research.org/volumes/vol2/4.

Hoem, Britta, and Jan M. Hoem. 1999. "Fertility Trends in Sweden up to 1996." *Population Bulletin of the United Nations*, nos. 40/41: 318–333.

Hoshi, Takeo, Anil Kashyap, and David Scharfstein. 1990. "The Role of Banks in Reducing the Costs of Financial Distress in Japan." *Journal of Financial Economics* 27: 67–88.

Hoshi, Takeo, Anil Kashyap, and David Scharfstein. 1991. "Corporate Structure, Liquidity, and Investment: Evidence from Japanese Industrial Groups." *Quarterly Journal of Economics* 106: 33–60.

Hrdy, Sarah Blaffer. 1981. *The Woman That Never Evolved*. Cambridge, MA: Harvard University Press.

Hrdy, Sarah Blaffer. 1991. The absence of estrus in *Homo sapiens*, in A. Brooks, ed., *The Origins of Humanness*. Washington, DC: Smithsonian Institution Press.

Hrdy, Sarah Blaffer. 1999. *Mother Nature: A History of Mothers, Infants, and Natural Selection*. New York: Pantheon.

Huber, Evelyne, and John D. Stephens. 2000. "Partisan Governance, Women's Employment, and the Social Democratic Service State." *American Sociological Review* 65: 323–342.

Huber, Evelyne, and John D. Stephens. 2001. *Development and Crisis of the Welfare State: Parties and Policies in Global Markets*. Chicago: University of Chicago Press.

Hwang, C. Philip, and Anders G. Broberg. 1992. "The Historical and Social Context of Child Care in Sweden," in Michael E. Lamb et al., eds., *Child Care in Context: Cross-Cultural Perspectives*. Hillsdale, NJ: Lawrence Erlbaum. 27–53.

Institute for Women's Policy Research. 2004. "Still a Man's Labor Market: The Long-Term Earnings Gap." Available at http://72.14.209.104/search?q=cache:Nvf6gL9yzooJ:www.iwpr.org/pdf/C355.pdf+75-80+percent+2003+2004&hl=en&gl=us&ct=clnk&cd=1.

Iversen, Torben. 2000a. "Decentralization, Monetarism, and the Social Democratic Welfare State," in Iversen, Pontusson, and Soskice, eds., *Unions, Employers, and Central Banks*. New York: Cambridge University Press. 205–231.

Iversen, Torben, Jonas Pontusson, and David Soskice, eds. 2000b. *Unions, Employers and Central Banks: Macroeconomic Coordination and Institutional Change in Social Market Economies*. New York: Cambridge University Press.

Iversen, Torben, and David Soskice. 2002. "Electoral Systems and the Politics of Coalitions: Why Some Democracies Redistribute More Than Others." Manuscript, Department of Government, Harvard University, and Department of Political Science, Duke University.

Iversen, Torben, and Frances Rosenbluth. 2006. "The Political Economy of Gender: Explaining Cross-national Variation in the Household Distribution of Labor, Divorce, and the Gender Preference Gap." *American Journal of Political Science* 50, 1: 1–19.

Jenson, Jane, and Rianne Maon. 1993. "Representing Solidarity: Class, Gender and the Crisis in Social-Democratic Sweden." *New Left Review*, no. 201: 76–100.

Jiyu minshuto (LDP). 1979. *Nihon-gata fukushi shakai* [The Japanese Model of a Welfare Society]. Tokyo: Jiyu minshuto koho iinkai shuppankyoku [LDP Press Committee, Publication Bureau].

Joliet, Muriel. 1977. *Japan: The Childless Society? The Crisis of Motherhood*. London: Routledge.

Katz, Lawrence F. 1997. Commentary on "Labor Supply Effects of State Maternity Leave Legislation," in Francine Blau and Ronald Ehrenberg, eds., *Gender and Family Issues in the Workplace*. New York: Russell Sage Foundation. 86–88.

King, Leslie. 2002. "Demographic Trends, Pronatalism, and Nationalist Ideologies in the Late Twentieth Century." *Ethnic and Racial Studies* 25(3): 367–389.

Kitschelt, Herbert, et al., eds. 1999. *Continuity and Change in Contemporary Capitalism*. Cambridge: Cambridge University Press.

Kjulin, Urban. 1995. "The Demand for Public Child Care in Sweden." Occasional paper, Goteborg University.

Klauder, Wolfgang. 1994. "Zukunft der Arbeit: Wirtschaftliche und gesellschaftliche Rahmenbedingungen [The Future of Work: Economic and Social Structural Conditions]." *Gewerkschaftliche Monatshefte* 12/1994: 764–782.

Klerman, Jacob Alex, and Arleen Leibowitz. 1997. "Labor Supply Effects of State Maternity Leave Legislation," in Francine Blau and Ronald Ehrenberg, eds., *Gender and Family Issues in the Workplace*. New York: Russell Sage Foundation. 65–85.

Knocke, Wuokko. 2000. "Integration or Segregation? Immigrant Populations Facing the Labour Market in Sweden." *Economic and Industrial Democracy* 21: 361–380.

Kono, Shigemi. 1996. "The Relation Between Women's Economic Activity and Child Care in Low Fertility Countries." *Population and Women: Proceedings of the United Nations Expert Group Meeting on Population and Women*, June 1992. 322–345.

Korpi, Walter. 2000. "Faces of Inequality: Gender, Class, and Patterns of Inequalities in Different Types of Welfare States." *Social Politics*. Summer: 127–191.

Koshiro, Kazutoshi. 1994. "The Employment System and Human Resource Management," in Kenichi Imai and Ryutaro Komiya, eds., *Business Enterprise in Japan*. MIT Press.

Kreyenfeld, Michaela. 2004. "Fertility Decisions in the FRG and GDR: An Analysis with Data from the German Fertility and Family Survey." Research article, Max Planck Institute for Demographic Research.

Kucera, David. 2000. *Gender, Growth, and Trade: The Miracle Economies of the Postwar Years*. London: Routledge.

Kuznets, S. 1955. "Economic Growth and Income Inequality." *American Economic Review* 45: 1–28.

Lamb, Michael, et al., eds. 1992. *Child Care in Context: Cross-Cultural Perspectives*. Hillsdale, NJ: Lawrence Erlbaum.

Lee, Richard, and Richard Daly, eds. 1999. *The Cambridge Encyclopedia of Hunters and Gatherers*. Cambridge: Cambridge University Press.

Lesthaeghe, Ron. 1995. "The Second Demographic Transition in Western Countries: An Interpretation," in Karen Oppenheim Mason and An-

Magritt Jensen, eds., *Gender and Family Change in Industrialized Countries.* Oxford: Clarendon. 17–62.

Lewis, Jane, and Gertrude Astrom. 1992. "Equality, Difference, and State Welfare: Labor Market and Family Policies in Sweden." *Feminist Studies* 18: 59–87.

Lindstrom, Ulf. 1995. "Social Democracy, Women, and the European Union," in Lauri Karvonen and Per Sell, eds., *Women in Nordic Politics: Closing the Gap.* Dartmouth, UK: Aldershot. 115–132.

Landsorganisationen I Sverige (L.O.). 2004. "Rate of Trade Union Organisation in Sweden." Available at http://www.lo.se/home, see English, Reports.

Lofstrom, Asa, and Thomas Westerberg. N.D. "Factors Behind Fertility Swings in Sweden, 1965–1998." Unpublished manuscript, Department of Economics, Umea University, Umea, Sweden.

Lundberg, Shelly, and Robert Pollak. 1996. "Bargaining and Distribution in Marriage." *Journal of Economic Perspectives* 10 (Fall): 139–158.

Luxembourg Income Study (LIS) Micro database. Accessed August 1–7, 2005. Harmonization of original surveys conducted by the Luxembourg Income Study, Asbl. Luxembourg, periodic updating.

Martin, Andrew. 2000. "The Politics of Macroeconomic Policy and Wage Negotiations in Sweden," in Iversen, Pontusson, and Soskice, eds., *Unions, Employers, and Central Banks.* New York: Cambridge University Press. 232–264.

McCubbins, Mathew, and Frances Rosenbluth. 1995. In Peter Cowhey and Mathew McCubbins, eds., *Structure and Policy in Japan and the United States.* Cambridge: Cambridge University Press.

McDonald, Peter. 1999. "Contemporary Fertility Patterns in Australia: First Data from the 1996 Census." *People and Place* 6(1): 1–13.

McDonald, Peter. 2000. "Gender Equity, Social Institutions and the Future of Fertility." *Journal of Population Research* 17(1): 1–16.

Meier-Braun, Karl-Heinz, and Martin A. Hilgus, eds. 1995. *40 Jahre "Gastarbeiter" in Deutschland* [40 Years of Guestworkers in Germany]. Baden-Baden: Nomos.

Mincer, Jacob. 1958. "Investment in Human Capital and Personal Income Distribution." *Journal of Political Economy* 66(4): 281–302.

Mincer, Jacob, and K. Ofek. 1982. "Interrupted Work Careers: Depreciation and Restoration of Human Capital." *Journal of Human Resources* 17:1.

Moen, Karl Ove, and Michael Wallerstein. 1995. "How Social Democracy Worked: Labor Market Institutions." *Politics and Society* 23(2): 185–211.

Mosesdottir, Lilja. 2000. "Pathways Towards the Dual Breadwinner Model: The Role of the Swedish, German, and the American States." *International Review of Sociology* 10(2): 189–205.

Nagase, Nobuko. 2000. "Standard and Non-standard Work Arrangements and Child-Bearing of Japanese Mothers." Manuscript, Upjohn Institute.

Organization for Economic Cooperation and Development. 2006. *Society at a Glance: OECD Social Indicators—2006 Edition*. Cheltenham, UK: OECD and Edward Elgar Publishing.

Osawa, Machiko. 1988. "Working Mothers: Changing Patterns of Employment and Fertility in Japan." *Economic Development and Cultural Change*, 36: 623–650.

Osawa, Mari. 2000. "Government Approaches to Gender Equality in the mid 1990s." *Social Science Japan Journal* 3(1): 3–19.

Persson, Lotta. 2002. "Reproduction and Employment Status." Statistics Sweden. Available at http://www.demography.scb.se.

Pontusson, Jonas. 2000. "Labor Market Institutions and Wage Distribution," in Iversen, Pontusson, and Soskice, eds., *Unions, Employers, and Central Banks*. New York: Cambridge University Press. 292–330.

Pross, Helge. 1972. "Zeugnis guten Willens—der neue Frauenbericht der Bundesregierung [Evidence of Good Will: The Federal Government's New Women's Report]." *Gewerkschaftliche Monatshefte* 11:708–715.

Ramseyer, Mark, and Frances Rosenbluth. 1993. *Japan's Political Marketplace*. Cambridge, MA: Harvard University Press.

Richter, Heinz. 1974. "DGB und Auslaenderbeschaeftigung [The DGB and Employment of Foreigners]." *Gewerkschaftliche Monatshefte* 1:35–40.

Rindfuss, Ronald R., Karin L. Brewster, and Andrew A. Kavee. 1996. "Women, Work, and Children: Behavioral and Ideational Change in the United States." *Population and Development Review* 22(3): 457–482.

Rogowski, Ronald, and Mark Kayser. 2001. "Majoritarian Electoral Systems and Consumer Power: Price-Level Evidence from the OECD Countries." Working paper, UCLA.

Rose-Ackerman, Susan. 1983a. "Unintended Consequences: Regulating the Quality of Subsidized Day Care." *Journal of Policy Analysis and Management* 3(1): 14–30.

Rose-Ackerman, Susan. 1983b. "Social Services and the Market." *Columbia Law Review* 83: 1405–1431.

Rosenbluth, F., and R.Schaap. 2002. "The Domestic Politics of Banking Regulation." *International Organization* 57(2): 307–336.

Rosenbluth, Frances, and Ross Schaap. 2003. "The Domestic Politics of Financial Regulation." *International Organization* 57 (Spring): 307–336.

Rubery, Jill, Mark Smith, and Colette Fagan. 1999. *Women's Employment in Europe: Trends and Prospects*. London: Routledge.

Ruhm, Christopher, and Jackqueline Teague. 1997. "Parental Leave Policies in Europe and North America," in Francine Blau and Ronald Ehrenberg, eds., *Gender and Family Issues in the Workplace*. New York: Russell Sage Foundation. 133–156.

Schoppa, Leonard. 2006. *Race for the Exits*. Ithaca, NY: Cornell University Press.

Schrag, Claudia. 2002. "Is Germany Revising Its Self-Understanding as an Ethnically Homogeneous Nation State? Recent Reforms in German Alien Law." Unpublished manuscript, Yale University.

Sen, Amartya. 1984. *Resources, Values, and Development.* Harvard University Press.

Sen, Amartya. 1987. *On Ethics and Economics.* Blackwell.

Sen, Amartya. 1990. "Gender and Cooperative Conflicts," in Irene Tinker, ed., *Persistent Inequalities: Women and World Development.* New York: Oxford University Press.

Sen, Amartya. 1992. *Inequality Reexamined.* New York: Russell Sage Foundation.

Shaffer, Harry G. *Women in the Two Germanies: A Comparative Study of a Socialist and a Non-Socialist Society.* New York: Pergamon Press.

Statistics Sweden. Available at http://www.scb.se/eng/index.asp.

Stephens, John D. 1996. "The Scandinavian Welfare States: Achievements, Crisis, and Prospects," in Gospa Esping-Andersen, *Welfare States in Transition: National Adaptations in Global Economies.* London: Sage. 32–65.

Sundstrom, Marianne. 1993. "The Growth in Full-Time Work Among Swedish Women in the 1980s," *Acta Sociologica* 36: 139–150.

Swenson, Peter, and Jonas Pontusson. 2000. "The Swedish Employer Offensive Against Centralized Bargaining," in Iversen, Pontusson, and Soskice, eds., *Unions, Employers, and Central Banks.* New York: Cambridge University Press.

Thelen, Kathleen A. 1991. *Union of Parts: Labor Politics in Postwar Germany.* Ithaca, NY: Cornell University Press.

Thelen, Kathleen. 2000. "Why German Employers Cannot Bring Themselves to Dismantle the German Model," in Iversen, Pontusson, and Soskice, eds. *Unions, Employers, and Central Banks.* New York: Cambridge University Press. 138–169.

Van Kersbergen, Kees. 1999. "Contemporary Christian Democracy and the Demise of the Politics of Mediation," in Herbert Kitschelt et al., eds., *Continuity and Change in Contemporary Capitalism.* Cambridge: Cambridge University Press. 346–370.

Walby, Sylvia. 2001. "From Gendered Welfare State to Gender Regimes: National Differences, Convergence, or Restructuring?" Paper presented to Gender and Society Group, Stockholm University, January.

Weinstein, David, and Yishay Yafeh. 1995. "Japan's Corporate Groups: Collusive or Competitive? An Empirical Investigation of *Keiretsu* Behavior." *Journal of Industrial Economics* (December). 43: 359–376.

Weinstein, David, and Yishay Yafeh. 1998. "On the Costs of a Bank Centered Financial System: Evidence from Changing Main Bank Relations in Japan." *Journal of Finance* (April): 635–672.

Wendt, Claus, and Mathias Maucher. 2000. "Mutter zweishen Kinderbetreuung und Erweerbstatigkeit: Institutionelle Hilfen und Hurden bei einem beruflichen Wiedereinstieg nach einer Kinderpaus [Mothers Between Care of Children and Gainful Employment." Institutional Assistance and Hurdles with a Vocational Reentrance After a Child Break]. http://www.mzes.uni-mannheim/de/publications/wp/wp_start.html.

Witte, James, and Gert Wagner. 1995. "Declining Fertility After Unification: A Demographic Response to Socioeconomic Change." *Population and Development Review* 21(2): 387–397.

Zenkoku bebishittaa kyokai, ed. 1997. *Zenkoku saitaku hoiku sabisu jisshi kokyo nado chosa jigyo* [*A Survey of National Babysitting Services*]. Tokyo.

CHAPTER 2

Women's Economic Status and Fertility: Japan in Cross-National Perspective

SAWAKO SHIRAHASE

Introduction

Drastic changes in Japan's demographic structure—that is, the decline in the fertility rate and the resulting growth in the aged population, and their possible consequences for Japan's fiscal health—have raised alarm in Japan's policy-making circles. The drop in the total fertility rate from 1.66 in 1988 to 1.57 in 1989 attracted public attention and became widely known as the "1.57 shock." Nothing the government has done so far has resulted in higher fertility, and the numbers seem to be edging ever downward. However we feel about fertility itself, the public spotlight on the fertility issue gives us an unprecedented opportunity to examine how women's lot might be improved.

Japan has been characterized by the least favorable work setting for women, as exemplified by the discontinuous pattern of work among mothers, the large wage gap between men and women, and the very low proportion of women holding managerial positions. In this chapter, I will examine the downward trend in the fertility rate, and provide an overview of recent studies on married women's labor force participation. Second, I will examine mothers' working patterns, especially on the continuation of work before and after the first childbirth in Japan. Third, I will compare mothers' work in Japan with that in other industrial nations, focusing on the extent of their contribution to the household economy. I will show how the wife's income affects the number of children in Japan and elsewhere.

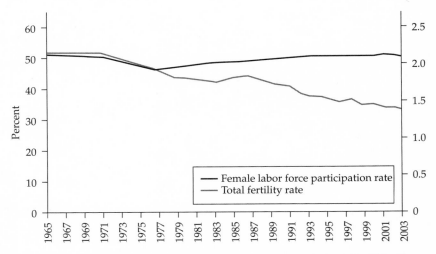

FIGURE 2.1 Female Labor Force Participation Rates and Total Fertility Rates since 1965

Trends in the Fertility Rate and Female Labor Force Participation in Japan

Figure 2.1 shows the female labor force participation rate and the total fertility rate since 1965. The rate of female participation in the labor force has not constantly increased in Japan since the end of World War II, unlike American and European societies. The rate decline until 1975 derived mainly from the fact that fewer and fewer married women worked as unpaid family workers in the farming sector, whereas the increase after 1975 is due to the fact that the influx of women as employees in the secondary and tertiary sectors surpassed the decline in the farming sector. The female labor force participation rate (measured as the percentage of working age population in the labor force) in Japan declined after World War II, hitting bottom in 1975, before reaching 48.5 percent in 2002.

Although the overall rate of female labor force participation has not strikingly increased, some significant changes are revealed by examining the economic activity of women in more detail. One is the growth of women's entry into the labor force as employees. As seen in Figure 2.2, the composition of employment status among the female labor force has changed substantially since 1960. About 60 percent of women in 1960

FIGURE 2.2 Distribution of Employment Status among Female Labor Force since 1960

were self-employed or family workers, but 40 years later, the percentage of family workers who were mostly unpaid declined dramatically. In 2000, more than 80 percent of working women were employees. Thus, the way women work, represented by the increase in the number of employees, has changed in Japan, while their overall level of economic activity has not changed much in that time. Women used to work on the family farms while taking care of the domestic duties, but the separation of the workplace from the family made it difficult for women to reconcile work with family responsibilities. The double-peaked pattern of Japanese women's economic activity by age group, known as the M-shaped curve, emerged in the 1960s and remained basically the same in the 1990s, as shown in Figure 2.3. The extent of the drop in the participation rate among the twenty-five to twenty-nine age group, however, has become less dramatic from 1975 to 1995.

The total fertility rate has continuously declined since 1965, as shown in Figure 2.1, as women have entered the labor force as employees. The labor force participation of mothers with small children is still limited in Japan. Among mothers who have children aged three years or younger, only 28 percent are engaged in employment, including part-time work. Among mothers who have children ages four to six, the percentage of

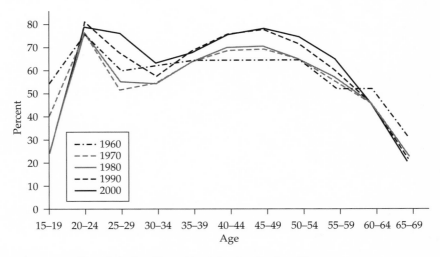

FIGURE 2.3 Female Labor Force Participation by Age Group
SOURCE: Ministry of Labor (Japan), *Labor Force Survey*, various years

those who work jumps to 50 percent, but 45 percent of them work part-time (Statistics Bureau 1997). For mothers who work on a full-time basis, 42 percent of those with children younger than four years relied on kinship ties for childcare in 1993, and 49 percent enrolled their children in daycare facilities (Fujin Shonen Kyokai 1994).

In order to encourage women to pursue their careers despite their family responsibilities, the Japanese government established parental leave policies. With the adoption of the Parental Leave Act in 1995, every employee is entitled to take childcare leave in order to take care of a child younger than one year. Following the amendment to the Employment Insurance Law, insured persons who take childcare leave are paid 40 percent of their wage before leave. In 1996, 44 percent of female workers in firms that had childcare leave policies took childcare leave, whereas less than 1 percent of men did (Ministry of Labor 1996). Clearly, workers who take childcare leave are overwhelmingly women.

Mother's Work at the Time of the First Childbirth

In this section, I analyze micro data to examine the determinants of mothers to work at the first childbirth. The data set I use here is the 1998 National Survey of Family in Japan (hereafter, NSFJ), a nationally representative survey on family in Japan, conducted by the National Institute of Population and Social Security Research. I focus on married women with child(ren) for this analysis.

Whereas in most industrial societies, including the United States, women and men show a similar working pattern, they are significantly different in Japan: women are more likely to drop out of the labor force. In fact, more than 70 percent of mothers stopped working at the time of giving birth to their first child. In response to the 1998 NSFJ questionnaire, about half of all married women stated that mothers should leave the labor market when their children are small. Fewer than 20 percent of the respondents said that women should stay in their jobs upon childbirth.

As far as married women are concerned, the belief that mothers should stay at home and take care of small children was still predominant even in the late 1990s. A national attitudes survey conducted in 2000[1] asked respondents what would be the ideal work pattern for mothers whose youngest child has not reached school age. Respondents who were in their twenties answered as follows: full-time work (6.8 percent), part-time work (24.8 percent), no work (43.2 percent), and don't know (25.2 percent). Even among the younger generation, then, conservative attitudes toward mothers' work prevail in contemporary Japan.

More than 80 percent of the women who withdrew from the labor market reported personal reasons for quitting their job (Statistics Bureau 1997). Among the women in their twenties and thirties, 42.8 percent said they stopped working because of marriage, and 37.7 percent said they stopped working because of childbearing. It appears that marriage and childbearing remain the primary reasons for being out of the labor market.

Table 2.1 shows the results of a logistic regression analysis of whether respondents stayed in the labor market or not at the time of birth of the first child, based on the 1998 NSFJ. The analysis is restricted to respondents who were married and had child(ren). The explanatory variables in the analysis are the age of the respondent, her husband's education measured by years of schooling, the urban area dummy, three dummy variables representing the occupation of the respondent before the first childbirth,[2] and a dummy variable indicating a government job before the first childbirth. Statistically significant variables are the age of the respondent, the husband's education, the urban dummy, the self-employed dummy, the white-collar dummy, and the government sector dummy. The older the respondents, the more likely they are to

TABLE 2.1

Logit analysis of the continuation of work after the birth of first child

	Coefficient
Constant	−0.355
Wife's age	0.017**
Husband's education	−0.068**
Urban dummy	−0.692**
Self-employed dummy	1.276**
Professional dummy	0.151
White-collar dummy	−0.394**
Government dummy	1.120**
Occupation missing dummy	−1.260**
Size missing dummy	0.175

SOURCE: Data from National Institute of Population and Social Security Research, 1998.

NOTE: Self-employed dummy includes family workers.

**$p < .01$

stay in the labor market at the time of their first childbirth. The net positive effect of age on the chances of continuing work probably derives from the fact that women who were married and had children in their twenties are more likely to hold conservative attitudes toward work and childrearing than young unmarried women in their twenties, who tend to delay their marriage, as well as married women in their thirties and forties. In other words, the positive effect of age on work continuity at the time of the first childbirth is probably due to the greater tendency of withdrawal from the labor market among young mothers in their twenties. The husband's education has a negative effect on whether or not a woman continues working. The higher the husband's educational attainment, the less likely the wife is to stay in the labor market. Since the socioeconomic status of the husband at the time of the first childbirth was not included in the survey, the educational level of the husband can be regarded as a proxy for the husband's socioeconomic status. The wife's decision about whether to stay in the labor force at the time of childbearing is associated more with the husband's socioeconomic status.

In addition to the husband's situation, a woman's own employment is also a critical factor in making the decision about her subsequent work trajectory. Women who work as self-employed or family workers before the first childbirth are more likely to stay in the labor force, compared with those who were blue-collar workers. This is consistent with

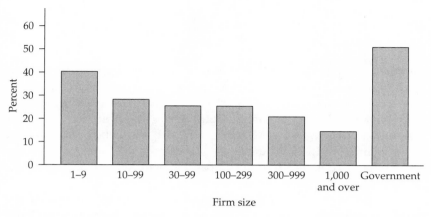

FIGURE 2.4 Proportion of Continuous Workers after the Birth of the First Child by Firm Size

the claim that the growth of employees among the female labor force leads to a discontinuous working trajectory. In fact, respondents who worked as white-collar employees are more likely to withdraw from the labor market after the childbirth than those who worked as blue-collar employees. White-collar work, which has expanded along with industrialization, is closely related to a discontinuous work profile.

Work experience in the government sector increases a mother's chances of staying in her job after childbirth, and this effect is probably associated with better fringe benefits related to childbearing. The government sector is considered to be one of the most favorable places for women to work due to gender equality in employment policies. According to the 1998 NSFJ, about 50 percent of those who worked in the government sector before the birth of their first child managed to stay in their job, which is an exceptionally high retention rate for Japan. When we examine women who worked in the private sector prior to giving birth to their first child, we find that firm size is negatively associated with the proportion of those who stayed in the labor market after their childbearing: the larger the firm, the lower the proportion of those who continued to work (Figure 2.4). Policy makers and managers are increasingly aware of the importance of family-friendly employment policy, and some large firms have a family-friendly work environment (Josei Rodo Kyokai 1999). Nevertheless, at the macro level, it is difficult to see the effect of better fringe benefits in large firms on the mothers' work behaviors, compared with those in smaller ones.

Determinants of Mother's Work
in Comparative Perspective

In this section, I compare the determinants of mothers' work in Japan with those in other nations. The data sets used in this analysis are the 1995 Social Stratification and Mobility Survey (hereafter, SSM) and the 1995 National Survey of Living Conditions (Kokumin Seikatsu Kiso Chosa),[3] conducted by the Ministry of Health and Labor in Japan, and the Luxembourg Income Survey data (hereafter, LIS data) for other nations. The LIS data is a highly comparable data set and is valuable for cross-national comparison.

Six countries from the LIS data set are selected for my analysis. They are Germany, Italy, Sweden, Taiwan, the United Kingdom, and the United States. I analyze the data sets collected in the mid-1990s for these countries. I chose Germany and Italy since the role of family is strong in these nations for welfare states. In contrast, Sweden has a high degree of gender equality, and it is generally regarded as a champion of the welfare state. Taiwan is included in the analysis because Japan is often compared with only European societies, leading to a highlighting of Japan's peculiarity. The United States is included because its growth in the number of mothers with small children is one of the most important social changes since the 1980s. The United Kingdom is included in our analysis because, like Japan, the proportion of part-time workers among married women is quite high.

Table 2.2 shows the work status of mothers by nation. In Japan, 51.2 percent of mothers are out of the labor force, and among working mothers, 12 percent are either self-employed or family workers. The proportion of Japanese mothers who do not work is close to the proportion of nonworking mothers in Italy. On the other hand, in the United Kingdom and the United States, more mothers are in the labor force than in Japan. The proportion of working mothers is even higher in Sweden than in the United Kingdom and the United States. More than 80 percent of mothers work as employees in Sweden.

In this section, my analysis is restricted to employees since, as we have already seen, the working patterns of employees and self-employed/family workers are different. I also restrict my analysis to only parents and unmarried children. Japan and Taiwan are characterized by a high proportion of multigenerational households (Shirahase 2001), which tend to provide their members with mutually beneficial services. For instance, elderly members enjoy economic security

TABLE 2.2
Mother's work status by nation

	Employees	Self-employed and family workers	Not working
Germany	56.7	4.5	38.8
Italy	37.5	9.2	53.3
Sweden	81.1	3.9	15.0
Taiwan	48.6	10.2	41.2
UK	53.9	4.7	41.4
U.S.	58.3	6.1	35.6
Japan	36.9	11.9	51.2

SOURCES: The data source for Japan is the 1995 National Survey of Living Conditions, and for other nations it is the Luxembourg Income Survey data. The survey year is 1994 for Germany and the United States and 1995 for the other countries.

NOTE: The figures in parentheses are the proportion of part-time workers among mothers who are employees. Other values are percentages of all mothers.

TABLE 2.3
Working mothers' contribution to household income by nation

Mother's income contribution	Germany	Italy	Sweden	Taiwan	UK	U.S.	Japan
Less than 20%	18.5	8.4	20.3	10	43.4	28.8	51.1
20–45%	23.1	47.0	36.6	76.7	39.5	42.4	35.2
45–55%	37.2	26.0	17.9	9.2	7.4	15.3	8.9
55–75%	11.8	11.5	22.1	2.6	5.5	9.6	3.4
75–100%	7.5	4.8	2.9	1.5	4.0	3.3	0.9
100%	1.8	2.2	0.2	0.0	0.1	0.6	0.4

through co-residence with the younger generation (Smeeding and Saunders 1998), and young parents benefit from asking grandparents to look after small children. In order to determine the importance of social support for childbearing and childrearing, I focus on mothers who do not enjoy services within the family and thus concentrate on mothers in nuclear households.

In Japan, the proportion of mothers who work as self-employed or family workers is higher than in the European nations at 11.9 percent. The proportion of working mothers as self-employed or family workers is even higher in Taiwan at 14.5 percent. This high proportion of working mothers as nonemployees characterizes these two Asian societies.

Table 2.3 shows the proportion of the mother's economic contribution to the household by nation. The figures calculated are the proportion of

TABLE 2.4
Mother's work status by age of youngest child

Age of youngest child	Germany	Italy	Sweden	Taiwan	UK	U.S.	Japan
<3	38.4 (70.6)	42.4 (41.9)	83.4 (50.2)	41.2	47.3 (65.6)	54.0 (33.6)	17.6
3 to 5	48.3 (56.9)	44.1 (43.3)	73.9 (64.6)	42.3	56.0 (72.7)	60.0 (33.7)	22.4
6 to 9	63.8 (54.1)	39.1 (36.7)	77.0 (63.0)	45.8	66.6 (71.0)	65.2 (36.9)	29.3
10 to 14	72.3 (42.3)	43.4 (36.5)	70.1 (45.1)	36.9	75.4 (71.4)	65.8 (34.8)	47.6
15 to 17	67.6 (36.5)	31.8 (36.7)	57.6 (47.3)	29.6	67.2 (70.2)	59.1 (37.7)	52.3

NOTE: The first values are the percentage of all mothers who work. Values in parentheses are the percentage of mothers working part-time out of all working mothers.

the mother's gross earnings as a share of household gross income. Japan shows the highest proportion of mothers who earn less than 20 percent of the household income, at 51.1 percent. Almost 90 percent of working mothers earn less than 45 percent of the household income in Japan. Japan is characterized by a high proportion of mothers who earn a low share of the household income, but other societies also show a similar gender-earning gap. Even in Sweden, a majority of mothers earn less than 45 percent of the household economy. The United Kingdom also shows a high proportion of mothers whose earnings comprise a small fraction of the total household economy; 43.4 percent of them earn less than 20 percent of the household economy.

A mother's propensity to work varies with the age of her youngest child. In Japan, the number of mothers with small children aged three and under is limited, as I have already pointed out. Even among the younger generation, a majority supports the idea that mothers should devote themselves to their children when they are younger than three. Table 2.4 presents the proportion of working mothers by the age of their youngest child. The highest proportion of working mothers with very small children younger than three can be found in Sweden; more than 80 percent of these mothers are in the labor force.

Only a small minority of mothers with small children are in the labor force in Japan. The proportion of Japanese working mothers with a child three or under is 17.6 percent, and the proportion of working mothers with children ages three to five is 22.4 percent. The proportion of working mothers with children aged six to nine also remains low, at 29.3 percent, the lowest among the seven countries.

In Taiwan and Italy working mothers with small children are in the minority, 41.2 percent and 42.4 percent, respectively. However, even as

TABLE 2.5
Wife's contribution to household income (%) by age of youngest child

Age of the youngest child	Germany	Italy	Sweden	Taiwan	UK	U.S.	Japan
<3	21.40	43.33	52.91	35.71	30.11	35.51	26.22
3 to 5	29.17	44.19	53.40	34.33	27.16	34.58	29.86
6 to 9	33.24	44.78	52.68	33.36	25.57	33.48	24.51
10 to 14	35.71	43.83	52.55	33.22	24.00	31.84	19.99
15 to 17	35.41	42.51	51.45	36.04	28.00	29.44	22.43
Total	32.63	43.89	52.72	34.18	26.88	33.48	22.9

the age of the youngest child increases, the proportion of working mothers does not increase substantially. It appears that the age of the youngest child does not affect a mother's economic behavior.

In the United States, workers have become a majority since the 1980s among mothers with small children (age three and younger), but mothers' work in the United States is not as common as in Sweden. Working mothers in the United States, however, are characterized by a high proportion of full-time workers: about two-thirds of working mothers are full-time workers. By contrast, the proportion of part-time workers among working mothers is high in the United Kingdom. More than 65 percent of working mothers with the youngest child age three and older are part-time workers in the United Kingdom. In Germany, the proportion of part-time workers among mothers with the youngest child younger than three is very high, but the proportion of part-time workers declines significantly as the age of the youngest child increases.

Table 2.5 shows the proportion of a wife's earnings in the household income by the age of the youngest child among dual-working couples. The proportions show how much the wife contributed to the household income and indicate the importance of the wife's work to household income. Let us look first at mothers with children younger than three. In Japan and Germany, where most mothers with the youngest child younger than three do not work, the proportion of the wife's income is also relatively small, 26.22 percent and 21.4 percent, respectively. On the other hand, Italy shows a high figure at 43.3 percent. Although the proportion of working mothers is relatively low in Italy, once Italian mothers decide to work while having a small child, their contributions to their household incomes are higher than in other societies. Working mothers are a minority in Italy, but this group of mothers probably faces a situation where they must continue their work in order to maintain the income level of the household.

In Sweden, where the majority of mothers with small children younger than three work, the extent of the mother's contribution to the household income is highest at 52.9 percent. The extent of mothers' contributions does not substantially change as the youngest child becomes older. This finding suggests that Swedish mothers' contributions to the household economy largely remain stable no matter how small their children are.

Japan stands out in Table 2.5 in that the contribution of the wife's earning is limited almost without regard to the age of the youngest child. The overall proportion of the mother's earning to the household income is smallest in Japan, at 22.90 percent. The highest value can be seen in Sweden, at 52.72 percent. This observation probably derives from three related points: first, the propensity of Japanese women to interrupt their careers; second, the fact that the increase in the proportion of working mothers with school-age children comes from those who return to work as part-time workers in lesser jobs; and third, the large gender wage gap. A large number of mothers who reenter the labor market do so with low pay, particularly as part-time workers, when their youngest child becomes older. Correspondingly, the number of mothers who stay in the labor market throughout the family formation process is still small in contemporary Japan.

The extent of the economic contribution of mothers to the household income overall does not differ much by the age of the youngest child among the seven countries except in Japan and Germany. According to our results in Table 2.5, mothers who continue working throughout the family formation process appear to be a relatively constant proportion. On the other hand, the extent of the average proportion of the mother's contribution to the household income fluctuates more with the age of her children in Japan than in the other nations. I plan to examine in more detail what such a relatively large fluctuation in the extent of mothers' contributions to the household economy in Japan means using longitudinal data in future research.

Matsuura and Shigeno (2001) and Nagase (1997) have already shown that in examining female labor force patterns, it is important to take into account the part-time or full-time work distinction. The husband's income level affects the likelihood of the wife's full-time work, but not of part-time work. Matsuura and Shigeno (2001) suggested that women assess the three alternatives of full-time work, part-time work, and not

TABLE 2.6
Multinomial logit analysis of mothers' work by nation

	Germany	Italy	Sweden	UK	U.S.	Japan
Full-time						
Constant	2.179	−2.931	−10.462**	−4.112*	−0.414	−10.228**
Age	0.141*	0.438**	0.542**	0.231**	0.291**	0.694**
Age squared	−0.177	−0.523**	−0.635**	−0.292**	−0.038**	−0.078**
Husband's earning	−0.550**	−0.368**	0.260**	−0.022	−0.329**	−0.977**
Higher education	1.474**	1.501**	2.093**	0.985*	1.660**	0.247
High school diploma	0.648**	2.022**	1.433**	0.376	1.263**	0.403
Child younger than 3	−2.412**	−0.082	0.626**	−0.669**	−0.499**	−1.275**
Part-time						
Constant	−7.414**	0.274	−11.495**	−1.782	−0.946	−7.936**
Age	0.328**	0.339**	0.623**	0.119*	0.025	0.403**
Age squared	−0.449**	−0.383**	−0.778**	−0.165*	−0.036	−0.049**
Husband's earning	0.080	−0.404**	0.254**	−0.010	0.054	−0.493*
Higher education	0.591**	2.052**	1.778**	0.386	0.987**	−0.515
High school diploma	0.808**	3.739**	1.565**	0.188	0.723**	0.180
Child younger than 3	−1.525**	−0.049	0.372**	−0.907**	−0.619**	−2.673**

*$p < .05$ **$p < .01$

working at the same time. Therefore, I resort to multinomial analysis to examine the determinants of these three outcomes: full-time work, part-time work, and not working.

Table 2.6 presents the results of a multinomial logit analysis on mothers' working behavior. In this analysis, I use the Social Stratification and Mobility Survey[4] (hereafter, 1995 SSM survey) because the National Survey of Living Conditions does not include the educational variables and full-time and part-time distinction. In the LIS data, I distinguish between full-time and part-time employment by using the working hours per week. If the working hours are shorter than 35 hours, the employment is regarded as part-time.[5] There are three hypotheses to be tested. The first hypothesis is the human capital hypothesis, in which mothers decide to work depending on their level of educational attainment. The higher the educational attainment, the more likely they are to work. The second hypothesis is the household income hypothesis, in which women's economic behavior depends on the level of the household income as represented by the husband's income. According to the Douglas-Arisawa hypothesis, a husband's income level is negatively associated with the probability that his wife works. The third hypothesis is the family-cycle hypothesis, in which having small children is critical for a mother's decision whether or not to work, regardless of her educational level and her husband's income. The presence of a small child discourages mothers from working, no matter how well they are educated or how much their husbands earn.

The dependent variable is the current work status of mothers with children: full-time workers, part-time workers, and not working (reference category). The explanatory variables are created with reference to the three hypotheses. The educational level is represented by two dummy variables: whether mothers obtained higher education or not, and whether they graduated from high school or not. Since the educational system differs greatly across societies, we constructed these dummy variables to present a wide range of educational systems. The log of the husband's income (referred to in our discussion as "husband's income") and whether or not the youngest child is younger than three years (referred to as "child dummy" or "small child") are the explanatory variables, corresponding to the second and the third hypothesis, respectively. We add the mother's age to take into account the age effect, and we also add the square of the age to take into account the nonlinearity in the age effect.

Let us start with the results for Japan. Age, age-squared, husband's income, and the child dummy variable are statistically significant for full-time work, and the same variables also show significant effects for part-time work. The probability of working full-time increases as mothers get older, up to a point, and then decreases at older ages. As Douglas and Arisawa predicted, husbands' incomes are negatively associated with their wives' working behavior. Whether they have a child younger than three significantly affects the mother's work. Having small children discourages mothers from being in the labor force. The educational level of mothers, on the other hand, does not exert any significant effect on whether mothers are in the labor market. The same pattern is found for the contrast between mothers working part-time and mothers not working. Thus, in Japan, the hypothesis about the negative impact of the husband's income level and the family-cycle hypothesis were supported, but the human capital hypothesis was not supported by our analysis.

In the United Kingdom, the effects of age, age-squared, higher education, and a small child are statistically significant in predicting if mothers work on a full-time basis. However, the husband's income does not show a statistically significant effect. In the United Kingdom, how much their husbands earn does not change the probability of mothers' work activity. In the analysis of predicting part-time work (as opposed to no work), only age and the child dummy are statistically significant.

In the United States, all explanatory variables are statistically significant for predicting full-time work (as opposed to no work). Even in the United States, the husband's income negatively affects the likelihood that mothers work full-time. The likelihood of working part-time is affected by the level of education and the presence of a small child. Mothers with high-school diplomas or higher education are more likely to have part-time jobs, and having a small child younger than three discourages mothers from having part-time work. However, the husband's income level does not exert a statistically significant effect.

In Sweden, all the explanatory variables affect the likelihood of working both on a full-time and a part-time basis. It is interesting to note that the husband's income level is positively associated with the wife's work, and having a small child increases the chances of work. I suspect that the positive effect of having small children on mothers' work is partly due to the cohort effect in which the younger generation is more likely to have small children and at the same time more likely to work than the older generation. In Germany, the likelihood of working full-time is affected by all the explanatory variables. Whereas educational attainment is positively associated with the mother's work, the husband's income and the child dummy are negatively associated with the mother's work. The effect of the husband's income disappears when we consider the likelihood of working part-time in Germany.

In sum, the husband's income is negatively associated with a mother's work in all of these countries except Sweden and the United Kingdom. The human capital of the mothers represented by educational level is also an important determinant to mothers' work in all societies except Japan. The lack of the impact of educational attainment among married women in Japan is peculiar among industrial societies, and probably reflects the ongoing constraints on women who would otherwise pursue career ambitions.

Female Income and Fertility

In this section, I analyze the impact of the wife's income level on the number of children she bears. In the previous section, Japanese mothers are characterized by the low level of labor force participation while their children are very small, and the very low level of their economic contribution to the household. In this section, focusing on working women, the effect of income level on the number of children will be examined.

TABLE 2.7
Regression analysis of the number of children among working women by nation

	Germany	Italy	Sweden	UK	U.S.	Japan
Constant	−0.083	0.471**	1.387**	−0.286	1.165**	0.962
Age	0.033**	0.021**	0.037**	0.046**	0.030**	0.043**
High school education	0.029	0.146*	−0.095	0.344*	−0.464**	−0.148*
Higher education	−0.023	0.054	−0.168	0.165	−0.645**	−0.850**
Professional job	−0.131	0.044	−0.065	−0.244**	−0.096**	0.179
Lower white-collar job	−0.269**	−0.154*	0.035	−0.140*	−0.043	0.205*
Farm job	0.334	0.196	0.163	−0.365	0.032	0.259
Own income	−0.032**	0.001	−0.138**	−0.054**	−0.068**	−0.010**
Other income	0.017**	−0.001	0.056**	0.010*	0.026**	−0.019

NOTE: "Own income" is the log of the respondent's own income. For women not working, the income is set at zero. "Other income" is the log of household income other than the wife's income.
*$p < .05$ **$p < .01$

The claim that the increase in the number of married women working outside the home is associated with the low fertility rate in Japan implies that if women are more likely to work and earn higher income, they are less likely to have children. Table 2.7 presents the results of a regression analysis of the number of children among working women who are married. Eight explanatory variables are included in the analysis: age of the respondents; the medium-level education dummy variable indicating whether their educational attainment reaches secondary education or not a higher-education dummy variable indicating whether their educational attainment reaches tertiary education; three occupational dummy variables (using the blue-collar occupation as the base category), representing professional and managerial occupation, lower white-collar occupation such as sale and clerical, and farm occupation; log of the woman's income; and log income of other members of the household that acts as a rough estimate of the husband's income.

The most important finding in Table 2.7 is that all societies, except Italy, show a statistically significant negative effect of women's income on the number of children. The higher a married woman's income, the fewer children she has. Furthermore, Germany, Sweden, the United Kingdom, and the United States show a positive effect of other household members' income on the number of children. Therefore, a relatively high economic power of the wife in the household lowers her fertility behavior. Women may be discouraged from having many children because it probably forces married women to depend more on other family members, most likely their husbands. Alternatively, this negative relationship may show that family is incompatible with career success. In

Japan, there is no significant effect of other members' income in determining the number of children, whereas the husband's income shows a negative effect on the mother's labor force participation (Matsuura and Shirahase 2002).

Educational attainment in Japan, as well as in the United States, negatively affects the number of children. We already know that Japan is peculiar in that higher education does not increase women's economic activity. In most other industrial nations, obtaining higher education increases women's attachment to the labor market while they have children. Some claim that the increased level of education among Japanese women contributes to increased human capital in their offspring (Brinton 1993). It may also signal, as we have mentioned, that women still find it more viable to marry into an income rather than trying to earn it themselves.

Our results suggest that how much wives earn and, consequently, how much they contribute to the household income are important in explaining their fertility levels. The economic power of the wife in the household is a crucial factor in determining the number of children. Therefore, even though the labor force participation rate of women might increase in response to better childcare support, if the gender gap in wages and career trajectories persists, the negative relationship between the wife's economic power in the household and fertility levels will not change.

It is no doubt an important policy issue to expand and improve the provision of childcare facilities and daycare centers, but an equally relevant policy issue deals with how to change the male-breadwinner model of employment and how to make the labor market more gender-equal.

Conclusions

In this chapter, I examined the work profile of married women and the extent of the mother's contribution to the household income in the late 1990s in Japan. Married women still tend to drop out of the labor force in Japan. The growth of employees working outside the family resulted in the physical separation of work and family and led to an emergence of a discontinuous work profile beginning in the 1960s. As they are currently configured, white-collar clerical and sales jobs discourage women from staying in the labor market because of the limited prospects for career advancement.

More than 70 percent of married women in Japan stopped working at the time of the birth of the first child. The probability of quitting their job was higher if they worked as a clerical worker or in any nongovernment job. Married women who were employed in large firms with more than 1,000 employees were more likely to stop working than those who were employed in small-scale firms. Even in the late 1990s, the majority of married women showed a discontinuous work pattern due to their family responsibilities.

The majority of working mothers return to work, after a temporary withdrawal due to childrearing, in order to supplement the household economy in Japan. In other words, most working mothers in Japan do not develop their own careers, and are simply secondary earners in the family to augment family income. This low proportion of mothers who invest in their career through continuous involvement in the labor force accounts for the persistence of the M-shaped curve of female labor force participation at the macro level. Furthermore, when the wives' economic contribution to the household budget is high, indicating that their incomes are relatively high, they tend to have fewer children. Offering the opportunity of better jobs for women and helping them stay at work throughout their family cycle will be crucial to lowering the high cost of marriage and childbirth in Japan.

Under the current work setting in many Japanese firms, there is no assumption that family responsibilities are shared by both the husband and the wife. A strong male-breadwinner model of employment has been firmly established since the era of high economic growth (Ochiai 1995; Mari Osawa 1993; Ueno 1990). The very important point that tends to be missed in arguments about family-friendly policies is how to make it possible for fathers as well as mothers to be involved in childrearing and caring for other family members. It is difficult for fathers to share family responsibilities given their extremely long working hours. In fact, one of the significant factors in explaining the extent of the husband's participation in household chores is his work time. The longer the husband's working hours, the less likely he is to do family chores (Shirahase 2000b). Therefore, making the workplace more family-friendly could be accomplished by making the employment system more flexible for men as well as for women. If a more flexible way of work, particularly during the early stage of family formation, is available for not only women but also men, the temporary withdrawal from the labor force or temporary shift to part-time work will probably not have the same detrimental effects on career development. Building a family-friendly welfare state requires reconstruction of the fundamental employment system, rather than simply providing childcare support services to women workers.

Notes

1. The data come from the National Survey of Welfare and Attitudes conducted by a group of sociologists (headed by Professor Shogo Takegawa, University of Tokyo) in April 2000.

2. I constructed three occupational dummy variables with "blue-collar occupation" as the reference. They were self-employed dummy including family workers, professional dummy, and white-collar occupation dummy, such as clerical and sales.

3. This research was conducted as part of a project entitled "A Study of the Future Social Security System in Response to Changes in the Family Structure and Employment Pattern," which was supported by the Health Science Grants (2001–2002), Japanese Ministry of Health, Labor, and Welfare.

4. The SSM surveys, which are national representative surveys, have been conducted by Japanese social scientists every ten years since 1955, and female respondents have been included in the survey since 1985. I would like to thank the 1995 SSM Survey committee for allowing me to analyze the data.

5. Taiwan is excluded from our analysis because I could not make the distinction between full-time and part-time employment given the data.

References

Atoh, Makoto. 2000. *Gendai Jinkogaku Shoshi-korei-ka no Kiso Chishiki* [Contemporary Demography: A Basic Knowledge of Aging Society with Low Fertility]. Tokyo: Nihon Hyron Sha.

Brinton, Mary C. 1993. *Women and the Economic Miracle: Gender and Work in Postwar Japan*. Berkeley: University of California Press.

Brinton, Mary C., and Hang-yue Ngo. 1993. "Age and Sex in Occupational Structure: A United States–Japan Comparison." *Sociological Forum* 8: 93–111.

Esping-Andersen, Gosta. 1990. *The Three Worlds of Welfare Capitalism*. Princeton: Princeton University Press.

Fujin Shonen Kyokai. 1994. *Yojiki no Kono Hahaoya no Seikatsu to Shugyo no Jittai ni kansuru Chosa* [Survey on the Living Conditions and Work Among Mothers with Small Children]. Tokyo: Fujin Shonen Kyokai.

Gauthier, Anne Helene. 1996. *The State and the Family: A Comparative Analysis of Family Policies in Industrial Countries*. Oxford: Clarendon Press.

56 *Sawako Shirahase*

Gelb, Joyce. 1988. "The Equal Employment Opportunity Law in Japan: A Decade of Change for Japanese Women?" *Yale Asia-Pacific Review* 1(Fall): 41–65.

Hanami, Tadashi. 2000. "Equal Employment Revisited." *Japan Labor Bulletin* 39:5–10.

Higuchi, Yoshio. 1991. *Nihon Keizai to Shugyo Kodo* [Japan Economy and Employment Behavior]. Tokyo: Toyo Keizai Shinpo sha.

———. 1994. "Ikuji Kyugyo no Jissho Bunseki [The Empirical Analysis on the Parental Leave]," in *Gendai Kazoku to Shakai Hosho* [Family and Social Security in the Contemporary Society], edited by the Institute of Social Security Research. Tokyo: University of Tokyo Press.

———. 1996. "Shokugyo Ido Bunseki [The Analysis of Occupational Mobility]," in *Shohisaikatsu nikansuru Paneru Chosa* [The Panel Survey of the Consumer Life], edited by Kakei Keizai Kenkyu Jo [Institute for Research on Household Economics], 129–155. Tokyo: Kakei Keizai Kenkyu Jo.

Higuchi, Yoshio, and Abe Masahiro. 1992. "Rodoujikan Seido to Jugyoin no Kigyo Teichakuritsu [Working Time System and the Retention Rate of Workers with the Firm]." *Keuzai Kenkyu* [Journal of Economics] 43: 203–213.

Higuchi, Yoshio, Masahiro Abe, and J. Waldfogel. 1998. "Nichieibei niokeru Ikuji Kyugyo / Shussan Kyugyo Seido to Josei Shugyo [Parental Leave and Maternity Leave Policies and Women's Work in Japan, the United States, and Great Britain]." *Jinko Mondai Kenkyu* [Journal of Population Problems] 53: 49–66.

Hirao, Keiko. 1999. "Joshi no Shoki Kyaria Keiseiki ni Okeru Rodo Shijo heno Teichakusei: Gakureki to Kazoku Ibento wo Megutte" [The Effect of Higher Education on the Rate of Labor-Force Exit for Married Japanese Women]. *Nihon Rodo Kenkyu Zasshi* [The Monthly Journal of the Japan Institute of Labor] 471:29–41.

Imada, Sachiko. 1996. "Josei Rodo to Shugyo Keizoku [Women's Work and Work Profile]." *Nihon Rodo Kenkyu Zasshi* [Japanese Journal of Labor Studies] 433: 37–48.

Institute for Health Economics and Policy. 1997. *Fukushi Jujitsu no Keizai Koka ni kansuru Kenkyu Hokokusho* [The Report on the Economic Effect of the Growth of Welfare].

Iwai, Hachiro. 1990. "Josei no Raifukosu no Dotai [The Dynamics of Women's Life Course]," pp. 155–184 in *Gendai Nihon no Kaiso Kozo Kyoiku to Shakai Ido* [The Stratification Structure in Contemporary Japan: Education and Social Mobility], edited by Joji Kikuchi. Tokyo: University of Tokyo Press.

Iwai, Hachiro, and Rinko Manabe. 2000. "M-jigata Shugyo Patan no Teichaku to sono Imi [The Stability of the M-shaped Pattern of Labor Force Participation and Its Meaning]," pp. 67–91 in *Nihon no Kaiso Shisutemu Jenda, Shijo, Kazoku* [Japan's Stratification Structure: Gender, Market, and Family], edited by Kazuo Seiyama. Tokyo: University of Tokyo Press.

Japan Institute of Labor. 1996. Ikuji Kyugyo Seido ga Koyo Kanri / Shugyo Kodo ni Oyobosu Eikyo nikansuru Kenkyu Kenkyuhokokusho [The Report on the Impact of Parental Leave Arrangement on Labor Management and Work Behavior]. No. 83.

Josei Rodo Kyokai. 1999. "Famiri Furendori Kigyo wo Mezashite [Toward the Family Friendly Firms]." Report on the research project. Tokyo: Josei Rodo Kyokai.

Knapp, Kiyoko Kamio. 1995. "Still Office Flowers: Japanese Women Betrayed by the Equal Employment Opportunity Law." *Harvard Women's Law Journal* 18:83–137.

Manabe, Rinko. 1998. "20 Saidai no Shurou Teishi to Kekkon/Shussan [Work Interruption at the 20s and Marriage/Childbearing]," pp. 31–45 in *The 1995 SSM Shosa Shiri-zu 13 Jenda to Raifukosu*, edited by Hachiro Iwai. Tokyo: 1995 SSM Survey Committee.

Matsuura, Katsumi, and Yukiko Shigeno. 1996. *Josei no Shugyo to Tomi no Bunpai* [Women's Work and the Distribution of Wealth]. Tokyo: Nihon Hyoron Sha.

———. 2001. *Josei no Sentaku to Kakei Chochiku* [Women's Choice and the Saving of the Household Income]. Tokyo: Nihon Hyoron Sha.

Matsuura, Katsumi, and Sawako Shirahase. 2002. "Kikonjosei no Shugyo Kettei to Kosodate—Korekara no Shakai Hosho Seisaku ni Mukete [Determinants of Married Women to Work and Childrearing: Toward the Future Social Security System]." *Quarterly of Social Security Research* 38(3): 188–198.

Ministry of Health and Welfare of Japan. 1997. *Annual Report on Health and Welfare 1995–96*. Tokyo: Japan International Corporation of Welfare Services.

Ministry of Labor. 1996. *Joshi Koyo Kanri Kihon Chosa* [Basic Survey on Personnel Management of Women Workers]. Tokyo: Roudo Tokei Kyokai.

———. 1998. *Hataraku Josei no Jitsujo* [Current Situation of Working Women]. Tokyo: 21 Seiki Shokugyo Zaidan.

Morita, Yoko. 2002. "Hoiku Seisaku to Josei no Shugyo [The Childcare Policy and Women's Work]," pp. 215–240 in *Shoshi Shakai no Kosodate Shien* [Childcare Support in the Society with Low Fertility], edited by the National Institute of Population and Social Security Research. Tokyo: University of Tokyo Press.

Morita, Yoko, and Yoshihiro Kaneko. 1998. "Ikujikyugyo Seido no Fukyu to Josei Koyosha no Kinzoku Nensu [The Prevalence of Parental Leave Arrangement and the Length of Work for Women's Workers]." *Nihon Rodo Kenkyu Zasshi* [Japanese Journal of Labor Studies] 459: 50–62.

Nagase, Nobuko. 1997. "Jose no Shugyo Sentaku: Kakeinai Seisan to Rokyo Kyokyu [Women's Choice to Work: Household Production and Labor Supply]," pp. 79–312 in *Koyo Kanko no Henka to Josei Rokyo* [The Change in Employment System and Women's Work], edited by Chuma Hiroyuki and Suruga Teruyuki. Tokyo: University of Tokyo Press.

————. 1999. "Shoshika no Yoin: Shugyo Kankyo ka Kachikan no Henka ka [Factors for the Decline of the Fertility Rate: Employment Conditions or the Change of the Attitude?]." *Jinko Mondai Kenkyu* [Journal of Population Problems] 55: 1–18.

Nakai, Miki, and Akachi Yumiko. 2000. "Shijo Sanka/Shakai Sanka [Participation in the Labor Force and in the Social Activity]," pp. 111–131 in *Nihon no Kaiso Shisutemu Jenda, Shijo, Kazoku* [Japan's Stratification Structure: Gender, Market, and Family], edited by Kazuo Seiyama. Tokyo: University of Tokyo Press.

National Institute of Population and Social Security Research. 1998. "The Eleventh National Family Survey: Marriage and Fertility in Japan." Tokyo: National Institute of Population and Social Security Survey.

————. 2000. Latest Demographic Statistics 2000. Tokyo: National Institute of Population and Social Security Survey.

Ochiai, Emiko. 1995. *21 Seiki Kazoku e* [Toward the Family in the Twenty-First Century]. Tokyo: Yuhikaku.

Osawa, Machiko. 1993. *Keizai Henka to Joshi Roko* [Economic Change and Women's Work]. Tokyo: Nihon Keizai Hyoron sha.

————. 1998. *Atarashii Kazoku no Tameno Keizaigaku: Kawariyuku Kigyoshakai no nakano Josei* [Economics for Families in the New Era: Women in the Changing Firm-oriented Society]. Tokyo: Chuou Koron sha.

Osawa, Mari. 1993. *Kigyo Chushin Shakai wo Koete* [Beyond the Firm-Oriented Society]. Tokyo: Jijitsushinsha.

Shigeno, Yukiko, and Yasushi Ogusa. 1998. "Ikuji Kyugyo Seido no Josei no Kekkon to Shugyo Keizoku heno Eikyo [The Impact of Parental Leave on Women's Marriage and Work Continuation]." *Nihon Rodo Kenkyu Zasshi* [Japanese Journal of Labor Studies] 459: 39–49.

————. 2001. "Ikuji Shiensaku no Kekkon / Shussan / Shugyo ni Ataeru Eikyo [The Impact of Parental Leave Policy on Marriage, Childbirth, and Work]," pp. 17–50 in *Shakai Fukushi to Kazoku no Keizaigaku* [Social Welfare and Economics of the Family], edited by Yasushi Iwamoto. Tokyo: Toyo Keizai Shinpo Sha.

Shintani, Yuriko. 1998. "Kekkon/Shussanki no Josei no Shugyo to sono Kitei Yoin—1980 nendai iko no Shussei Kodo no Henka tono Kanren yori [Women's Work at the Time of Marriage and Childbirth and Its Determinant Factor with the Change in Childbirth Behavior Since the 1980s]." *Jinko Mondai Kenkyu* [Journal of Population Problems] 54: 46–62.

Shirahase, Sawako. 1997. "Women in the Labour Market: Mobility and Work Life in Japan." PhD thesis, Oxford University.

————. 1999. "Kaikyu/Kaiso, Kekkon to Jenda: Kekkon ni itaru Kaiso Ketsugo Patan [Class, Marriage, and Gender: The Pattern of the Process to Marriage as Class Matching]." *Riron to Hoho* [Journal of Mathematical Sociology] 14: 5–18.

————. 2000a. "Women's Increased Higher Education and the Declining Fertility Rate in Japan." *Review of Population and Social Policy* 9: 47–63.

————. 2000b. "Kateinai Seibetsu Yakuwari Bungyo to Shakaiteki Shien nikannsuru Ichikosatsu [A Study of Gender Division of Labor Within the Household and Expectation to Social Support]." *Kikan Shakai Hosho Kenkyu* [Quarterly of Social Security Research] 34: 256–268.

————. 2001. "Japanese Income Inequality by Household Type in Comparative Perspective." Luxembourg Income Studies Working Paper no. 268.

Shirahase, Sawako, and Ishida Hiroshi. 1994. "Gender Inequality in Occupational Structure in Japan, Great Britain, and the United States." *International Journal of Comparative Sociology* 35(3–4): 188–206.

Siaroff, Alan. 1994. "Work, Welfare, and Gender Equality: A New Typology," in *Gendering Welfare States*, edited by Diane Sainsbury. London: Sage.

Smeeding, Timothy, and Peter Saunders. 1998. "How Do the Elderly in Taiwan Fare Cross-Nationally? Evidence from the Luxembourg Income Study (LIS) Project." Luxembourg Income Study Working Paper no. 183.

Statistics Bureau. 1997. *Rodoryoku Chosa Tokubetsu Chosa* [Special Edition of Labor Force Survey]. Tokyo: Management and Coordination Agency, Japan.

Tomita, Yasunobu. 1994. "Josei ga Hatarakitsuzukeru kotono dekiru Shokuba Kankyo: Ikuji Kyugyo to Rodo Jikan Seido no Yakuwari [The Workplace Environment That Allows Women to Continue to Work]." *Osaka Furitsu Daigaku Keizai Kenkyu* [Journal of Economic Studies at Osaka Furitsu Daigaku] 40: 43–56.

Tsumura, Atsuko. 2002. "Kazoku Seisaku no Kokusai Hikaku [Crossnational Comparison of Family Policies]," pp. 19–46 in *Shoshi Shakai no Kosodate Shien* [The Childcare Support in the Society with Low Fertility], edited by the National Institute of Population and Social Security Research. Tokyo: University of Tokyo Press.

Tsuya, Noriko. 1999. "Shusseiritsu no Teika to Kosodate Shien [The Decline in the Fertility Rate and Childcare Support]." *Kikan Shakai Hosho Kenkyu* [Quarterly of Social Security Research] 34: 348–360.

Ueno, Chizuko. 1990. *Kafuchosei to Shihonsei* [Patriarchy and Capitalism]. Tokyo: Iwanami Shoten.

————. 1998. "Shusshoritsu Teika: Dareno Mondai ka [The Decline of the Fertility Rate: For Whom Is It the Problem?]" *Jinko Mondai Kenkyu* [Journal of Population Problems] 54: 41–62.

Yamagami, Toshihiko. 1999. "Shussan/Ikuji to Joshi Shugyo tono Ryoritsu Kanosei nitsuite [The Chances for the Reconciliation Between Childbearing/Childrearing and Work]." *Kikan Shakai Hosho Kenkyu* [Quarterly of Social Security Research] 36:52–64.

Zenkoku Hoiku Dantai Renrakukai to Hoiku Kenkyujo. 1997. *Hoiku Hakusho* [White Paper on Childrearing]. Tokyo: Sodo Bunka.

PART TWO

Constraints on the Demand for Female Labor

Gendering the Varieties of Capitalism: Gender Bias in Skills and Social Policies

MARGARITA ESTÉVEZ-ABE

Introduction

Despite recent improvements, gender inequality in the labor market still persists even in the most advanced industrial societies. Women are generally less likely to hold positions of responsibility; women tend to be segregated into a narrower range of occupations; and women are paid less. Even in Scandinavian countries, otherwise known for their success in achieving gender equality, women are segregated into "female jobs." This chapter seeks to explain why such gender inequality persists.

To this end, this chapter focuses on national skill profiles. It argues that the degree to which countries rely on specific skills rather than general skills produces labor market bias against women. In explaining gender inequality, this chapter draws together two separate literatures: one, the literature on *gendering* the welfare state (hereafter referred to as GWS); and two, the literature on varieties of capitalism (hereafter VOC). The GWS literature has produced the most vibrant and exciting research on welfare states in recent years. It has identified gender bias in welfare programs, recategorized welfare states in a more gender-sensitive perspective, and identified the impact of the welfare state on employment patterns of women. I argue that such *gendering* perspective needs to be extended beyond the welfare state if we are to fully understand the status of women in the labor market. This is where I bring in the VOC literature.

The VOC literature has improved our understanding of how different market economies operate. It has identified how key institutions of the economy work in conjunction with one another to form a web of institutional complementarities (see Hall and Gingerich 2001; Hall and Soskice 2001). The most important message of this literature is that—contrary to what economic textbooks suggest—an economically efficient choice depends on the availability of specific sets of institutions. Let me use an example to illustrate this point. The effectiveness of seniority wages as work incentives is contingent on the institutional context. If the future of the firm is uncertain, seniority wages will fail to motivate rational young workers. Certain kinds of institutions, however, can affect the motivation of young workers by reducing future uncertainty. Industrial regulations that limit competition, financial regulations that make takeovers virtually impossible, and employment regulations that make layoff costly can all contribute to making seniority wages highly attractive.

This VOC approach, I argue, has two important ramifications for the study of gender. One, the institutional complementarities that sustain different national skill regimes affect patterns of gender segregation, because some types of skills are more gender segregating than others (Estévez-Abe 2005; Estévez-Abe, Iversen, and Soskice 2001). Two, we need to examine the effects of women-friendly policies in the broader institutional context that sustains a particular model of capitalism.

This chapter is organized in three sections. The first section introduces in greater detail the puzzles that motivate this chapter. The second section presents an analytical framework that identifies the gender bias of different skills and how particular types of social policy exacerbate or mitigate the bias. The third section examines whether the framework put forth in the second section can account for the cross-national patterns of occupational segregation by gender.

Gender and the Welfare State: Unsolved Puzzles

Recent scholarly efforts to *gender* the welfare state have contributed to a better understanding of how different social policy regimes affect women. Traditionally, scholars have shown little interest in understanding the gender implications of different welfare states. Esping-Andersen's taxonomy of three worlds of welfare capitalism, which distinguishes welfare states in terms of the degree of *decommodification* and *stratification*, is a classic example (Esping-Andersen 1990).[1] Feminists criticized Esping-Andersen for his exclusive concern for the fate of male workers. As Ann Orloff (1993) aptly points out, Esping-Andersen failed to see that *decommodification* mainly concerned men since the work of

many women was yet to be *commodified*. For instance, since a large number of women in advanced industrial societies engaged in unpaid work,
conservative welfare states that link benefits to work categorically dis-
advantage women more than welfare states based on social rights. Yet
Esping-Andersen (1990) neglected such potentially important gender
consequences of welfare states. Neither did he pay attention to social
policy that mattered for supporting working mothers such as public
provision of childcare and maternity and parental leaves.

A decade of *gendering* the welfare state has taught us that welfare
states differ from one another in terms of how they treat women and
family (Daly 1994; Orloff 1993; Sainsbury 1994). On the one hand, there
are welfare states that are geared to protecting breadwinners' wages
and the traditional family (i.e., the breadwinner husband and his dependent housewife and children). Other welfare states, on the other
hand, provide more social services to socialize domestic care based on
the two-earner family. On the basis of feminist insights, scholars have
begun to explore the origins of different gender policies and also to
explain patterns of female employment in advanced industrial societies (see Esping-Andersen 1999; Gornick 1999; Gornick et al. 1996, 1997;
Huber and Stephens 2001, 2002; Sainsbury 1994).

At first, scholars expected women-friendly Scandinavian countries
to score high on gender equality. Despite their well-known commitment to egalitarian agenda, a closer examination of international data
shows that women-friendly social democratic countries are not necessarily the only ones that have succeeded in promoting gender equality
(Anker 1998; Melkas and Anker 1997). Neither are they always the best
performers regarding gender equality. Ironically, liberal countries that
provided little support to working mothers perform well on various
gender-equality scores.

Figures 3.1, 3.2, and 3.3 demonstrate how countries compare on the
following three dimensions of gender equality: (a) female labor force
participation; (b) occupational segregation by gender; and (c) gender wage gap. Figure 3.1 indicates that, despite their meager—or nonexistent at times—maternity leave benefits and public childcare provisions, some of the liberal countries actually do very well on female
labor force participation. Figure 3.2 focuses on one aspect of occupational segregation measured as concentration of women into female-
dominated jobs. Again, we observe that Scandinavian welfare states
are not always high performers. On the contrary, as far as occupational
segregation is concerned, Scandinavian states do worse than some of

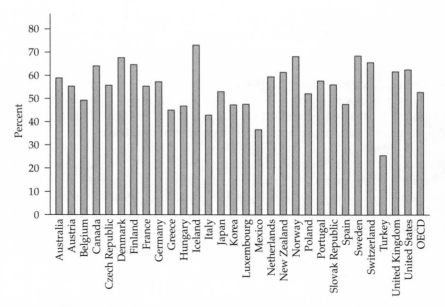

FIGURE 3.1 Female Labor Force Participation Rate, 2002

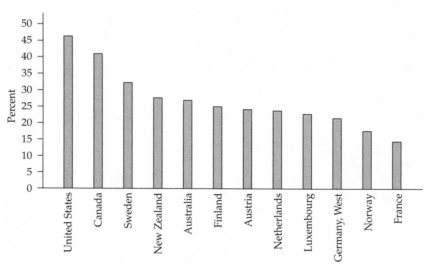

FIGURE 3.2 Percentage of Women Employed in Female-Dominated Occupations

SOURCE: Data from Anker 1998

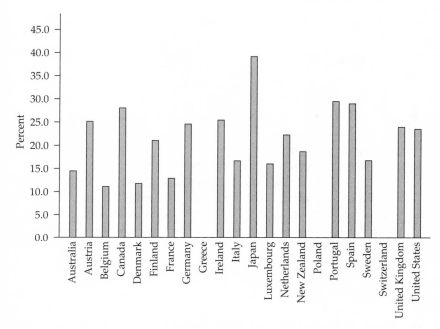

FIGURE 3.3 Gender Wage Gap (How Much More Full-Time Men Make Relative to Full-Time Women)

the conservative countries, which uphold the traditional family. When we turn to the gender wage gap, Scandinavian states are far from alone in narrowing the gender wage gap (Figure 3.3). Here we see Italy and Australia, for example, doing as well as Scandinavian countries, although their welfare states differ significantly from the social democratic model.

These comparative patterns of gender inequality do not readily square with the conventional wisdom. This chapter is particularly interested in two puzzles that emerge: (1) Why have liberal welfare states, with their scant support for working women, achieved high levels of gender equality? (2) Why does occupational segregation persist in Scandinavian countries? Some scholars have provided partial explanations.

Esping-Andersen attributes high female participation rates to the degree of *defamiliarization* in his newer book (Esping-Andersen 1999). In this later work, he responds to his feminist critics by expanding the scope of analysis to include the family as a unit of welfare provision in addition to the state and the market. He notes that some welfare regimes *defamiliarize* care, whereas others do not. *Defamiliarization*, so he argues, can occur either through socialization of family care by the welfare state or through creating a market for it. Therefore, both public provision of social services and the availability of relatively cheap private care services in liberal welfare states lead to *defamiliarization*. Esping-Andersen uses the high degree of *defamiliarization* to explain why not only social democratic welfare states but also liberal ones have achieved high female labor participation rates.

Esping-Andersen's original thinking about the postindustrial employment trajectories of his three worlds of welfare capitalism is intact in his analysis of *defamiliarization*: it is precisely the meagerness of liberal welfare states that explains the supply of cheap labor, which is vital for the growth of cheap service jobs (Esping-Andersen 1990, 1999).[2]

Esping-Andersen's new framework, however, still leaves the aforementioned puzzles unresolved. It does not provide a satisfactory answer as to why gender segregation should persist or even be higher in social democratic welfare states and why women in some liberal welfare states (Australia and New Zealand) do better than their Scandinavian counterparts in achieving wage parity with men. Let us look at occupational segregation first. Esping-Andersen sees more than mere *defamiliarization* in social democratic welfare states: they also generate public sector jobs for women. This view is not unique to him. Others have also noted that social democratic welfare states generally create lots of stable public sector jobs for women (Klausen 1999; Huber and Stephens 2001; OECD 1994; Pontusson and Swenson 1996). The Organization for Economic Cooperation and Development (OECD) report on female employment patterns indicates that the public sector provided more general skill jobs that suited women (OECD 1994).

This explanation accounts for why women are overrepresented in public sector jobs, but does not explain why highly educated Scandinavian women have not been able to do as well in private sector firms in resuming managerial positions as their North American counterparts have. Esping-Andersen's argument about high rates of labor force participation of women in liberal countries is based on the assumption that the equivalent services of care have been provided by the market in liberal countries. If that is the case, we should see a degree of segregation of women in care jobs equivalent to the overrepresentation of women in Scandinavian public sector jobs. Nonetheless, despite the growth of service jobs that similarly require general skills, women in liberal welfare states seem to have done better in advancing to managerial positions than Scandinavian women.

Neither does Esping-Andersen explain why some liberal welfare states should achieve high levels of gender wage parity. This is based on the idea that liberal welfare states have deregulated labor markets with greater wage dispersion. It follows from Esping-Andersen's argument that it is the presence of cheap, low-skill service jobs in liberal welfare states that makes market-based personal services available to working mothers and wives. The combination of the high female labor force participation and wage parity in liberal Australia and New Zealand remains a puzzle.

An alternative approach exists. A number of scholars began to pay attention to differences in the legal environment such as the presence of laws on equal opportunity, affirmative action, and labor standards geared to protecting women's health—prohibition of women's nighttime work, for instance (Chang 2000; O'Connor, Orloff, and Shaver 1999). This approach very effectively explains: (1) why patterns of segregation change in certain countries at particular points in time; and (2) why some countries that are otherwise similar might have very different employment patterns. However, it does not explain how countries with similar legislative conditions (Scandinavian countries legally mandate equality of access as strongly as the United States and Canada do) still may display different patterns of segregation.

This chapter takes altogether a different approach in answering the aforementioned unresolved puzzles by integrating insights from the VOC literature. As the VOC literature elaborates, market economies form distinctive clusters of specific institutions. The gender effects of welfare states need to be placed in this broader institutional context. This chapter looks at the interaction between different skill regimes that characterize different models of capitalism and different welfare states. Comparatively speaking, some market economies display different compositions of skills among their workforce. Soskice (1990, 1991) has shown that vocational training systems vary significantly from country to country because countries are endowed differently in terms of institutions that are necessary to efficiently invest in particular kinds of skills. Estévez-Abe et al. (2001) demonstrated that welfare programs are among those institutions that are necessary to sustain certain types of skill regimes.

These skill regimes are highly relevant to patterns of occupational segregation by gender. As labor economists have argued, differences in human capital endowment between the two sexes are important sources of occupational segregation (see Becker 1985). I argue that some skills are inherently biased against women. Hence those skill regimes that rely on and reward investments in such skills exacerbate the gender skill gap. This, I claim, explains cross-national patterns of occupational gender inequality better than explanations that solely look at the degree of policy support for working mothers and the scope of service sector employment.

Skills, Welfare States, and Gender

This section lays out the logic of gender bias in skills and discusses how different types of social policy might exacerbate or mitigate it. Before we can discuss gender bias in skills, it is necessary to introduce crucial qualitative differences between different types of skills.

Although political scientists generally speak of a skilled/unskilled dichotomy, differences between skills are more complex. We can distinguish three skills following Estévez-Abe et al. (2001): general, industry-specific, and firm-specific skills. These skills vary in terms of portability across employers, the locus of training, and atrophy rate, to borrow Polachek's terminology (i.e., some skills become obsolete or decline when not used for a long period of time) (Polachek 1981). General and industry-specific skills possess high levels of portability because employers other than a person's current employer value them. Portability is especially high when these skills are certified in an objectively recognizable form (i.e., school diploma, vocational certification). Firm-specific skills, in contrast, are very limited in portability, as only the current employer finds them valuable.

Another important dimension in which skills vary is the locus of training. General skills are acquired through school-based education or through off-the-job training (e.g., leadership courses). Training for industry-specific skills can either take place in schools or be acquired through vocational schools or apprenticeship programs, depending on the country. Firm-specific skills are, however, solely provided by on-the-job training, and are never certified (at least in a manner that makes sense to outside employers). Compared to general and industry-specific skills, firm-specific skills involve the highest degree of employer commitment because employers directly plan, provide for, and supervise the skill acquisition by the worker.

Furthermore, skills can vary in terms of what Polachek calls "atrophy rate." Some skills can become obsolete more rapidly than others. This is likely to be the case for skills that are affected by rapid technological and market changes. According to Polachek's calculation, engineering jobs and managerial jobs record a higher rate of atrophy whereas service jobs suffer much less from atrophy.

Gender Bias of Skills

Women are more likely than men to interrupt their work life in order to tend to their family needs. For this reason, skill qualities such as portability, locus of training, and atrophy affect women differently from men. Firm-specific skills are biased against women most. Limited portability of firm-specific skills makes such skills unattractive for women who plan to interrupt their career in the future, since their potentially short tenure at the same firm renders their firm-specific skill investment useless every time they exit and reenter the labor force. Furthermore, any work discontinuity early in one's career can jeopardize the process of firm-specific skill acquisition, because the critical skill acquisition period coincides with a woman's childbearing years.

Even when women themselves are determined to put their career first, problems still persist due to employers' discrimination against women, which labor economists have named "statistical discrimination" (Mincer and Polachek 1974). Since employers have to pay for the cost of recruitment and the training of new workers, they are sensitive to turnover rate. Because women generally quit more often than men, employers discriminate against women when hiring in order to minimize the loss of their search costs and training costs. This occurs independently of whether a particular female job applicant plans to quit or not. Instead of gathering more information, which is costly, employers simply assume all women are equally likely to quit. Because employers have to bear the large portion of the cost of on-the-job training, the tendency for statistical discrimination will be more acute for jobs that require firm-specific skills. Such discrimination denies women a chance to acquire firm-specific skills.

School-based vocational education is much more gender-neutral because it does not involve employers. Women can enroll in vocational programs of their choice if they meet the academic criteria. Most certified general skills (including high school diploma, BA, MBA) and some industry-specific skills (e.g., certified nurses, schoolteachers, computer programmers) fall into this category. In some countries, training for industry-specific skills is provided through apprenticeship programs.

This again opens the door for statistical discrimination as employers get to choose among applicants for apprenticeship slots.

These skill biases suggest that—other things being equal—women are more likely to invest in general skills and skills that are shielded from technological changes. We can thus expect to find fewer women in occupations that require firm-specific skills and apprenticeship-based skills than in general skill jobs.

Gender Bias of Welfare States

Welfare states come back into our story here because they affect the skill investment decisions of workers and employers (Estévez-Abe et al. 2001). We have already discussed how general, industry-specific, and firm-specific skills carry different degrees of "investment risks" due to their respective portability from one employer to another. The more limited the portability of her skill, the more vulnerable the worker is to potential employment termination. Welfare states provide an important insurance mechanism that safeguards skill investments (Mares 1997, 2003).

Welfare states, for instance, can interfere to make layoffs very costly or provide public wage subsidies for redundant workers. Such provisions, when institutionalized, send strong signals to workers that their investments in firm-specific skills will be safeguarded. Similarly, generous unemployment benefits can protect industry-specific skill investments. Unemployed skilled workers can collect benefits that are tied to their skilled wages while they wait for job openings that pay the same skill premium as before. The other side of the story is that, in the absence of generous unemployment benefits and employment protection, workers are more likely to invest in general skills rather than specific skills.

In short, welfare programs constitute important components of institutional complementarities that sustain distinctive skill regimes that rely on specific skills. Hall and Gingerich (2001) have demonstrated how measures of employment protection and other institutions with similar effects (i.e., legal barriers to mergers and acquisitions, anticompetitive regulations that protect market shares of existing firms) correlate with abundance in specific skills.

These complementarities that sustain skill regimes are far from gender-neutral, because specific skills—firm-specific skills, in particular—are gender-biased. When institutions do little to level the playing field for women to overcome the bias, they de facto exacerbate occupational segregation by gender. Employment protection and generous unemployment benefits, for instance, treat men and women differently. They reduce uncertainties that men face, but they do little to address additional uncertainties that women face in making career choices. Let us elaborate on this point.

Men only have to calculate the relative merits of career investments in terms of prospective lifetime earnings, employment security, and the maintenance of skilled wages during unemployment spells. In contrast, for a woman to commit to skill investments, she needs to consider a whole range of uncertainties such as: (1) whether she will be able to keep her job after childbirth; (2) whether she will be compensated for the loss of income (i.e., returns on her skill investments) during pregnancy and childrearing; and (3) whether her skills will become obsolete during her career interruptions for childrearing. Employment protection that aims at preventing layoffs hence fails to address the employment risks facing women. Neither do generous unemployment benefits during business downturns address women's need for compensation during time off work due to their biological and social roles. As a consequence, these policy measures facilitate male skill investments while worsening women's relative positions.

In short, in occupations that require firm-specific skills we can expect high levels of employment security with high levels of firm-specific skill acquisition by men, and underrepresentation of women. Employment security and generous unemployment benefits are, for similar reasons, likely to exacerbate underrepresentation of women in occupations that require gender-biased industry-specific skills (i.e., those available only through apprenticeships and those with high atrophy rates).

Women-Friendly Policies and Skill Bias

We have so far argued that the greater uncertainties that women face in the labor market (i.e., discontinuity of work) explain the gender skill gap largely responsible for occupational segregation. In other words, policy measures that level the playing field for women, enabling them to acquire skill profiles similar to men's, would ultimately reduce occupational segregation by gender. This section evaluates whether women-friendly policies level the playing field for women or not.

To reiterate, women face three types of uncertainties: (1) possibility of dismissal due to pregnancy and other family-related contingencies;

(2) loss of income during work interruptions; and (3) declining skills during work interruptions. Statutory maternity leave serves as extra-employment protection by prohibiting unfair dismissal due to pregnancy. In its strongest form, statutory maternity and parental leave guarantees mothers' return to the jobs they held before childbirth. A generous paid maternity and parental leave protects women against loss of income during pregnancy and childrearing. Thus these policies are almost equivalent to what generous unemployment benefits are to men. Publicly subsidized childcare, in turn, reduces women's time off work.

It is important to note that different women-friendly policies possess different skill effects—sometimes just the opposite. Although both generous paid leaves and childcare might promote women's attachment to employment (i.e., higher female labor force participation), the former keeps women off work whereas the latter reduces women's time off work. When the take-up rate of paid leave is higher for women than for men, paid leave can exacerbate existing gender bias.

For firm-specific skill investment, a long paid leave can be detrimental. Because accumulation of firm-specific skills takes place through on-the-job training, time off work during the early years of a woman's career interrupts her skill acquisition, leading to lower earnings. The length of statutory maternity and parental leaves also affects employers' costs and hence their willingness to hire women.[3] When leaves are long, employers face three options: (1) hire replacement workers; (2) share the work among existing employees; and (3) get rid of the job. The longer the leave, the more difficult will be option 2. However, when the employee who takes the leave possesses large amounts of firm-specific skills, option 2 is the only solution available to the employer because it would be impossible to recruit replacement workers from outside the firm.

Hiring replacement workers is less problematic for occupations based on industry-specific and general skills. Even in these cases, however, employers incur search costs and training costs. These costs are not trivial. According to studies conducted in Scandinavian countries, these costs can run up to five to nine times the monthly wages of the worker on leave. Furthermore, aside from the costs associated with replacement, retraining will have to be provided when the employee returns to work from parental leave. In occupations with a rapid pace of technological change, the high cost of retraining is likely to make cost-conscious private sector employers averse to hiring women in the first place. It is important to note that public sector employers do not face the same cost constraints in hiring decisions that private sector employers face.

The potential negative effects on private sector employment not-withstanding, long statutory leaves will motivate women to enter the labor market. When this increased supply is met with public sector demand, it will raise the female labor participation rate. Nonetheless, any gain in the labor force participation rate is likely to result in under-representation of women in the private sector. The greater the reli-ance of private sector employees on firm-specific skills and technologi-cally sensitive skills, the greater the underrepresentation of women will be. Overrepresentation of women is also likely to occur in occupations whose skills are less vulnerable to atrophy and where replacement workers are relatively abundant, strengthening gender bias in "female-dominated jobs" and hence exacerbating occupational segregation.

In contrast to the gender-segregating effects of long parental leaves (unless they mandate long leaves to be taken by fathers as well), the provision of affordable childcare helps narrow the gender skill gap between men and women. Although extensive provision of childcare might create female-dominated childcare jobs, it will enable women to advance into occupations with firm-specific skills (and technologically sensitive skills).

Explaining Occupational Segregation by Gender: Evidence

This section presents comparative data from advanced industrial so-cieties to demonstrate how the framework put forth in the preceding section accounts for the gender segregation patterns we observe.

Gender Bias of Skills

The second section of this chapter argued that women are more likely to invest in general skills than in firm-specific skills when compared to men. It also predicted that women are likely to be underrepresented in technologically sensitive skills due to problems of atrophy. Although direct measurements do not exist, we can use enrollment in general education programs as a proxy for general skill investment and enroll-ment in vocational training and apprenticeship programs as proxies for industry-specific skill investments. The female-male ratio in enrollment can be used to examine gender skill bias. Similarly, for the gender gap in firm-specific skills, we can use the difference in enterprise tenure

TABLE 3.1
Vocational education: Percentage of female enrollment

	Art, Religion	Commerce, Service	Health	Craft, Industry, Engineering	Agri- culture	Home Economics
Japan		70.1	99.6	6.3	30.8	96.4
Austria	58.7	63.4	86.5	13.2	42.5	96.1
Denmark		62.4	95.7	20.9	38.7	90.3
Finland	70.5	69.4	91.8	16.5	41.9	97.9
Germany	66.7	68.2	98.5	13.5	47.1	89.1
Ireland		80.4		53.2	25.3	
Italy	69.9	61.3		11.7	23.8	90.4
Netherlands		53.0	93.9	10.5	30.7	86.9
Norway	72.9	59.4	95.1	10.7	36.4	84.7
Spain	62.1	68.3	83.5	8.9	22.4	98.6
Sweden	66.9	56.6	88.5	14.5	43.4	72.4
Switzerland	60.0	65.0	90.4	13.1	29.3	90.8

SOURCE: UNESCO, "Secondary Technical and Vocational Education," *Statistical Issue*, March 1995. Data on the size and the breakdown of vocational training for the United States are not available in UNESCO data.

rate between men and women, since length of tenure is typically used as a proxy for the amount of firm-specific skills.

Table 3.1 shows the percentage of women among all students enrolled in vocational training calculated from UNESCO statistics. Unfortunately, the UNESCO data include only data for enrollment in school-based vocational training and exclude apprenticeship programs. Neither do the UNESCO data include vocational–general education breakdowns for Australia, Canada, New Zealand, the United Kingdom, and the United States. Despite these limitations, Table 3.1 shows that women are less likely than men to enroll in vocational education in nine out of twelve countries. We can supplement this information with OECD data available for two countries: Among people ages twenty to twenty-four in Australia and the United Kingdom, 2.7 percent and 9.9 percent, respectively, of the women enrolled in vocational training, whereas 15.1 percent and 24.4 percent, respectively, of the men did so. This further supports our view that women choose general-skill education over vocational training.

When we look at the breakdown by subject, we see a much wider gender gap: women are much more likely than men to enroll in vocational training for occupations that require more general skills such as clerical training (commerce) and service. Vocational training in health (mainly nurses) is very popular among women. It is worth noting that Polachek's calculations indicate that atrophy rates are very low for clerical staff and

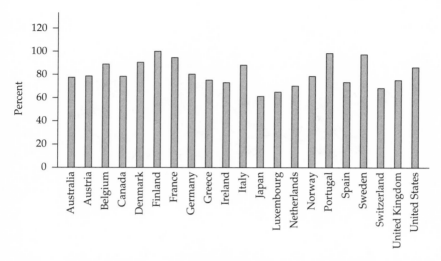

FIGURE 3.4 Gender Gap in Enterprise Tenure (Female Average Tenure as Percentage of Male Average Tenure)

SOURCE: OECD *Employment Outlook* 1993, 1997

nurses. In the case of home economics, although it is listed as vocational training, what occupation it leads to in the labor market is unclear, suggesting that it has a very weak vocational component.

We can also examine the gender breakdown of apprenticeship programs in a number of countries for which national data are available. Based on country reports, we have the gender breakdown of apprenticeship programs in Australia, Austria, Germany, and Switzerland. In Australia, the percentage of men who pursued apprenticeships and traineeships was significantly greater than the percentage of women who did so—the ratio was three to one in late 1980s (OECD 1988). In Germany, the female ratio of vocational apprentices fluctuated between 35 percent and 40 percent (CEDEFOP 1991). Apprenticeship programs showed extremely high levels of gender concentration. The five most popular traineeships for men included different types of mechanics; and usually men accounted for around 98 percent of enrollment (CEDEFOP 1991; 1995a). The top three most heavily female-dominated apprenticeships were doctor's assistant (99.9 percent of enrollees were females), hairdresser (94.3 percent), and office clerks (81 percent). Austria displayed similar patterns (CEDEFOP 1995b).

Figure 3.4 shows the gender gap in firm-specific skills. Again, for most countries, women's enterprise tenure is shorter than men's tenure,

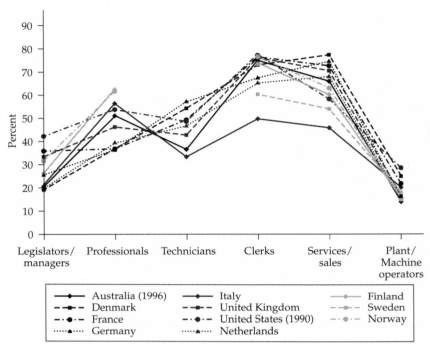

FIGURE 3.5   Percentage of Women in Major Occupational Categories

confirming our view that it is more difficult for women to accumulate firm-specific skills.

Let us now turn to occupational segregation. The second section of this chapter argued that the gender skill gap was responsible for the patterns of occupational segregation. Figure 3.5 shows general patterns of the proportion of females in major occupational categories. As predicted, we find favorable female ratios in occupations that mostly require general skills such as clerical, service, and professional occupations in all countries, whereas women fare less well in occupations that require firm-specific skills to a greater degree, such as managerial occupations and production-related jobs. However, the major occupational categories set by the International Standard Categories of Occupations (ISCO) still consist of many occupations that vary from one another. For instance, ISCO major categories (called one-digit-categories) treat medical doctors and nurses as the same category. The occupational category for production workers does not distinguish skilled foremen from assembly line workers.

Explaining Cross-National Variations
in Occupational Segregation

Although general patterns of female skill investment help us understand universal trends among advanced industrial economies, they do
not explain why countries display different degrees of occupational
segregation by gender. In order to examine cross-national differences
in occupational segregation, we need more detailed data at the disag-
gregate level. We use data compiled by Richard Anker, an economist
at the International Labor Organization, which is based on three-digit-
level data. Given that ILO only published one-digit data, and that national data are often very difficult to attain and compare, Anker's data
constitute the best source for standardized comparisons of advanced
industrial countries.

First, let us examine how countries differ in terms of the degree of
vertical segregation by gender. In some countries, women are overrepresented at the bottom of the occupational ladder and men occupy
higher-level occupations, which are much better paid. If we follow the
argument developed in the second section, skill regimes that value firm-
specific skills are more likely than others to discriminate against women
in higher levels of occupational hierarchy, since promotion to higher
positions of responsibility within the work organization likely depends
more on firm-specific skills in these countries. As a proxy for national
reliance on firm-specific skills, we use the percentage of workers with
enterprise tenure of twenty or more years. We measure vertical segregation as a percentage of females in managerial ranks.

Figure 3.6 illustrates the relationship between national reliance on
firm-specific skills and how well women fare in the organizational
hierarchy at work. It clearly shows that women do significantly better in
countries where the overall levels of firm-specific skills are low. Thus,
the skill regime perspective explains national variations in terms of female advancement within the company. Figure 3.7 shows, as predicted
in the second section, that policy measures such as employment protection impact women negatively as they contribute to the building up of
firm-specific skills by men but not necessarily by women.

In short, these two figures both support the view that skill regimes
in favor of firm-specific skills tend to discriminate against women.
Do generous long leaves exacerbate the gender bias whereas childcare provisions mitigate it? Although we cannot reasonably measure
interactive effects given the small number of observations, we can

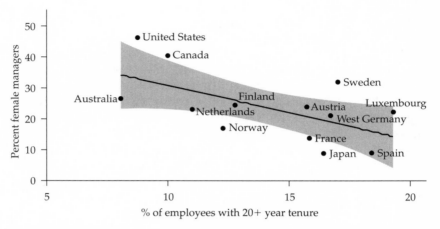

FIGURE 3.6 The Relationship between Skill Regimes and Vertical Segregation (% of Female Managers)
SOURCE: See Estévez-Abe (2005)

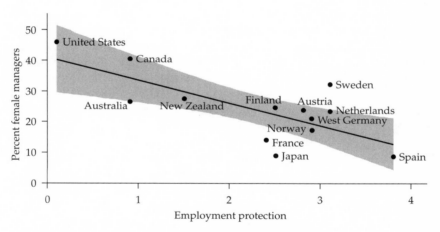

FIGURE 3.7 Employment Protection and Vertical Segregation (% Female Managers)
SOURCE: See Estévez-Abe (2005)

compare countries that are within the same skill regimes but differ in terms of their policy package for working mothers. We have two sets of regime variations that are convenient to our objective here: variations within the group with high firm-specific skills, and variations within the group with low firm-specific skills.

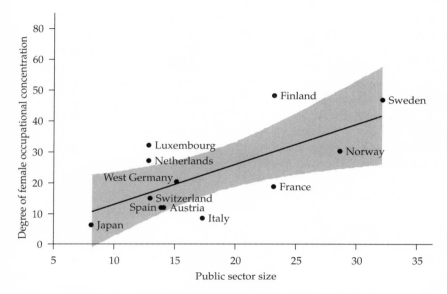

FIGURE 3.8 Public Sector and Female Occupational Concentration
SOURCE: See Estévez-Abe (2005)

Norway presents an important case to explore the effect of generous leave and the relative deficiency in childcare provision on the gender gap in firm-specific skills. Gornick (1999) and Meyers, Gornick, and Ross (1999) reveal that Norway differs from other Scandinavian countries in an important way: although it offers relatively generous paid leave, it falls short of providing an equivalent level of childcare. As a result, despite the largesse of the public sector, Norwegian women are more disadvantaged than Swedish and Finnish women in firm-specific skill acquisition relative to men, resulting in a lower percentage of female managers compared to Sweden and Finland.

Figure 3.6 does not explain the variation in the percentage of female managers among low tenure (i.e., low firm-specific-skill regimes). The United States, Canada, Australia, and New Zealand all score lower than other countries in terms of firm-specific skills, yet women in Australia and New Zealand are significantly worse off when it comes to moving into managerial positions.

Of these four countries, Canada and New Zealand distinguish themselves as they do have paid maternity and parental leaves, which the other two countries lack. Canada and New Zealand also provide some public childcare, unlike the other two countries. Since the levels of public childcare provision remain low even in Canada and New Zealand, availability of affordable private childcare is indispensable for women in these countries to reduce time off from work. This is where the United States and Canada seem to do better than New Zealand and Australia, making a decisive difference for the fate of their women. We can use the intragender wage gap as a proxy for the availability of low-skill women's labor for those women who earn significantly more. In other words, the intragender wage gap measures the relative availability of formal or informal private childcare. Canada and the United States score higher in intragender gap, whereas Australia and New Zealand show a more egalitarian wage distribution among women. Hence women in North America who are career-oriented can purchase care services in order to work more "like men," giving them advantages not available to women in Australia and New Zealand.[4]

Now let us turn to occupational segregation that occurs due to the overrepresentation of women in general skills. Service sector jobs require mostly general skills—which are biased in favor of women (OECD 1994, 124). For this reason, the larger the service sector in the economy, the more women enter the labor force, as demand for general skills will be met by female supply. At the same time, it will exacerbate the segregation of women into female-dominated jobs (Figure 3.8).

We can explain the particularly high levels of segregation of women into female-dominated occupations in Finland and Sweden in terms of their extremely generous policy packages for women. To follow our earlier argument, generous leaves will lead to the overrepresentation of women in the public sector, as private sector employers will be averse to hiring women.

Conclusion

This chapter has explored a new theoretical terrain linking the impact of skills and social policies on occupational segregation by gender. Most of the literature on gender equality at work has tended to focus on the beneficial effects of women-friendly policies, such as equal employment opportunity law, affirmative action, generous maternity and parental leave, and public provision of childcare. This chapter has argued that we need to include cross-national differences in labor market institutions to understand gender inequality in advanced industrial economies. The central claim of the chapter is that different types of skills—that is, firm-specific and general skills—possess different gender implications independently of social policies for working mothers. Furthermore, this chapter argued, in some cases the otherwise women-friendly policies such as generous leaves can exacerbate gender inequality when introduced to jobs that rely heavily on firm-specific skills.

Notes

1. Social democratic welfare states in Scandinavia provide tax-financed generous flat-rate benefits as social rights of citizens. Citizens gain some means of subsistence outside the market; hence those have become decommodified. Conservative welfare states in continental European countries, through benefits that are tied to one's occupation and earnings, stratify citizens rather than promote equality. Finally, liberal welfare states—in Anglo-American countries—neither decommodify nor actively stratify, as they only offer meager benefits, relying heavily on private welfare provision.

2. Also see Iversen and Wren (1998) for a variant of the argument concerning the relationship between service sector growth and the welfare state.

3. Even in an otherwise gender-egalitarian Sweden, employers are wary of labor costs associated with generous leaves (Haas and Hwang 1999).

4. For a more detailed account of how intragender wage inequality compensates for the absence of public policy for working mothers, see Estévez-Abe and Linos (2003).

References

Anker, Richard (1998). *Gender and Jobs: Sex Segregations of Jobs in the World* (Geneva: ILO).

Becker, Gary (1985). "Human Capital, Effort and the Sexual Division of Labor." *Journal of Labor Economics*, January Supplement, S33–S58.

Blossfeld, Hans-Peter (1987). "Labor-Market Entry and the Sexual Segregation of Careers in the Federal Republic of Germany." *American Journal of Sociology*, 89–118.

Brinton, Mary (1993). *Women and the Economic Miracle: Gender and Work in Postwar Japan* (Berkeley: University of California Press).

CEDEFOP: *See* European Center for the Development of Vocational Training.

Chang, Mariko (2000). "The Evolution of Sex Segregation Regimes." *American Journal of Sociology* 105(6): 1658–1701.

Daly, Mary (1994). "A Matter of Dependency? The Gender Dimension of British Income Maintenance Provision." *Sociology* 28(3): 779–797.

Esping-Andersen, Gosta (1990). *The Three Worlds of Welfare Capitalism* (Princeton: Princeton University Press).

Esping-Andersen, Gosta (1999). *Social Foundation of Postindustrial Economics* (Oxford: Oxford University Press).

Estévez-Abe, Margarita (2005). "Gender Bias in Skills and Social Policies: The Varieties of Capitalism Perspective on Sex Segregation." *Social Politics* 12(2): 180–215.

Estévez-Abe, Margarita, Torben Iversen, and David Soskice (2001). "Social Protection and the Formation of Skills: A Reinterpretation of the Welfare State" in Peter A. Hall and David Soskice, eds., *Varieties of Capitalism: The Institutional Foundations of Comparative Advantage* (Oxford: Oxford University Press), 145–183.

Estévez-Abe, Margarita, and Katerina Linos (2003). "Women Against Women: The Effects of Intra-Gender Wage Inequality on Womens' Employment." Unpublished paper, Harvard University.

European Center for the Development of Vocational Training, ed. (1991). *Vocational Training in the Federal Republic of Germany* (Berlin: European Center for the Development of Vocational Training).

European Center for the Development of Vocational Training, ed. (1995a). *Vocational Education and Training in the Federal Republic of Germany* (Berlin: European Center for the Development of Vocational Training).

European Center for the Development of Vocational Training, ed. (1995b). *Vocational Education and Training in the Republic of Austria* (Thessaloniki, Greece: European Center for the Development of Vocational Training).

Gornick, Janet (1999). "Gender Equality in the Labour Market," in Diane Sainsbury, ed., *Gender and Welfare State Regimes* (Oxford: Oxford University Press), 210–242.

Gornick, Janet C., Marcia K. Meyers, and Katherin E. Ross (1996). "Supporting the Employment of Mothers: Policy Variation Across Fourteen Welfare States." Luxembourg Income Study, Working Paper No. 139.

Gornick, Janet C., Marcia K. Meyers, and Katherin E. Ross (1997). "Supporting the Employment of Mothers: Policy Variation Across Fourteen Welfare States." *Journal of European Social Policy* 7(1), 45–70.

Haas, Linda, and Philip Hwang (1999). "Parental Leave in Sweden," in Peter Moss and Fred Deven, eds., *Parental Leave: Progress or Pitfall?* (The Hague/Brussels: NIDI/CBGS Publications, vol. 35), 45–68.

Hakim, Catherine (1992). "Explaining Trends in Occupational Segregation: The Measurement, Causes, and Consequences of the Sexual Division of Labour." *European Sociological Review* 8(2): 127–152.

Hakim, Catherine (1993). "Refocusing Research on Occupational Segregation: Reply to Watts." *European Sociological Review* 9(3): 321–324.

Hall, Peter, and Daniel W. Gingerich (2001). "Varieties of Capitalism and Institutional Complementarities in the Macroeconomy: An Empirical Analysis." Paper presented at the Annual Meeting of the American Political Science Association, San Francisco.

Hall, Peter A., and David Soskice, eds. (2001). *Varieties of Capitalism: The Institutional Foundations of Comparative Advantage* (Oxford: Oxford University Press).

Huber, Evelyne, and John D. Stephens (2001). *Development and Crisis of the Welfare State: Parties and Policies in Global Markets* (Chicago: University of Chicago Press).

Huber, Evelyne, and John D. Stephens (2002). "Globalization, Competitiveness, and the Social Democratic Model." *Social Policy and Society* 1(1): 47–57.

Iversen, Torben, and Anne Wren (1998). "Equality, Employment and Budgetary Restraint: The Trilemma of the Service Economy." *World Politics* 50 (July): 507–546.

Klausen, Jytte (1999). "The Declining Significance of Male Workers: Trade-Union Responses to Changing Labor Markets," in Herbert Kitschelt, Peter Lange, Gary Marks, and John Stephens, eds., *Continuity and Change in Contemporary Capitalism* (New York: Cambridge University Press), 261–290.

Mares, Isabela (1997). "Is Unemployment Insurable? Employers and the Institutionalization of the Risk of Unemployment." *Journal of Public Policy* 17(3): 299–327.

Mares, Isabela (2003). *The Politics of Social Risk: Business and Welfare State Development* (New York: Cambridge University Press).

Melkas, Helina, and Richard Anker (1997). "Occupational Segregation by Sex in Nordic Countries: An Empirical Investigation." *International Labour Review* 136(3): 341–363.

Meyers, Marcia, Janet Gornick, and Katherin E. Ross (1999). "Public Childcare, Parental Leave, and Employment," in Diane Sainsbury, ed., *Gender and Welfare State Regimes* (Oxford: Oxford University Press), 117–146.

Mincer, Jacob, and Solomon Polachek (1974). "Family Investments in Human Capital: Earnings of Women." *Journal of Political Economy* 82 (March/April 1974): S76–S108.

Nicoletti, Giuseppe, Stefano Scarpetta, and Oliver Boylaud (1999). "Summary Indicators of Product Market Regulation with an Extension to Employment Protection Legislation." OECD, ECO Working Paper No. 226.

O'Connor, Julia, Ann Shola Orloff, and Sheila Shaver (1999). *States, Markets, Families: Gender, Liberalism and Social Policy in Australia, Canada, Great Britain and the United States* (Cambridge: Cambridge University Press).

OECD: *See* Organization for Economic Cooperation and Development.

Organization for Economic Cooperation and Development (1988). *Employment Outlook* (Paris: OECD).

Organization for Economic Cooperation and Development (1993). "Enterprise Tenure, Labour Turnover and Skill Training." *Employment Outlook* (Paris: OECD), 119–148.

Organization for Economic Cooperation and Development (1994). *Women and Structural Change* (Paris: OECD).

Organization for Economic Cooperation and Development (1997). *Employment Outlook*. Paris: OECD.

Orloff, Ann Shola (1993). "Gender and Social Rights of Citizenship: State Policies and Gender Relations in Comparative Research." *American Sociological Review* 58(3): 303–328.

Polachek, Solomon (1981). "Occupational Self-Selection: A Human Capital Approach to Sex Differences." *Review of Economics and Statistics* 63(1): 60–69.

Pontusson, Jonas, and Peter Swenson (1996). "Labor Markets, Production Strategies, and Wage Bargaining Institutions: The Swedish Employer Offensive in Comparative Perspective." *Comparative Political Studies* 29(April): 223–250.

Sainsbury, Diane, ed. (1994). *Gendering Welfare States* (London: Sage).

Sainsbury, Diane, ed. (1999). *Gender and Welfare State Regimes* (Oxford: Oxford University Press).

Soskice, David (1990). "Wage Determination: The Changing Role of Institutions in Advanced Industrial Countries." *Oxford Review of Economic Policy* 6:36–61.

Soskice, David (1991). "The Institutional Infrastructure for International Competitiveness: A Comparative Analysis of the UK and Germany," in Anthony Atkinson and Renato Brunetta, eds., *The Economics of the New Europe* (London: Macmillan).

CHAPTER 4

Gendered Offices: A Comparative-Historical Examination of Clerical Work in Japan and the United States

MARY C. BRINTON

Introduction

The second half of the twentieth century was marked by dramatic changes in women's economic participation in the United States and other Western industrial countries (Bergmann 1986; Davis 1984; Oppenheimer 1970, 1994). The most important departure from previous decades was the rapid rise in labor force participation among married women. In the United States, this trend began in the 1940s and early 1950s; in each subsequent decade, white married women's labor force participation increased by about 10 percentage points, reaching 60 percent by the end of the century (Blau and Kahn 2005).

There are many reasons for this change. One of the most important was a transformation in the nature of labor demand. The rapid development of the service sector in the early part of the twentieth century produced great increases in the demand for white-collar workers, in particular clerical workers. Compared to manufacturing and domestic service, the sectors that had employed the majority of working women in earlier periods, office work opened up the possibility of cleaner, less hazardous, "respectable" wage-earning labor. The opportunity to work in the clerical sector was especially important for white middle-class married women, as factory and domestic service jobs were viewed by the majority of these women and their husbands—as well as by some working-class families—as beneath their dignity (Cohen 1992; Degler 1980; Goldin 1990). The demand for office workers played an important role in drawing more women into the labor force and, even more importantly for the eventual narrowing of the male-female wage gap, transforming the *composition* of the female labor force in full-time jobs into a more highly educated group comprised of both single and married women.

Stated simply, participation in clerical work increased American women's labor force attachment. As early as 1940, the labor force participation rate among married women who had worked in the clerical sector while single was higher than for women who had been in the manufacturing sector before marriage (Goldin 1990). The clerical sector also played a historical role in heightening women's educational aspirations, because office work required more education than the jobs that had been open to women in earlier periods. Women with more human capital were increasingly drawn into the labor market, resulting in a "virtuous cycle" of continual upgrading of the human capital stock of working women from the mid-twentieth century on. This eventually had positive repercussions for the narrowing of the overall male-female wage gap in the United States: the narrowing of the gap since 1980 has been due in part to the cumulative effect of the increased economic participation of successive cohorts of highly educated women (Bianchi and Spain 1986; Blau and Kahn 2005; Goldin 1990; McLaughlin et al. 1988; O'Neill and Polachek 1993; Wellington 1993).[1]

Expansion of the clerical sector and its increasing openness to women therefore played a very important role in the transformation of the female labor force in the twentieth-century United States (Goldin 1990; Oppenheimer 1970). Many studies have documented the transformation of clerical work from being a male job to being culturally defined as "female" within the space of a few decades early in the century (Goldin 1990; Oppenheimer 1970; Reskin and Roos 1990). It is not clear whether the nearly complete feminization of clerical work was critical to its transformative role for the female labor force or whether the gender integration of clerical work would have been sufficient; certainly, what *was* required was that clerical work change from being culturally labeled as an occupation suitable only for men. But feminization of clerical roles was tied inextricably to a second, more structural, change: these roles became bracketed off from internal labor markets. The intertwining of these two processes rendered clerical jobs unattractive to the vast majority of men and in effect created a cultural space that was female. At first almost entirely occupied by single females, these jobs eventually expanded to include large numbers of married women because the supply of single women eventually became insufficient to meet the volume of employer demand for secretaries, filing clerks, and other clerical positions.

The important influence of clerical sector expansion on the dramatic increase in American married women's full-time labor force participation across the twentieth century can be contrasted with the Japanese experience, where expansion of the clerical sector has had more muted effects. Two distinct differences mark these national cases. First, a great deal of clerical work in Japan remains embedded in career ladders in internal labor markets—career ladders that remain occupied almost entirely by men (Brinton 1993; Ishida et al. 2002; Spilerman and Ishida 1996). Second, and closely related, clerical jobs have not become feminized to the extent that occurred in the United States in an earlier historical period, nor have full-time positions in the Japanese clerical sector become as open to *married* women. This has dampened the positive effect of service sector expansion on labor force participation and labor market rewards for Japanese married women overall.

The next section outlines the historically transformative role of the clerical sector in increasing American female labor force participation, especially for the married population. I show that the early cultural labeling of clerical work as "female" and women's subsequent near-monopolization of most of the numerically largest clerical occupations opened up a culturally sanctioned space for women in the American labor force that was preserved even when demands were high for full employment for men, as in the early post-WWII era. In the third section I outline recent historical trends in women's clerical sector participation in Japan and show that although large numbers of women do hold clerical jobs, their presence in these positions does *not* increase their lifetime labor force attachment. In the final section I discuss in more general terms what the contrast between the United States and Japan tells us about the conditions necessary for clerical sector expansion to have a transformative effect on married women's labor force participation and rewards.

The Rise of Married Women's Labor Force Participation in the United States: The Contribution of Clerical Work

Women's participation in the American labor force was heavily concentrated in a handful of low-level jobs in manufacturing and service occupations at the turn of the twentieth century.[2] But in the course of the

TABLE 4.1

Percentage of working women over time in the clerical sector, United States

Birth cohort	AGE								
	20–24	25–29	30–34	35–39	40–44	45–49	50–54	55–59	60–64
1896–1900			28.0		21.8		23.6		22.1
1901–1905		34.0		26.6		23.9		26.7	
1906–1910	37.1 (1930)		30.2		26.9		28.0		28.0
1911–1915		30.1		26.9		29.0		29.8	
1916–1920	31.2 (1940)		30.8		31.2		33.3		32.6
1921–1925		40.2		35.3		36.5		34.1	
1926–1930	49.3 (1950)		38.1		37.0		35.1		
1931–1935		41.9		36.7		35.4			
1936–1940	51.6 (1960)		37.1		34.5				
1941–1945		38.8		32.9					
1946–1950	48.8 (1970)		34.3						
1951–1955		35.5							
1956–1960	42.4 (1980)								

SOURCE: James P. Smith and Michael P. Ward. 1984. "Time-Series Growth in the Female Labor Force." *Journal of Labor Economics* 3: 559–590.

NOTE: Figures are for white women.

first thirty years of the century, the proportion of working women who occupied clerical jobs increased fivefold; fully one-quarter of all working women in 1930 were employed in this sector (Goldin 1990). Table 4.1 shows the proportion in clerical work for each five-year age group of American working women, starting with the cohort born in 1906–1910. Because the layout of the table is rather nonintuitive, it bears explaining why the numbers are presented in this way and how they can help us understand how the age structure of women's participation in clerical work changed over the first 60 years of the twentieth century.

Work-history data are the ideal type of data to show how individuals respond to opportunities in the labor market across their life cycle. These can be collected by asking individuals in late middle age, for example, to recall the jobs they have held throughout their working life, or they can be collected by asking a large sample of individuals every year about their current jobs, allowing the researcher to compile a record of the jobs an individual has held across his or her life cycle. But neither of these options is generally available to economic historians, labor economists, or sociologists who want to study the historical patterns of individuals' work over the life cycle; such data were very rarely collected historically by anyone.

In lieu of individual work-history data, we can create "synthetic cohorts" by piecing together cross-sectional data (data gathered at one point in time) for a large number of individuals across different age groups and compiling these cross sections to infer life-cycle work patterns from them. This is the method I rely upon here. Table 4.1 shows the figures compiled by Smith and Ward (1984) for the proportion of each five-year age group of working women in the United States who were in clerical work, beginning in 1930. The left-hand column shows when a given group of women was born (beginning at the top of the table with the cohort born in 1896–1900 and ending at the bottom of the table with the cohort born in 1956–1960). The row across the top of the table follows members of each cohort as they age, and the cells in the table show the proportion of the working women in each cohort who were in the clerical sector at each age. As an aid, I have added to the first data column the calendar years in which a given cohort reached ages twenty to twenty-four. (For instance, the cohort born between 1906 and 1910 reached ages twenty to twenty-four in 1930.)

The table allows us to see three principal changes over time in the ages of American female clerical workers. First, the proportion of working women in each age group employed in clerical work generally grew over time. This can be seen by reading the figures in each column from top to bottom. The proportion of working women ages twenty to twenty-four in 1930 who were in clerical work was 37 percent, and this had increased to 42 percent for this age group by 1980. The proportion of women in clerical work at each life-cycle stage, as indicated by the ages across the top of the table, increased over the decades. Second, this increase was *the greatest for middle-aged women*—those in their forties and early fifties. Whereas only about 22 percent of working women ages forty to forty-four in the early period were in the clerical sector, this had increased to 35 percent for women in this age group in 1980. This shows the secular change over time in the proportion of American middle-aged women who worked in the clerical sector. Although these figures unfortunately are not available by marital status, it is likely that a large proportion of women in this age group were married. The increase is similar for women ages forty-five to forty-nine and fifty to fifty-four. In contrast, the participation of younger women in clerical work reached its peak around 1960 and has declined slightly thereafter. This is probably due to the increased educational opportunities that became available to women, especially pre-professional school programs in business and medicine; starting one's work life in the clerical sector has become less appealing for highly educated American women since other opportunities have opened up.

Third, over historical time there has been a gradual "leveling" in the age distribution of clerical work, starting from a point early in the century when it was chiefly the domain of young women. This is a different way of stating the second point, that clerical work gradually became less and less monopolized by younger women. This can be seen by following each historical time point upward and to the right on its diagonal line. In 1940, 31 percent of women ages twenty to twenty-four were in clerical work compared to almost 10 percent fewer women (22 percent) ages forty to forty-four. By 1980, these figures had changed to 42 percent and 35 percent, respectively.

One need not rely solely on aggregate data to see the dramatic shift in the United States from a historical situation where clerical work was mainly an arena for young, single women to the more contemporary situation where working women across the age spectrum are almost equally likely to hold such jobs. Using establishment surveys conducted by the Women's Bureau of the U.S. Department of Labor, Goldin (1990) shows that about half of female office workers in the 1930s and 1940s were in firms that had a policy of not hiring married women or a policy of leaving this to the discretion of the department head. These so-called "marriage bars" were not removed for clerical work until the 1950s. This happened because the supply of young single women to fill these jobs became insufficient and employers quite simply *had* to hire married women. There were three principal reasons for this change.

First, the birth rate rapidly declined beginning in the early 1930s in the United States (Cherlin 1992). This produced smaller cohorts of young women entering the labor force from the mid-1950s on. Second, there was a decline in women's age at first marriage in the 1950s, partly related to the end of World War II and the beginning of a period of postwar prosperity. This also translated into fewer single women in their twenties. Third, the increase in female educational attainment beginning around 1900 meant that ever-larger numbers of young women remained in school (and, consequently, out of the labor force) for longer periods, gradually reducing further the available labor supply for these jobs. The last of these reasons—the historically early and continuous expansion of education for American women—meant that when employers faced a shortage of clerical workers in the 1950s there existed a ready supply of high school–educated, middle-aged married women.

Historically, then, the expanding clerical sector in the United States had a positive effect on the labor force participation of married women in two ways. First, young women who had begun their work lives in clerical jobs were more likely than others to be gainfully employed as married women. Although our contemporary image of clerical work tends to be a series of dead-end jobs with no, or at most a shallow, promotional trajectory, the rise of clerical work half a century ago in the United States provided women at that time with the possibility of safe and "respectable" work vis-à-vis the previous era's concentration of labor power in manufacturing and domestic service work. This was especially significant for white middle-class married women who otherwise very likely would not have participated in the labor force. Second, clerical sector expansion had a feedback effect on young women's incentives to pursue their education. If a young woman completed a high school education, the world of white-collar work was at least open to her, even if the work itself did not lead directly into a long and promising career ladder. Women became better-educated in order to gain the skills and credentials to enter the white-collar sector (Cohen 1992; Smith and Ward 1984; Walters and O'Connell 1988). By the 1950s, middle-aged married women were increasingly drawn into office work because the labor supply of young single women could not meet the economy's demands (partly because women were in fact spending longer in school). These middle-aged women had the requisite education and some prior work experience, generally from the period before they had married. The fit was therefore good between employers' labor needs on the one hand and the desire of educated women in their late thirties and forties on the other hand to continue working or to reenter the labor force after having left at marriage or childbirth.

But we can still ask why American employers turned to *married women* to fill their clerical needs in the mid-twentieth century rather than to *young men* (whether single or married). The answer lies in the fact that many types of clerical jobs had essentially become "female jobs" in the early twentieth century. This laid the cultural groundwork for clerical job openings to be filled by married women rather than by men, if single women came to be in short supply. To understand why this occurred and to provide a backdrop against which the contrasting development of Japanese offices can be compared, it is necessary to look at how the division of labor and the structuring of jobs in American offices radically changed in the first half of the twentieth century.

The Feminization of Clerical Work in the United States

In the closing years of the nineteenth century, office clerks and secretaries in the United States, Canada, and Great Britain were almost always male (Cohn 1985; Davies 1975; Lowe 1980, 1986). Census data for the

United States in 1870 document that women were a mere 2.5 percent of the clerical labor force (Hooks 1947). Offices were typically small, entrepreneurial enterprises with young men serving as "right-hand men" to business owners (Edwards 1979; Kanter 1977). But by 1890, the proportion of clerical workers who were women was 21 percent and by 1920 the figure had more than doubled, to 50 percent (Davies 1975). Why?

Along with the expansion of the administrative work of businesses in the early part of the twentieth century came the extension of scientific management techniques from factories to offices, as well as innovations in office technology. The introduction and rapid spread of the typewriter around 1900 created differentiation in clerical work and gave rise to the new job category of typist. Women were believed to have high manual dexterity and, furthermore, to be willing to perform repetitive activities and to be closely monitored. Typing soon became a female occupation. By the early post-WWII period, the office division of labor was so advanced that the National Office Management Association in Canada could meticulously outline the specific duties of job categories such as typist, junior stenographer, stenographer, secretary, and private secretary as well as the progression among these (Lowe 1986). Similarly, the advent of the adding machine followed by Hollerith (precomputer) technology created a more fragmented division of labor compared to the more unified responsibilities of the turn-of-the-century office clerk. As Lowe writes:

Nineteenth-century office routines are often portrayed as craft-like work. The traditional male bookkeeper was an experienced generalist who at any given moment could report to his boss on the state of the business. But with industrial expansion and increasingly complex business dealings, the rise of large-scale office bureaucracy after 1900 wrought fundamental changes in the division of administrative labour. The mounting volume of routine work induced employers to hire women largely because they could be paid much less than men. As the scope of administration widened, the focus of individual clerical tasks narrowed. By the 1920s, the generalist male bookkeeper had become a relic of the past in most large offices, succeeded by teams of female functionaries monotonously processing financial data with the aid of machines. (Lowe 1986, 194)

This illustrates a complex interplay between the increased mechanization and specialization of many office tasks and their delegation to women, who could be hired more cheaply than men. As I will argue below, the compartmentalization of office tasks has not occurred to this degree in Japan, and this is one of the principal reasons behind the limited possibilities for married women to participate full-time in office work, especially in large firms.

American women were willing to put up with lower wages than men in the clerical sector. First, descriptions of office work in the early twentieth century all emphasize that it was safer, cleaner, and more respectable than almost all other jobs open to women except for the handful of professions (such as teaching and nursing) that were available only to highly educated women. Second, the pay was relatively good, certainly not compared to men's jobs but compared to the other jobs open to women with a high school education. And third, channels of upward mobility were open to at least some female clerical workers, although it is important to note that this depended on individual initiative and was not built-in, in the sense of clear promotional trajectories in firm-internal labor markets. As Kessler-Harris writes, "File clerks who normally began work at twelve dollars a week could aspire to run offices, where they might create classification systems, index, and keep records at eighty dollars per week. Cash girls could become sales clerks or even buyers. Telephone operators could be supervisors" (Kessler-Harris 1982, 227). The expansion of personnel departments after 1910 is a particularly good example of a class of jobs considered especially appropriate for women to move into, involving skills such as the maintenance of good interpersonal relations that were considered to be natural among women's arsenal of abilities (Kessler-Harris 1982).

The fact that over half of all clerical jobs were filled by women by the onset of the Great Depression had an ironic effect on the employment of American women versus men. Aside from the first three years of the Depression, women actually fared better than men in employment (Cohen 1992; Kessler-Harris 1982; Milkman 1987). The industries hit hardest in the 1930s were those such as heavy industry that employed very few women. And the industries that recovered the most quickly and then expanded (social services and education) had large clerical needs—and many jobs that had already been culturally labeled as "female." The return of American men to the economy after WWII therefore had less effect on women's labor force participation than might have been expected, because so much low-level office work had become labeled as "women's work." The Women's Bureau reported shortages of stenographers and typists in 1953; these shortages were subsequently filled by women, not men (Goldin 1990).

Nevertheless, it would be a definite mistake to suggest that women's increased participation in clerical work in the first half of the twentieth century quickly helped narrow the overall male-female wage gap in the U.S. economy. This chapter does not advance such an argument. To the contrary, the overall male-female wage gap remained stubbornly resistant to change until the 1980s (Bernhardt et al. 1995; Goldin 1990). Rather, what the feminization of office work accomplished was to gain for married women a permanent foothold in white-collar work and to encourage subsequent cohorts of women to increase their human capital through educational attainment. As stated earlier, by 1940 educated married women were on average more likely to be in the labor force than their less-educated counterparts, and they were highly visible in the office.[3] The historical comparison of women's to men's wages in clerical work is not a positive one; male and female starting wages tended to be very similar, but the wage gap increased substantially with experience. However, the earnings slope for female clerical workers with substantial (more than 15 years) work experience was greater than for women in manufacturing by 1940 (Goldin 1990). It is this comparison—with women's other occupational alternatives—that is significant for the argument posed here. Women had occupational choices available, albeit across a limited and culturally defined range, and clerical work had become a very positive choice relative to the others available.

In conclusion, the rapid expansion and feminization of clerical work in the early twentieth century created a female ghetto in American offices. But at the same time, this very feminization led ever-greater numbers of women to complete high school in order to enter office work, eventually producing a critical mass of middle-aged, educated women. Members of this new labor pool were increasingly hired from the 1940s on because the supply of young single women for these jobs, now designated by employers as female jobs, had become insufficient.

It is also highly likely that the exposure of a broad age spectrum of educated women to corporate environments eventually made women's comparison of their wages relative to *men's* ever more natural and more frustrating. Further education, always a distinctly "American" solution to individuals' aspirations for upward mobility, was pursued fervently by women in American universities' rapidly expanding MBA programs from the 1970s on. This option was available not just to young women but to those who had had some work experience and perhaps marriage and childrearing experience as well. By 1980, nearly 30 percent of American administrators/managers were female, as were nearly 80 percent of clerical workers (Brinton and Ngo 1993). Women's increased educational attainment and labor force attachment had so permeated successive cohorts that both factors finally had some effect on reducing the overall male-female wage gap.

I turn now to the experience of Japan as a distinctly different case, where clerical sector expansion has not exerted as transformative an effect on the economic status of married women as occurred in the United States.

The Expanding Clerical Sector in Japan

In East Asia as in the United States and other Western economies, industrialization and the expansion of the white-collar and service sectors led to an irreversible rise in female labor force participation. But women's rates of labor force exit upon marriage, as well as the male-female wage gap, remain much greater than in Western industrial countries (Brinton 1993; Brinton et al. 1995; Hirao 2002; Shirahase 2002). This is especially the case in Japan and South Korea. As pointed out by Yamaguchi (1997), the deepening of the "M-shaped" curve of female labor force participation by age in postwar Japan contrasts with the historical experience in the United States, where the trough in the M-shaped curve has virtually disappeared. The same can be said for South Korea (Brinton et al. 1995). Moreover, the link between women's education and their probability of labor force participation, evident in U.S. data as far back as half a century ago (Goldin 1990; Smith and Ward 1984), has repeatedly shown up as weak or absent in analyses of married women's employment in these two countries (Brinton 1993; Brinton et al. 1995; Hirao 1997; Osawa 1988; K. Tanaka 1987; S. Tanaka 1998). Why has an expanded clerical sector apparently not strengthened married women's labor force attachment, not produced a close relationship between married women's education and labor force participation, and therefore not helped narrow the gender wage gap as it did in the United States?

Trends over Time

Expansion of the clerical sector in Japan has occurred at a steady pace throughout the post-WWII period. Forty years ago about 15 percent of the nonagricultural labor force (including males and females) were in clerical jobs, compared to 21 percent currently. Table 4.2 shows the proportion in clerical work for five-year age groups of Japanese working women across historical time. A comparison with the trends for U.S. women (Table 4.1) shows a number of similarities.

TABLE 4.2
Percentage of working women over time in the clerical sector, Japan

Birth cohort	AGE							
	20–24	25–29	30–34	35–39	40–44	45–49	50–54	55+
1899–1903								
1904–1908								4.5
1909–1913							7.7	4.9
1914–1918						7.7	11.1	6.0
1919–1923					7.7	11.1	10.4	12.3
1924–1928				15.4	11.1	15.2	15.0	13.3
1929–1933			15.4	16.0	16.6	17.5	18.4	16.1
1934–1938		23.0	15.9	16.3	18.4	18.5	18.1	
1939–1943	34.9 (1963)	27.5	20.6	21.5	22.0	22.5		
1944–1948	42.6 (1968)	32.6	26.9	26.2	26.0			
1949–1953	45.5 (1973)	36.1	26.9	26.4				
1954–1958	49.6 (1978)	38.9	31.0					
1959–1963	50.2 (1983)	42.0						
1964–1968	48.0 (1988)							
1969–1973								

SOURCE: *Rôdôryoku chosa* (Survey of the Labor Force), various years.

The proportion of Japanese working women in each age group employed in clerical work has consistently increased over historical time. Women ages twenty to twenty-four increased their participation in clerical work from 35 percent in 1963 to 48 percent in 1983, above the American rate. But just as in the United States, the most dramatic increase was among middle-aged women. In the early 1960s, less than 8 percent of Japanese women in their forties worked in the clerical sector. By the late 1980s, the rate had more than tripled among women in their late forties as well as their early forties. Thus a very substantial change had occurred in the space of just a few decades.

Yet substantial differences are also observable in the comparative data for the United States and Japan. The probability that an American working woman over age twenty-five was in a clerical occupation in 1980 could not have been predicted very well by her age, as shown if we follow the line for 1980 in Table 4.1 across ages (upward to the right): between 32 and 35 percent of women in every age group (save the youngest) were clerical workers. In contrast, over 40 percent of Japanese working women ages twenty-five to twenty-nine were in clerical work in 1983 compared to just over 20 percent of women in their late forties and many fewer in the older cohorts.[4]

In sum, the movement of women out of clerical work as they age is much more evident in Japan than in the United States. The late-1980s life-cycle pattern for clerical work that we can infer for Japanese women from these data is similar to the pattern that existed for American women in the late 1940s, before marriage bars were dismantled in the United States. This can be seen by comparing the last diagonal, upward-sloping line in Table 4.2 with the line for 1950 in Table 4.1. Also, the proportion of young women (ages twenty to twenty-four) in clerical work in the United States peaked in 1960 at over 50 percent and then declined by about 10 percentage points over the next twenty years, consistent with young American women's increasing rates of university and professional school attendance. In contrast, once young Japanese women began exhibiting high rates of clerical sector participation in the late 1960s, the figure continued to rise and appears to have become quite stable since the late 1970s. The difference between these rates and those of women in their early thirties and beyond is suggestive of the continued importance of youth and singlehood among female Japanese clerical workers.

Work-Career Implications of Clerical Work for Japanese Men and Women

To look in greater detail at Japanese women's life-cycle employment patterns and the role of clerical jobs within those patterns, I use data from the Japanese Survey on Social Status and Mobility (SSM) conducted in 1995 by the Social Status and Mobility Survey Research Group. The survey was distributed in two versions to a national random sample of 8064 individuals. I use the version that includes information on the complete work histories of individuals. Because the survey was carried out for both men and women, we can examine the implications of clerical work for the work lives of both sexes, which is an additional advantage of the data. These implications are strikingly different.

Of all ever-worked women in the sample, the proportion of women who entered clerical work as their first job nearly doubled from 26 percent for women who were over age sixty in 1995 (who would have entered the labor force in the early 1950s) to 47 percent for women ages twenty to twenty-nine in 1995 (who would have started work in the late 1980s to early 1990s).[5] Interestingly, these figures from individual-level data are very consistent with the aggregate figures in Table 4.2 for these cohorts.

The great majority (93 percent) of ever-worked women in the sample have had at least some work experience prior to marriage. Among these, clerical work was the most common first job; employing 41 percent of women.[6] Among women who started their first job after marriage, only 20 percent were in clerical work. Instead, these women were more likely to work in manufacturing jobs. Virtually no women (or men) started their working lives as administrators/managers.[7]

Although American women in the mid-twentieth century who began their work lives in clerical jobs were more likely to be employed after marriage than women who had started out in manufacturing, it is striking that the *opposite* is true for Japanese women. Calculating the proportion of Japanese women in the labor force at ages thirty, forty, and fifty as well as the occupational distribution of working women at each age shows that among women whose first job was clerical, the majority (54 percent) were not in the labor force at age thirty. This figure is higher than for women who started out in any other occupation, although sales occupations are close behind. Similarly, fewer women who had started out in clerical than in other work had reentered the labor force by age forty or fifty, a stark contrast with the United States.

Among women who had initially entered the labor force as clerical workers, 30 percent were also in clerical work at age thirty. This figure increases to 34 percent for women working at age forty and a similar proportion at age fifty.[8] In sum, although about one-third of the women who began their work lives in office work were also engaged in that type of work at ages thirty, forty, and/or fifty, much larger proportions at each age (54 percent, 39 percent, and 42 percent, respectively) were not in the labor force at all. The data also demonstrate that clerical experience almost never produces female administrators/managers in Japan. By ages thirty, forty, and fifty, respectively, only minuscule percentages—0.5 percent, 1.0 percent, and 1.3 percent—of initial female clerical workers had become administrators/managers (see also Ishida et al. 2002).

The experience of Japanese men is very different. About 20 percent in every cohort started their work lives in jobs classified as clerical. At age thirty, all of these men were employed and nearly 80 percent remained in clerical work. An additional 4 percent had become administrators/managers. By age forty, about 60 percent were still clerical workers and about 20 percent had moved into management; an additional 10 percent were in sales. The proportion who had moved into management by age fifty was 34 percent, and a remaining 50 percent and 9 percent, respectively, remained in clerical or sales work.

In sum, three occupational categories (administrative/managerial, clerical, and sales) are the career destination points at age fifty for over 90 percent of Japanese men who start out as office workers. In contrast, these white-collar occupations are the destination points at age fifty for fewer than half as many women (42 percent); moreover, an equivalent proportion of women who initially held clerical jobs are not in the labor force at all at age fifty. Even more stark is the fact that whereas about one-third of Japanese men who start out in low-level office work eventually become managers or administrators—many of them by age forty—the corresponding figure for women is just *1 percent*.[9] This finding is very similar to what Spilerman and Ishida report in their study of a large Japanese financial firm; there were so few women in managerial positions that the researchers needed to delete them from the statistical analysis of promotional trajectories (Spilerman and Ishida 1996). In contrast, women occupied 46 percent of the managerial positions in the comparable American firm the authors studied, and posting and bidding provisions in the company (a nonexistent practice in Japanese companies) translated into about one-half of all managerial entrants having started out as clerical staff (Ishida et al. 2002).

Clerical and Managerial Work Throughout Men's and Women's Working Lives

Given that a significant proportion of Japanese men continue to be classified as clerical workers at ages thirty, forty, and fifty, what is the nature of the clerical work that the two sexes do at these different ages? Calculation of the distribution of men and women across clerical categories at these ages as well as the percentage of females in each category shows that male clerical workers' distribution across job titles varies little with age. Women's distribution shows slightly more variation, the major shift being that the proportion of female clerical workers who are account clerks goes up considerably among older women workers. Notably, Japanese women do not monopolize (by occupying 85 percent or more of the positions) any categories of clerical work at any age, except for the categories of receptionist and typist/stenographer/keypuncher, which together comprise less than 5 percent of the clerical labor force in Japan.

The workplaces and employment statuses of Japanese male and female clerical workers also increasingly diverge over the life cycle.[10] The distribution of first jobs for the two groups of workers across different firm sizes is similar; women are slightly more likely to be in small firms of fewer than thirty workers, and men are considerably more likely to be in government jobs.[11] But nearly half of the women working in the clerical sector at age forty work for firms of fewer than thirty people;

this is true for only 15 percent of men. In contrast, about one-third of male clerical workers are in large firms of 1,000 or more employees, whereas only 12 percent of women are. Men also continue to be more heavily represented in government than women. Perhaps even more striking is the fact that whereas men in clerical fields at age forty overwhelmingly remain full-time employees, the rate of women working as full-time employees in clerical fields drops to one-half what it was on first jobs. At age forty, 46 percent of female clerical workers are full-time employees, another 23 percent are part-time or temporary workers, and 24 percent are classified as family enterprise workers.

To conclude, although the job classifications of Japanese male and female clerical workers remain fairly stable across different ages, the workplaces become more and more different for the two sexes. Women become heavily concentrated in small firms and distributed almost equally between full-time workers on the one hand and part-time, temporary/family enterprise workers on the other. These trends are not at all evident for Japanese men. It is especially important to emphasize the divergence of the two sexes into firms of different sizes as they age. Given the large discrepancy in wages by firm size among middle-aged Japanese employees, men's greater presence in large firms in and of itself creates a significant gender wage advantage (Brinton 1993; Kalleberg and Lincoln 1988).

Critical National Distinctions in the Gendered Division of Labor in Office Work

In both the United States and Japan, clerical work among women was historically concentrated among the young and single. But I have argued that once we acknowledge this historical similarity, the two national situations look quite different. Although larger proportions of married Japanese working women over age thirty have gradually come to participate in the clerical sector, the transformative effect of clerical work for the status of married women in the economy is less evident than in the United States. The clerical sector opened up the possibility of normatively approved employment for older American married women with a high school education or greater who wished to reenter the labor force. Perhaps more importantly, it also offered a long-term career for younger women starting out in the working world—a phenomenon that is not evident in Japanese data. Whereas some clerical jobs in the United

States lead into management positions for American women as well as men, this occurs for Japanese men but virtually never for women (Ishida et al. 2002).

To understand the differences in the implications that the clerical sector has held for middle-aged married women in these two countries, it is not enough to argue that this sector expanded much later in Japan and therefore has not yet incorporated married women to the degree that it did in the United States. The higher labor force participation of middle-aged American married women who had been in clerical work before marriage became a phenomenon by the mid-twentieth century. In contrast, as the data examined in this chapter have shown, Japanese women who work in the clerical sector prior to marriage are currently the *least likely* of any occupational group to be in the labor force when they are married. Middle-aged female clerical workers in Japan are also much more likely than their male counterparts to work in small enterprises, and a large percentage of them work part-time rather than full-time. There is not a sense in Japan that clerical work is a "career" for women. Why is this the case?

I suggest that there are three fundamental reasons: (1) basic differences in the social organization of office work in the United States and Japan, which include whether clerical work remains built into male-dominated internal labor markets or not, (2) differences in labor supply—namely, dramatic historical changes in the supply of young single women in the United States but not in Japan, and (3) the greater cultural significance of age and gender hierarchies in Japan.

The Organization of Office Work: Embedded in Firm-Internal Labor Markets or Not?

As discussed by many Japanese and American social scientists who have written about the Japanese workplace, white-collar jobs have remained much more ambiguous bundles of tasks and responsibilities than in American work settings (Clark 1979; Cole 1979; Lincoln and Kalleberg 1990; Spilerman and Ishida 1996). Large Japanese companies clearly had set the template for the ideal profile of the full-time worker by the mid-twentieth century: a generalist who was hired straight out of school and who aspired to stay with the company until retirement. Anticipating a long tenure on the part of new graduates, employers set them on a track that would involve rotation through the company in various job assignments in order that they would gain a general understanding of the operation of different sections and their interplay (Ishida et al. 2002). Clerical tasks were bundled into the mix of job responsibilities performed by male white-collar workers in their twenties. Young men who are in *sôgôshoku* (management-track) positions and are therefore potential permanent employees of the company engage in a wide variety of tasks during their first several years on the job, competing with others in their age cohort to get promoted into the lower ranks of management (Imada and Hirata 1994; Spilerman and Ishida 1996; Yashiro 1995). Young women play subsidiary office roles and are very rarely in the management track, nor do they monopolize key office functions as is common of more experienced secretaries in the United States. Clerical positions guarantee Japanese women neither indispensability to the company nor progression up even a highly truncated job ladder (Ogasawara 1998). This includes not only young women, but also older women with extensive experience in the office environment.

Changes in Labor Supply

Married women in the United States were increasingly drawn into clerical work only after the sector had feminized and after the supply of young female labor had declined to the point where marriage bars were no longer feasible for employers. Such a decline in the labor supply of single women has been barely visible in Japan. Marriage age continues to increase, and by 2005 it stood at an all-time high of over twenty-seven years for women. Although the Japanese population is rapidly aging, the slowdown in economic growth from the early 1990s on has *increased* the ratio of available new female graduates at all levels of schooling to job openings. Japanese media reports since the mid-1990s have often depicted the long lines of female university and junior college graduates waiting to interview for clerical jobs; were the supply of these highly-educated young women exhausted, new high school graduates would gladly take their place, as such jobs are highly desired by female high school seniors (Rosenbaum and Kariya 1989). Under such conditions, even if the complete feminization of certain clerical jobs were to occur, the increased entrance of married women into those jobs would proceed much more slowly than in the United States.

Cultural Significance of Age and Gender Hierarchies

Finally, whereas a beautiful young receptionist may be valued at corporate headquarters in the United States or at major law firms or other types of offices that deal with an elite client base, age and appearance are otherwise not as important commodities as skill and experience for female American clerical staff. Age is not as important a status-defining characteristic in the United States as in Japan. A young manager who has an MBA from a prestigious business school may have an older, experienced secretary. In such a situation, his educational credentials and status in the firm clearly override the fact that the secretary is more senior to him in terms of age; it does not matter for their interactions with each other. In Japan, status in the work environment is much more related to age. Older women in the workplace constitute an anomaly vis-à-vis younger men. As women, they generally have lower status, but their age gives them higher status. This produces a situation that can be disconcerting for everyone. This cultural difference between the United States and Japan is important because it has ramifications for the work roles that are considered acceptable for older married women in each country. It is more comfortable for Japanese men if the low status attributed to women simply by their gender is complemented by youth as well as by placement in the lowest-level clerical jobs. This produces comfortable status consistency among gender, age, and job status. Older married women disrupt this consistency because culturally they should command more respect due to their age (see also Ogasawara 1998 on the difficulties that female office workers encounter in their interactions with each other when status indicators such as age, education, and work experience are inconsistent). An exception to this discomfort may be work situations such as the small manufacturing company described by Kondo (1990), where older female workers act in a motherly fashion toward young male apprentices. Such logic may work better in the traditional small-scale manufacturing settings Kondo studied than in the sleek corporate offices of Tokyo and other major business centers of Japan.

Looking toward the future, it is clear that the increasing trend toward outsourcing and the rapid development of temporary clerical services in the Japanese economy signal changes in the structure of clerical work in Japanese offices (Houseman and Osawa 1995; Osawa and Kingston 1996). Some categories of clerical work may become more feminized in Japan. But due to the three reasons discussed above, this feminization will not necessarily be coupled with the conversion of full-time clerical jobs into ones culturally designated as appropriate for married women. Instead, it is rapidly becoming apparent that the clerical work performed by Japanese women is becoming more concentrated in part-time and temporary work, and the clerical functions performed by men are remaining within firm-internal career ladders. Despite its low pay compared to professional and managerial jobs, clerical work guaranteed American women a permanent place in the corporate world—a place they would not be required to leave when they married, and a place from which they might launch a different sort of career if they had the skills and initiative to do so. The significance of this fact lies in its profound effect on the continuity of American women's labor force participation across their lives. It is not at all clear that this transformation is occurring in Japan.

This chapter has demonstrated that the historical circumstances of occupational feminization can have important implications in terms of drawing women into the labor force and giving them incentives to form strong labor force attachments that persist long after they marry. Much gender stratification research underemphasizes or denies the positive role that newly feminizing occupations can play in drawing women into the labor force and affecting successive cohorts' human capital investment decisions. When the clerical sector expanded and feminized in the United States in the early decades of the twentieth century it represented good jobs relative to the other choices faced by all but the tiny minority of college-educated American women. It thereby contributed strongly to the possibilities for middle-class married women to participate in the labor force in a culturally acceptable way.

As legal, medical, business, and academic professions have increasingly become more open to American women in successive decades, the relative status and appeal of clerical work has of course declined, but it remains a white-collar sector that is female-typed and has few age barriers. Much has been written about the career squeeze for American women in professions such as law and academics that have rigid requirements for tenure that temporally coincide with women's prime childbearing years. But what if a much wider range of white-collar occupations—such as clerical work—were relatively closed to women who temporarily leave the labor force during the prime childrearing years? One need only look at a case such as Japan or, less widely known, South Korea, to see the result. These cases demonstrate that employers' strong preference to employ young single women in full-time clerical work, especially in the higher-paying large firms, is detrimental to the chances for middle-class married women to participate in occupations that befit their tastes. Just as American middle-class married women earlier in this century were loath to enter the labor force if manufacturing jobs and petty sales jobs were their principal options, so too are married women in these and many other countries. Because of this, researchers of comparative gender stratification need to pay greater attention to the historical and cultural context of female-typed occupations in the occupational structure and to the occupational *age segregation* practiced by employers as well, which often takes place within the context of highly structured internal labor markets designated primarily for men.[12]

Notes

I am grateful to Lungyu Tsai for his research assistance in the preparation of the first draft of this paper, and to Margarita Estévez-Abe and Frances Rosenbluth for helpful suggestions on a later draft.

1. Bernhardt et al. (1995) convincingly argue that the polarization in white men's earnings by educational level was also important in narrowing the male-female wage gap since 1980.

2. Because the labor force participation rates and occupational distribution of white and nonwhite women vary considerably in some historical periods, I restrict the discussion in this paper to white women.

3. Many women gained some specialized clerical skills such as typing in the natural course of their high school education, and some also attended postsecondary secretarial schools. The utility and importance of education and a certain amount of occupational training prior to entering the American office were established early in the century and have continued (Osawa 1988).

4. The extent of leveling in the age distribution of clerical work in Japan is at once considerably less pronounced than in the American data and yet more pronounced than one might expect given the popular image that all Japanese clerical workers are "office ladies," a euphemistic term for young single women in office work (McLendon 1983; Ogasawara 1998).

5. The figures are even higher if we exclude from the denominator women working in agriculture, self-employment, or family enterprises.

6. Among women not working in agriculture, self-employment, or family enterprise, the proportion is even higher (47 percent).

7. There were only two men and one woman in this category in the entire sample.

8. There is no job category except clerical at any of these ages into which more than 10 percent of initial clerical workers move.

9. More than half of the males who started out in clerical work and became managers/administrators by age forty or fifty originated as operations or sales clerks or as "other" clerical workers. Very few women started out as operations or sales clerks; the "other" category was heavily female at young ages but became less so at older ages.

10. This is consistent with findings reported by Brinton (1989) using a different data set.

11. Over 90 percent of both sexes who start out in clerical work do so as full-time employees.

12. Japan has a low index of occupational sex segregation relative to many other industrial and postindustrial economies (Brinton 1993; Charles 1992; Charles and Grusky 2005). But as mentioned earlier in the paper, it also has one of the lowest rates of married women's labor force participation and one of the highest male-female wage gaps.

References

Bergmann, Barbara. 1986. _The Economic Emergence of Women_. New York: Basic Books.

Bernhardt, Annette, Martina Morris, and Mark S. Handcock. 1995. "Women's Gains or Men's Losses? A Closer Look at the Shrinking Gender Gap in Earnings." _American Journal of Sociology_ 101, 2: 302–328.

Bianchi, Suzanne M., and Daphne Spain. 1986. _American Women in Transition_. New York: Russell Sage Foundation.

Blau, Francine D., and Lawrence M. Kahn. 2005. "Do Cognitive Test Scores Explain Higher U.S. Wage Inequality?" _Review of Economics and Statistics_, February.

———. 2006. "Going, Going . . . But Not Gone." Pp. 37–66 in _The Declining Significance of Gender?_ edited by Francine D. Blau, Mary C. Brinton, and David Grusky. New York: Russell Sage Foundation.

Brinton, Mary C. 1989. "Gender Stratification in Contemporary Urban Japan." _American Sociological Review_ 94, 2: 300–334.

———. 1993. _Women and the Economic Miracle: Gender and Work in Postwar Japan_. Berkeley: University of California Press.

Brinton, Mary C., Yean-Ju Lee, and William L. Parish. 1995. "Married Women's Employment in Rapidly Industrializing Societies: Examples from East Asia." _American Journal of Sociology_ 100, 5: 1099–1130.

Brinton, Mary C., and Hang-yue Ngo. 1993. "Age and Sex in the Occupational Structure: A United States–Japan Comparison." _Sociological Forum_ 8, 1: 93–111.

Charles, Maria. 1992. "Cross-National Variation in Occupational Sex Segregation." _American Sociological Review_ 57: 483–502.

Charles, Maria, and David Grusky. 2005. _Occupational Ghettos_. Stanford: Stanford University Press.

Cherlin, Andrew J. 1992. _Marriage, Divorce, Remarriage_. Cambridge, MA: Harvard University Press.

Clark, Rodney. 1979. _The Japanese Company_. New Haven: Yale University Press.

Cohen, Miriam. 1992. _Workshop to Office: Two Generations of Italian Women in New York City, 1900–1950_. Ithaca: Cornell University Press.

Cohn, Samuel. 1985. *The Process of Occupational Sex-Typing: The Feminization of Clerical Labor in Great Britain.* Philadelphia: Temple University Press.

Cole, Robert E. 1979. *Work, Mobility, and Participation.* Berkeley: University of California Press.

Davies, Margery. 1975. "Woman's Place is at the Typewriter: The Feminization of the Clerical Labor Force." Pp. 279–296 in *Labor Market Segmentation,* edited by Richard C. Edwards, Michael Reich, and David M. Gordon. Lexington, MA: D.C. Heath.

Davis, Kingsley. 1984. "Wives and Work: The Sex Role Revolution and Its Consequences." *Population and Development Review* 10, 3: 397–417.

Degler, Carl. 1980. *At Odds.* Oxford: Oxford University Press.

Edwards, Richard C. 1979. *Contested Terrain: The Transformation of the Workplace in the Twentieth Century.* New York: Basic Books.

Goldin, Claudia. 1990. *Understanding the Gender Gap.* New York: Oxford University Press.

Hirao, Keiko. 1997. "Work Histories and Home Investment of Married Japanese Women." Ph.D. dissertation, University of Notre Dame.

Hirao, Keiko. 2002. "The Privatized Education Market and Maternal Employment in Japan." Paper prepared for a conference on The Political Economy of Maternal Employment in Japan, Europe, and the U.S., Yale University, July 22.

Hooks, Janet M. 1947. *Women's Occupations through Seven Decades.* U.S. Department of Labor Women's Bureau Bulletin 218. Washington, DC: U.S. Government Printing Office.

Houseman, Susan, and Machiko Osawa. 1995. "Part-Time and Temporary Employment in Japan." *Monthly Labor Review* 118 (10): 10–18.

Imada, Sachiko, and Shuichi Hirata. 1994. *Howaito-karaa no shoshin kozo* (The promotional structure of white-collar workers). Tokyo: Japan Institute of Labor.

Ishida, Hiroshi, Kuo-Hsien Su, and Seymour Spilerman. 2002. "Models of Career Advancement in Organizations." *European Sociological Review* 18: 179–198.

Ishida, Hiroshi, Seymour Spilerman, and Kuo-Hsien Su. 1997. "Educational Credentials and Promotion Chances in Japanese and American Organizations." *American Sociological Review* 62: 866–882.

Kalleberg, Arne L., and James R. Lincoln. 1988. "The Structure of Earnings Inequality in the United States and Japan." *American Journal of Sociology* 94 (Supplement): S121–S153.

Kanter, Rosabeth Moss. 1977. *Men and Women of the Corporation.* New York: Basic Books.

Kessler-Harris, Alice. 1982. *Out to Work: History of Wage-Earning Women in the United States.* New York: Oxford University Press.

Kondo, Dorinne. 1990. *Crafting Selves: Power, Gender, and Discourses of Identity in a Japanese Workplace.* Chicago: University of Chicago Press.

Lincoln, James R., and Arne L. Kalleberg. 1990. *Culture, Control, and Commitment*. Cambridge: Cambridge University Press.

Lowe, Graham. 1980. "Women, Work and the Office: The Feminization of Clerical Occupations in Canada, 1901–31." *Canadian Journal of Sociology* 5: 354–365.

———. 1986. "Mechanization, Feminization, and Managerial Control in the Early Twentieth-Century Canadian Office." Pp. 177–209 in *On the Job: Confronting the Labour Process in Canada*, edited by Craig Heron and Robert Storey. Montreal: McGill-Queen's University Press.

McLaughlin, Steven, Barbara D. Melber, John O. G. Billy, Denise M. Zimmerle, Linda D. Winges, and Terry R. Johnson. 1988. *The Changing Lives of American Women*. Chapel Hill: University of North Carolina Press.

McLendon, James. 1983. "The Office: Way Station or Blind Alley?" Pp. 156–182 in *Work and Lifecourse in Japan*, edited by David W. Plath. Albany: State University of New York Press.

Milkman, Ruth. 1987. *Gender at Work: The Dynamics of Job Segregation by Sex during World War II*. Urbana: University of Illinois Press.

Ogasawara, Yuko. 1998. *Office Ladies and Salaried Men*. Berkeley: University of California Press.

O'Neill, June, and Solomon Polachek. 1993. "Why the Gender Gap in Wages Narrowed in the 1980s." *Journal of Labor Economics* 11: 205–228.

Oppenheimer, Valerie Kincaid. 1970. *The Female Labor Force in the United States*. Berkeley: Institute for International Studies.

———. 1994. "Women's Rising Employment and the Future of the Family in Industrial Societies." *American Journal of Sociology* 93: 659–687.

Osawa, Machiko. 1988. "Changing Role of Education and Women Workers in Japan." *Keio Business Review* 24, 5: 87–101.

Osawa, Machiko, and Jeff Kingston. 1996. "Flexibility and Inspiration: Restructuring and the Japanese Labor Market." *Japan Labor Bulletin* (January 1): 4–8.

Reskin, Barbara, and Patricia Roos. 1990. *Job Queues, Gender Queues*. Philadelphia: Temple University Press.

Rosenbaum, James, and Takehiko Kariya. 1989. "From High School to Work: Market and Institutional Mechanisms in Japan." *American Journal of Sociology* 94: 1334–1365.

Shirahase, Sawako. 2002. "Women's Working Pattern and the Support to Working Mothers in Contemporary Japan." Paper presented at Workshop on Political Economy of Childcare and Female Employment: Japan in Comparative Perspective, New Haven, CT, Yale University, January 18.

Smith, James P., and Michael P. Ward. 1984. "Time-Series Growth in the Female Labor Force." *Journal of Labor Economics* 3: 559–590.

Spilerman, Seymour, and Takeshi Ishida. 1996. "Stratification and Attainment in a Large Japanese Firm." Pp. 317–342 in *Generating Social Stratification*, edited by Alan C. Kerckhoff. Boulder: Westview.

Tanaka, Kazuko. 1987. "Women, Work, and Family in Japan: A Life Cycle Perspective." Ph.D. dissertation, University of Iowa.

Tanaka, Shigeto. 1998. "Kogakurekika to seibetsu bungyo: josei no raifutaimu danzetsu shugyo ni taisuru gakko kyoiku no koka (Higher education and the sexual division of labor: the schooling effect on women's continuous full-time employment)." Pp. 1–16 in *Josei no kyaria kozo to sono henka* (Changing career structures of women), edited by Kazuo Seiyama and Sachiko Imada. Volume 12 of *SSM Survey Series*. Tokyo: SSM Chosa Kenkyukai.

Walters, Pamela Barnhouse, and Philip J. O'Connell. 1988. "The Family Economy, Work, and Educational Participation in the United States, 1890–1940." *American Journal of Sociology* 93, 5: 1116–1152.

Wellington, Allison J. 1993. "Changes in the Male/Female Wage Gap, 1976–1985." *Journal of Human Resources* 28: 83–141.

Yamaguchi, Kazuo. 1997. "Continuing Major Disruption: Determinants of Historical Changes in the Rate of Job Separations Due to Marriage or Childbirth/Childcare among Japanese Women." Working paper, Department of Sociology, University of Chicago.

Yashiro, Atsushi. 1995. *Daikigyo howaito karaa no kyaria* (White-collar careers in large firms). Tokyo: Japan Institute of Labor.

CHAPTER 5

Employment Options: Japan in Comparative Perspective

EIKO KENJOH

Introduction

Despite a general pattern of declining female labor force participation with childbirth, there is still substantial and intriguing variation across industrialized countries in this relationship. We know, for example, that there is a pronounced "M-curve" in Japan in female labor force participation, where many women drop out of the labor force with the birth of their first child. In some other countries, many women continue to work, largely wiping out the drop in market participation that produces the M shape. Public policies can affect a woman's choice to stay in the market or to leave at childbirth by creating different economic incentives surrounding this choice. Generous parental leave and accessible childcare can ease a woman's transition between work and parenting, thereby making it more possible for mothers to maintain their careers across their life cycle (Kenjoh 2004).

Estévez-Abe and Brinton (this volume) have argued that Japan's labor markets are so inhospitable to women that parental leave and childcare policies alone are likely to be insufficient to boost dramatically a woman's ability to balance family and career. By implication, these policies are also likely to be insufficient to induce women to strive both for career success and to give birth to a larger number of children. Japan may indeed require a fundamental overhaul of its labor markets to put women on equal footing with men and to motivate higher fertility at the same time. In this chapter, I take on a smaller piece of the problem by showing how high-quality part-time work can go some distance toward helping women achieve their goals.

The rest of the paper is organized as follows. The next section presents a vignette of the Netherlands, where government policies supporting high-quality part-time work seem to have increased the labor market attachment of Dutch women in comparison with Japan. The third section presents some statistical analysis of work decisions after the birth of a first child in Japan, the Netherlands, Britain, Germany, and Sweden. The results seem to confirm my hunch that the availability of good part-time jobs might help Japanese women's efforts to balance family and career.

Maternal Employment in the Netherlands and Japan

Let us first look at Figures 5.1 through 5.4, which show the employment patterns of Dutch and Japanese mothers around the birth of their first child, using household panel data sets from the two countries. I have selected the sample of women who gave birth to their first child in the 1980s and the 1990s and matched with the information on labor force status (see Kenjoh 2004 for more detailed explanation of the data). For the Netherlands, the labor force status of the first-time mothers is organized so that month zero represents the month in which the child was born. Month 12 then represents the month when the child was one year old and month −12 represents one year before the child was born. For Japan, the results are based on yearly information. Thus, −1

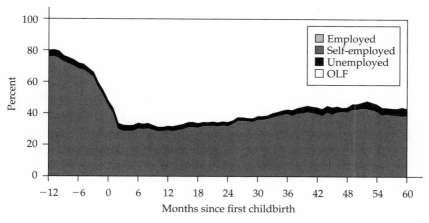

FIGURE 5.1 Monthly Employment Status after Childbirth in the Netherlands, 1980s

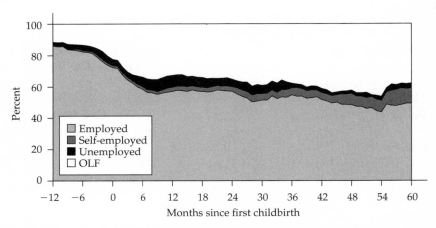

FIGURE 5.2 Monthly Employment Status after Childbirth in the Netherlands, 1990s

indicates one year before the child was born. Note that the birth took place at different calendar times for each woman during the 1980s and the 1990s.

Comparing Figures 5.1 and 5.3, we can see that there is rather surprisingly large resemblance of the employment patterns between Dutch and Japanese mothers who had their first child in the 1980s. In both countries, nearly 90 percent of women participate in the labor market before pregnancy, whereas around the time of childbirth only 30 percent of them are employed. Further, as the child grows older, the employment rate of mothers gradually increases, up to 40 percent at the time when the first child reaches five years old.

Figures 5.2 and 5.4, however, present very different development between the two countries. In Japan, women's employment rates after childbirth hardly changed from the 1980s to the 1990s. By contrast, in the Netherlands, it increased dramatically between the two decades. For instance, the employment rate of Dutch women five years after childbirth was about 60 percent in the 1990s. Unfortunately, there is no information on the division between part-time and full-time employment on a monthly basis in the Dutch data set (OSA).[1] However, it is reasonable to assume that most of the employed women with young children are working part-time in the Netherlands. For example, in the 1998 OSA, among 178 female employees with children younger than six years old, 158 women (89 percent) worked less than 35 hours per week (own computation based on OSA 1998).

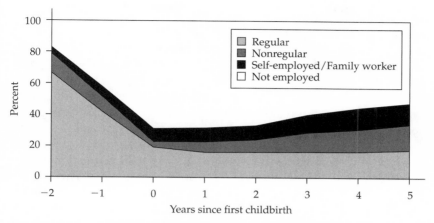

FIGURE 5.3 Yearly Employment Status after Childbirth in Japan, 1980s

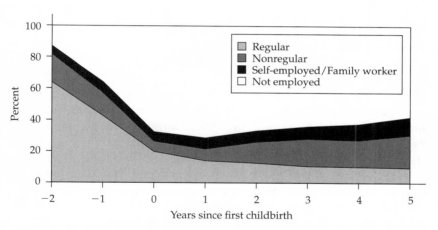

FIGURE 5.4 Yearly Employment Status after Childbirth in Japan, 1990s

The large increase in the employment rate from the 1980s to the 1990s can be explained not only by the wider social acceptance of mothers who work, but also by the revolution of part-time employment in the 1990s. In the Netherlands, the status of part-time employees improved significantly in the 1990s. The 2000 Act on Adjustment of Working Hours ensures the right of employees in firms with more than ten employees to shorten or increase work hours on request if they have been employed for at least one year. This is the most advanced treatment of part-time employment in the Organization for Economic Development and Cooperation (OECD). Moreover, hourly wages of part-time workers are as high as those of full-time workers for both men and women, holding other characteristics of workers constant (Gustafsson, Kenjoh, and Wetzels 2003; Visser 1999).

Additionally, Dutch family policies such as childcare and parental leave have shown relatively modest improvement. For example, in 1995, 12.2 percent of children under four years of age attended day care centers, while most of these children came only a few days a week. If children were to come the whole week, only half as many children, 6.7 percent rather than 12.2 percent, would have a space. This is not a high percentage compared to Japan (Kenjoh 2004). Furthermore, the Dutch parental leave scheme was established in 1991, but only provided a legal right to working part-time for six months. It was as late as in 1997 that mothers obtained an option to stay at home full-time for three months (Wetzels 2001; Kenjoh 2004).

First-Time Mothers' Employment Choice After Childbirth

This section analyzes women's employment choices in the five years after the birth of the first child in Japan, the Netherlands, Britain, Germany, and Sweden. The main question of this analysis is whether labor force participation behavior of first-time mothers with the same human capital differs or is similar in the five countries under different family policies in the 1980s and 1990s. The latter three countries, in addition to Japan and the Netherlands, are examined because they present a considerable variation of family-friendly policies, especially for the period from the 1980s to the 1990s (Gustafsson 1994, Wetzels 2001, and Kenjoh 2004 for information on family policies in these countries). I estimate multinomial logit models of employment choices of first-time mothers, using yearly data for Japan and monthly data for the four European countries. These data are constructed based on household panel data sets from each of the five countries. After her childbirth, an individual woman is assumed to choose her employment status. Depending on data availability, for Britain, Germany, and Sweden, employment status is classified into full-time employment, part-time employment, and not at work (including being on leave, unemployed, and out of the labor force). For Japan, an additional category of "self-employed or family workers"[3] is added

as an option, since this employment status applies to significant proportion of women, as can be seen from Figures 5.3 and 5.4. For the Netherlands, employment status distinguishes between being employed and
not being employed, thus there are two choices for Dutch women: being
employed and not being employed.

The Estimation Results

Tables 5.1 through 5.5 present the results of the multinomial logit analyses for Britain, Germany, Sweden, and Japan and the binary logit analysis for the Netherlands. The results are reported in the form of the relative risk ratio (RRR). The interpretation of a RRR of smaller (or larger)
than one is that the variable in question decreases (or increases) the
probability of taking an employment status in comparison to the base
value of that variable. In the following, I discuss the effects variable by
variable for all the models across the five countries.

The first set of variables in the tables indicates the effect of education

TABLE 5.1
Multinomial logit model of mothers' employment status after birth of first child in Britain

	FULL-TIME		PART-TIME	
	RRR	Z-value	RRR	Z-value
Education medium	1.66	2.5**	1.51	2.5**
Education high	2.20	4.4***	1.58	2.7***
Mother's age at first birth	1.28	2.2**	1.69	3.8***
Mother's age at first birth, squared	1.00	−1.5	0.99	−3.5***
First child born in 1990s	1.84	4.0***	1.58	3.4***
Age of first child	1.30	7.7***	1.49	13.2***
Presence of second child	0.29	−7.3***	0.50	−5.3***
Unemployment rate	0.95	−1.9*	1.00	0.2
Number of observations (woman-months)	59,045			
Number of women	1,128			
Wald chi^2 (16)	341			
Prob > chi^2	0.00			
Pseudo R^2	0.077			
Log likelihood	−48,812			

SOURCE: Author's own computations based on BHPS 1991–1998.

NOTE: Robust variance estimates are calculated by controlling for personal identification. Self-employed
workers are not included in the sample. Education high: obtained qualification requiring 15 years or more of
schooling; Medium: between 12 years and 14 years of schooling; Low: less than 12 years of schooling.

*$p < .10$ **$p < .05$ ***$p < .01$

TABLE 5.2

Multinomial logit model of mothers' employment status after birth of first child in West Germany

	FULL-TIME		PART-TIME	
	RRR	Z-value	RRR	Z-value
Education medium	1.00	0.0	0.91	−0.3
Education high	1.78	1.9*	1.54	2.0**
Mother's age at first birth	1.50	1.9*	1.27	1.4
Mother's age at first birth, squared	0.99	−1.9*	1.00	−1.4
First child born in 1990s	0.39	−3.8***	0.73	−1.9*
Age of first child	1.51	7.8***	1.72	14.6***
Presence of second child	0.18	−5.3***	0.22	−8.1***
Unemployment rate	1.13	1.5	0.93	−1.5
Number of observations (woman-months)	31,754			
Number of women	632			
Wald chi^2 (16)	250			
Prob > chi^2	0.00			
Pseudo R^2	0.080			
Log likelihood	−24,253			

SOURCE: Author's own computations based on GSOEP 1984–1998, Sample A = Germans in the former West Germany.

NOTE: Robust variance estimates are calculated by controlling for personal identification. Education high: obtained qualification requiring 15 years or more of schooling; Medium: between 12 years and 14 years of schooling; Low: less than 12 years of schooling.

*$p < .10$ **$p < .05$ ***$p < .01$

TABLE 5.3

Multinomial logit model of mothers' employment status after birth of first child in Sweden

	FULL-TIME		PART-TIME	
	RRR	Z-value	RRR	Z-value
Education medium	1.12	0.3	0.69	−1.5
Education high	1.34	0.9	0.79	−1.0
Mother's age at first birth	0.68	−1.6	0.86	−0.7
Mother's age at first birth, squared	1.01	1.8*	1.00	0.8
First child born in 1990s	0.91	−0.2	0.77	−0.7
Age of first child	2.14	7.1***	2.17	9.6***
Presence of second child	0.20	−4.3***	0.25	−5.7***
Unemployment rate	0.98	−0.4	1.01	0.2
Number of observations (woman-months)	10,086			
Number of women	259			
Wald chi^2 (16)	144			
Prob > chi^2	0.00			
Pseudo R^2	0.094			
Log likelihood	−9,000			

SOURCE: Author's own computations based on HUS 1984–1998.

NOTE: Robust variance estimates are calculated by controlling for personal identification. Education high: obtained qualification requiring 15 years or more of schooling; Medium: between 12 years and 14 years of schooling; Low: less than 12 years of schooling.

*$p < .10$ **$p < .05$ ***$p < .01$

TABLE 5.4

Binary logit model of mothers' employment status after birth of first child in the Netherlands

	EMPLOYED	
	Odds	Z-value
Education medium	1.80	3.4***
Education high	4.11	5.7***
Mother's age at first birth	1.50	2.2**
Mother's age at first birth, squared	0.99	−1.9*
First child born in 1990s	1.86	2.9***
Age of first child	1.05	1.3
Presence of second child	0.80	−1.3
Unemployment rate	0.89	−1.9*
Number of observations (woman-months)	24,679	
Number of women	569	
Wald chi^2 (8)	97	
Prob > chi^2	0.00	
Pseudo R^2	0.097	
Log likelihood	−15,305	

SOURCE: Author's own computations based on OSA 1985–1998.

NOTE: Robust variance estimates are calculated by controlling for personal identification. Education high: obtained qualification requiring 15 years or more of schooling; Medium: between 12 years and 14 years of schooling; Low: less than 12 years of schooling.

*$p < .10$ **$p < .05$ ***$p < .01$

TABLE 5.5

Multinomial logit model of mothers' employment status after birth of first child in Japan

	REGULAR		NONREGULAR		FAMILY WORKERS	
	RRR	Z	RRR	Z	RRR	Z
Education medium	1.43	1.8*	1.05	0.3	0.82	−0.8
Education high	3.27	4.0***	0.38	−1.7*	1.02	0.0
Mother's age at first birth	0.71	−1.2	0.42	−3.0***	1.90	1.4
Mother's age at first birth, squared	1.01	1.3	1.01	2.6***	0.99	−1.4
First child born in 1990s	0.73	−1.4	2.59	4.1***	0.79	−0.8
Age of first child	1.12	2.9***	1.74	12.3***	1.23	4.6***
Presence of second child	0.51	−3.8***	0.25	−7.7***	0.79	−1.2
Unemployment rate	0.82	−1.3	0.66	−2.4**	0.91	−0.5
Living with parents or in-laws	3.87	7.3***	1.53	2.4**	4.21	6.9***
Number of observations (woman-years)	4,818					
Number of women	913					
Wald chi^2 (27)	361					
Prob > chi^2	0.00					
Pseudo R^2	0.090					
Log likelihood	−4,589					

SOURCE: Author's own computations based on JSPC 1993–1997.

NOTE: Robust variance estimates are calculated by controlling for personal identification. Education high: obtained qualification requiring 16 years or more of schooling (four-year university graduates or above); Medium: between 13 years and 15 years of schooling (junior college or vocational school graduates); Low: less than 13 years of schooling (high school graduates or less than high school).

*$p < .10$ **$p < .05$ ***$p < .01$

on the probability of working in paid labor compared to being a full-time housewife after becoming a mother. Women's education is expected to have a positive effect on female labor force participation after the birth of the first child, since higher-educated women on average earn more than lower-educated women.[4] If childcare services are available in the private market with no subsidies, affordability of childcare will solely depend on the earning powers of the family. A positive effect of education is detected in Japan, the Netherlands, Britain, and the former West Germany, albeit to differing degrees. The most prominent effect is found for the Netherlands; the probability of being employed for highly educated women is four times as large as that for women with less than a high school diploma, holding other variables constant. On the other hand, there is no statistically significant effect of education in Sweden, which I assume is on account of the egalitarian access to subsidized daycare and paid parental leave.

The positive effect of education is stronger on full-time employment than part-time employment in Britain and, to lesser extent, in Germany. However, in Japan, although better-educated women are more likely to work in full-time regular employment, they are less likely to work in nonregular employment such as part-time and temporary employment. This peculiar result for nonregular work can be explained by the fact that part-time employment provides significantly lower wages and other disadvantageous labor conditions compared with full-time regular employment in Japan (Houseman and Osawa 2003; Kenjoh 2004). Therefore, mothers with higher education levels have almost no incentive to work part time.

A mother's age at first childbirth and its square enter the regressions in order to examine the effect of human capital accumulation at first birth. The hypothesis is that a higher age implies the acquisition of a larger amount of human capital that steps up the likelihood of full-time or part-time employment. Similar to the effect of education, a mother's age at first birth has a positive effect on being employed in the Netherlands and Britain and on full-time employment in Germany. In these countries, older mothers are more attached to the labor market than younger mothers. In Sweden, the mother's age has no statistically significant effect, as was the case for the educational variables. In Japan, the coefficient of this variable for nonregular work again shows an effect opposite to what would have been expected. That is, older mothers are less likely to work as nonregular workers than younger mothers, which can be explained by Japanese labor market characteristics.

The next variable captures developments over time by comparing the employment status of mothers who had their first child in the 1990s with that of mothers who had their first child in the 1980s. In order to interpret this variable as a proxy for the effect of policy changes from the 1980s to the 1990s, I control for the labor market situation by including the monthly unemployment rate (the yearly unemployment rate for Japan). On the one hand, the number of British and Dutch mothers working in paid employment in the 1990s nearly doubled compared to the 1980s, holding other variables constant. On the other hand, German mothers in the 1990s stayed at home more after childbirth than in the 1980s, which is in line with the expansion of maternity leave from the mid-1980s to the mid-1990s.[5] In Sweden, there was no significant change between the 1980s and the 1990s, because the relevant policies had been in effect since the 1970s: paid parental leaves shared between fathers and mothers during the child's first year, subsidized day care for preschool children, full-day schools that accommodate parents' working hours, and separate individual taxation of earnings. In Japan, this variable is only significant for nonregular employment. Mothers who gave birth to their first child in the 1990s are nearly three times as likely to be nonregular workers compared to those who gave birth in the 1980s.

The age of the first child has a positive effect on employment for mothers after birth in all the countries examined except the Netherlands. As the child grows older, women are more likely to work in paid labor. The effect of this variable was the largest in Sweden, followed by Germany, Britain, and Japan. In Sweden, where the most generous and flexible parental leave system is offered to parents, a larger proportion of women return to paid work as the child becomes older. In contrast, in the Netherlands, this variable has no effect, which indicates a clear distinction between workers and nonworkers. Considering the above results on the strong influence of education and mother's age at first childbirth, it is typical that Dutch mothers with larger human capital—namely better-educated and older mothers—have been working continuously in the labor market for five years after childbirth, whereas those with smaller human capital have been staying at home during this period.

Moreover, the effect of the age of the first child is slightly stronger for working part-time than for working full-time. In other words, during the first five years after childbirth, mothers (re)enter the labor market more often as part-time workers than as full-time workers. This is unsurprising, since part-time work may be more compatible with caring for children. The difference in the size of the effect between full-time and part-time employment is particularly large in Japan. In terms of the M-curve, not only is the second "hump" smaller, but it is of a different quality as well. That is, most of the mothers who reenter paid work after giving birth are not full-time regular workers but nonregular workers such as part-time and temporary workers. This can also be attributed to the fact that the availability of full-time regular jobs is limited for potential reentrants with children under Japanese employment practices.

I enter a variable to control for the presence of the second child in the household.[6] This variable is expected to have a negative effect on mother's employment, since having another very young child raises a mother's time cost at home. If she works in the labor market, additional childcare would be required. This expectation is confirmed in all the countries studied here except in the Netherlands. The negative effect is particularly strong in Sweden and Germany, where longer job protection is available after childbirth so that women are likely to take parental leave after giving birth to the second child. Having the second child decreases the probability of being in the labor market more for full-time employment than for part-time work in Britain, Germany, and Sweden. This finding suggests that part-time employment is more compatible than full-time employment with caring for two children. On the contrary, in Japan the negative effect is stronger on nonregular employment than regular employment, which again indicates the peculiarity of part-time employment in Japan.

In the estimations for Japan, a (time-variant) variable of living with parents or in-laws is included, since many adults still live with their parents.[7] A positive effect of this variable on married women's labor force participation, especially on full-time employment, is repeatedly observed in previous studies on Japan (Ogawa and Ermisch 1996; Shimada and Higuchi 1985). This is due to the fact that under less-developed public policies, a childcare role for grandparents, especially grandmothers, has been traditionally very important for mothers to combine market work and family responsibility. In my data set, 40 percent of mothers are living with their parents or in-laws. The expected positive effect on mothers' employment is confirmed in Table 5.6. Women living with their parents or in-laws are four times more likely to be regular workers or family workers compared to those who do not live with their parents or in-laws.

TABLE 5.6
Predicted probability of employment status of mothers

	1980s			1990s		
	Low	Medium	High	Low	Medium	High
Britain						
Full-time	0.17	0.23	0.28	0.24	0.31	0.36
Part-time	0.25	0.31	0.30	0.31	0.35	0.33
Not at work	0.58	0.47	0.43	0.45	0.34	0.30
West Germany						
Full-time	0.19	0.20	0.25	0.10	0.10	0.13
Part-time	0.36	0.34	0.41	0.33	0.31	0.41
Not at work	0.45	0.47	0.34	0.57	0.60	0.46
The Netherlands						
Employed	0.31	0.45	0.65	0.46	0.61	0.78
Not employed	0.69	0.55	0.35	0.54	0.39	0.22
Sweden						
Full-time	0.17	0.23	0.25	0.19	0.24	0.27
Part-time	0.53	0.43	0.44	0.47	0.37	0.39
Not at work	0.29	0.34	0.31	0.34	0.38	0.35
Japan						
Regular	0.11	0.15	0.30	0.07	0.10	0.23
Nonregular	0.11	0.11	0.03	0.25	0.25	0.09
Self-employed	0.09	0.07	0.07	0.06	0.05	0.06
Not employed	0.70	0.67	0.59	0.62	0.60	0.62

SOURCE: Author's own computations based on BHPS 1991–1998, GSOEP 1984–1998, OSA 1985–1998, HUS 1984–1998, and JPSC 1993–1997.

NOTE: A hypothetical woman who was 27 years old at the birth of the first child when the child is 36 months (3 years for Japan) old and who does not have a second child. Unemployment rates are set at the sample average in each country. For Japan, the woman does not live with her parents or in-laws.

Predicted Probability of Employment of New Mothers

In order to further clarify the difference in employment choices of first-time mothers according to educational levels and whether the child was born in the 1980s or the 1990s, the predicted probability of taking employment is calculated from the results of the multinomial logit analyses (binary logit analysis for the Dutch data). The probability is computed for a hypothetical woman who is twenty-seven years of age at the birth of the first child and whose child is thirty-six months old (three years old for Japan) and who does not have a second child. The unemployment rate is set to the mean for each country. Additionally, for Japan I assume that the woman does not live with her parents or in-laws.

Table 5.6 presents the predicted probabilities. The table reveals that the probability of being employed is higher in Sweden than in the other countries, especially in the 1980s. For mothers in the 1990s, this probability increased sharply in Britain and the Netherlands. In contrast, the probability has decreased in Germany and Sweden and only increased to a limited extent in Japan. Again, this points to the beneficial effects of policies designed to support working parents. The decrease in Germany reflects the extension of statutory parental leave. In Sweden, policies remained advantageous, and the decrease is likely to be due to the increase in the general level of unemployment.

Table 5.6 further shows the importance of part-time employment as an employment status for mothers during the five years following the first birth. In Germany, Britain, and Sweden, the probability of being in part-time employment is 30–50 percent for women who gave birth to the first child both in the 1980s and 1990s, no matter what their educational level. In Sweden, many mothers make use of a parent's right to shorten her working hours to 30 hours as a regular worker. Moreover, in the Netherlands, it is inferred that a majority of mothers work in part-time employment. However, in Japan, the probability of being a nonregular worker (part-time or temporary worker) is not as high as in the other countries. The probability is particularly low for women with the highest educational level. Given the limited availability of daycare for children under age three and the less generous and inflexible parental leave arrangements, the low employment rate of Japanese mothers can also be attributed to the lack of part-time employment opportunities with reasonable pay.

Conclusions

This chapter analyzed women's employment after the birth of the first child in Japan, compared to Britain, Germany, the Netherlands, and Sweden. Social policies aimed at helping women balance family and career apparently matter. The length of parental leave, the level of the benefit paid during the leave, the flexibility of leave arrangements, and the availability of affordable childcare all seem to have a positive effect on the employment status of new mothers. But the level of government support required in order for significantly more women to reenter the labor market will vary by how much the labor market penalizes women for interrupting their careers in the first place. Given the rigid internal labor markets that typify the large firm sector in Japan, it is hard to imagine a level of government subsidy for leave and childcare that will put women on equal footing with men in the absence of labor market changes.

Improving the quality of part-time work, as the Dutch government has done in recent years, may be a first step to helping Japanese women stay in the labor market after the birth of their first child. I am not advocating the use of women as low-status buffers in insecure, low-skill part-time jobs. I mean instead the possibility of high-quality part-time jobs in professions—such as medicine, law, and accounting—as has become fairly common in the Netherlands. The increased ability to combine motherhood with paid full- or part-time employment might well encourage more women to have children. Particularly if men also reduce their employment hours to help in the home when their children are young, this kind of labor market flexibility holds some promise for increasing gender equality.

Notes

I am grateful for the support of the EU MOCHO project, The Rationale of Motherhood Choices: Influence of Employment Conditions and of Public Policies (Contract No. HPSE-CT2001-0096), and partly the European Centre for Analysis in the Social Sciences (ECASS) at the Institute for Social and Economic Research, University of Essex, and the Access to Research Infrastructure action of the EU Improving Human Potential Programme.

1. I use the Labour Force Supply Panel collected by Organisatie voor Strategisch Arbeidsmarktonderzoek (OSA) 1985–1998 for the Netherlands and the Japanese Panel Survey of Consumers (JPSC) 1993–1997 for Japan.

2. The Dutch and Japanese data are the sub-sample of the data used in the graphical analysis in Figures 5.1 through 5.4. For Britain, I have used the British Household Panel Survey (BHPS) 1991–1998, for the former West Germany, Sample A (Germans in the former West German area) of the German Socio-Economic Panel (GSOEP) 1984–1998, and for Sweden, the Hushållens ekonomiska levnadsförhållanden (HUS) 1984–1998.

3. In the following, I often refer to this category as family workers for brevity.

4. The effect of an increase in women's wage rate on their labor supply theoretically depends on the size of the negative income effect and the positive substitution effect. However, the bulk of empirical research on the female labor supply in North America and Europe demonstrates that the positive substitution effect dominates the negative income effect, resulting in a positive gross effect of women's wages (see, for instance, Killingsworth 1983; Killingsworth and Heckman 1986).

5. The parental leave period in the former West Germany was extended

from six months in 1979 to 24 months in 1993, by which time the country was reunified (Wetzels 2001). However, leave benefits are low compared to Sweden. During the period covered by this analysis most women were only entitled to leave benefits for up to six months after childbirth. In addition, childcare services are very limited in the former West Germany: only 2 percent of children under 3 years old went to childcare in 1994 (Kreyenfeld, Spiess and Wagner 2000).

6. This is a time variant variable, which takes on the value one from the birth of the second child, and zero, otherwise.

7. In the Japanese data set, JPSC, there is a detailed question on living arrangements with parents or in-laws. The dummy variable of living with parents or in-laws equals one in cases where respondents reported that they lived in the same household as their parents or in-laws or lived on the same building site but in a separate building. This information has been available every year since the first wave of 1993. For years before 1993, the value for 1993 is assigned.

References

Gustafsson, S. S. (1994). "Childcare and Types of Welfare States," in D. Sainsbury, ed., *Gendering Welfare States*. London: Sage.

Gustafsson, S. S., E. Kenjoh, and C. Wetzels (2003). "Employment Choices and Pay Differences between Nonstandard and Standard Work in Britain, Germany, the Netherlands, and Sweden" in Houseman, S. and M. Osawa, eds. (2003), *Nonstandard Work in Developed Economies: Causes and Consequences*. Kalamazoo, MI: Upjohn Institute.

Houseman, S. N., and M. Osawa, eds. (2003). *Nonstandard Work in Developed Economies: Causes and Consequences*. Kalamazoo, MI: Upjohn Institute.

Kenjoh, E. (2004). *Balancing Work and Family Life in Japan and Four European Countries: Econometric Analyses on Mothers' Employment and Timing of Maternity*. Timbergen Institute Research Series. Amsterdam: Thela Thesis.

Killingsworth, M. (1983). *Labour Supply*. Cambridge: Cambridge University Press.

Killingsworth, M., and J. J. Heckman (1986). "Female Labor Supply: A Survey," in O. Ashenfelter and R. Layard, eds., *Handbook of Labor Economic*, Volume I. North Holland: Amsterdam. 103–204.

Kreyenfeld, M., K. C. Spiess, and G. G. Wagner (2000). "A Forgotten Issue: Distributional Effects of Day Care Subsidies in Germany." *IZA Discussion Paper Series*, No. 198.

Ogawa, N., and J. F. Ermisch (1996). "Family Structure, Home Time Demands, and the Employment Patterns of Japanese Married Women." *Journal of Labor Economics* 14(4): 677–702.

Shimada, H., and Y. Higuchi (1985). "An Analysis of Trends in Female Labor Force Participation in Japan." *Journal of Labor Economics* 3(1), Part 2, S355–S374.

Visser, J. (1999). "The First Part-Time Economy in the World: Does It Work?" Working paper, Department of PSCW, University of Amsterdam.

Wetzels, C. M. M. P. (2001). *Squeezing Birth into Working Life: Household Panel Data Analyses Comparing Germany, Great Britain, Sweden and The Netherlands*. Aldershot: Ashgate.

PART THREE

Constraints on Women's Supply of Labor

CHAPTER 6

Policies to Support Working Mothers and Children in Japan

PATRICIA BOLING

Introduction

This chapter provides a guide to current family policies in Japan. In the following section, I lay out public policies that govern child allowances, tax breaks for dependents, public childcare, and childcare leaves. The Japanese government's public subsidies of childcare look positively generous compared to lower government spending in the United States, where childcare needs are more commonly met by low-paid workers in the private sector. But Japan's declining fertility has led to a great deal of soul searching in government circles, and has prompted regular reviews of childcare policies and attempts to squeeze more effectiveness out of limited funds. While fertility continues to slide and the search for the magic policy bullet continues, the problem remains larger than the amount of taxes the government is willing to commit. The third section examines the policy process that produces and amends these policies over time, with attention to who benefits and who pays. In conclusion, I suggest explanations for why these policies have developed as they have.

Public Policies

Analysts of policies to support working mothers commonly look to an array of related measures: cash benefits given as family allowances; public support for and regulation of childcare services; use of the public school system to provide usable supervision of children while parents work; childrearing leaves; pensions; and tax measures that allow deductions or credits for dependents or for dependent care expenses, or that other-wise affect families or women who work outside the home. Following this rubric, I focus here on family allowances, the childcare system, maternity and parenting leaves, and tax policies, and the possibility that these might change.

Childcare Allowances

Child allowances were established in Japan in 1972. Initially they applied only to large families, since they covered only the third and subsequent children below 18 years of age. The allowance was extended to apply to the second child in 1988, and to all children in 1994, but with the stipu-lation that it would only apply to children under the age of three. The family income threshold that is required to be eligible for this benefit is related to how many dependents there are and to whether the head of household is an employee or self-employed.[1]

The most recent revision was enacted in 2000, when the system was expanded to cover children up to the age of six. This measure had its be-ginnings in December 1999, when the Liberal Democratic Party, Komeito (affiliated with the Soka Gakkai Buddhist sect), and the Democratic Party of Japan agreed after intense discussions to expand child allow-ance payments to children up to age six. This decision was a compromise between the LDP and Komeito, the latter of which had been pushing for even more extensive expansions in the program: coverage of children up to age sixteen, a significant increase in the amount of the allowance, and elimination of income requirements so that all families would receive it. The payment remained at the same level as before, ¥5,000 per child per month for the first two children, ¥10,000 for third and subsequent chil-dren, payable as long as the youngest child is under age six (equivalent to $43 and $86, or to €37.4 and €74.8 at current exchange rates). Receipt is not automatic; the benefit must be applied for at the local town hall, which determines whether the family meets the income threshold. Re-cipients of child allowances must submit a yearly "notice of current situ-ation" in order to continue to receive the allowance (Abe 2002, S69).

Curiously, the uptake rate for the child allowance is rather low: only 20 percent of households with children under the age of three that met the income threshold received this benefit in 1996 (Abe 2002, S72). Aya Abe speculates that the reason for this low uptake rate might have to do with the bother and expense of applying for the benefit, which requires a family member to take a day off from work, gather together some paperwork, and take it in person to the town hall. The trade-off between forgone wages and the small benefit may not seem worthwhile. Abe also suggests that lack of awareness of the benefit may explain why so few people apply for it (Abe 2002, S76).

Indeed, before 1999, Ministry of Health and Welfare officials repeatedly discounted the importance of the child allowance, calling into question the efficacy of such a small monthly payment for relieving the financial stresses of childrearing or encouraging people to have (more) children. Liberal Democratic Party (LDP) politicians also made this argument frequently in the debates about expanding the family allowance program that continued from late 1999 through the summer of 2000. But Komeito insisted on a more generous family allowance program as a condition for its continued support of the governing coalition, and it was able to force the LDP to make concessions to keep it on board. Initially, income requirements to qualify for the family allowance payment meant that only 72.5 percent of families with children under age six would receive it, but that was later revised so that now 85 percent of these families may receive the payment (Foundation for Children's Future 2002a; Study Group 2000b).

The mechanism for funding these expanded family allowance payments has also drawn criticism. Rather than simply fund expanded child allowance payments out of general tax revenue (as Komeito would have preferred), the LDP was able to insist that the money come from cuts in dependent child tax deductions, which were trimmed by ¥100,000 ($862, from ¥480,000 to ¥380,000) per child under the age of sixteen. In theory, the tax cut and the increase in family allowances roughly balance out; the net impact of the change in policy is to take money from relatively better-off families with older children and transfer it to somewhat poorer families with younger children (Honda 2001). The revised family allowance policy appears to be the result of a political compromise between Komeito's desire to support families with young children, and LDP concerns about keeping tight control over the budget during an era of recessions and strapped budgets.

Tax Breaks and the Employment System

Japanese income tax law allows significant deductions for both dependent children and dependent spouses. Both deductions offer support to families by supplementing the earnings of the primary wage earner, but the spousal deduction (*haigusha tokubetsu kōjō*) has been fiercely attacked by feminists and analysts who see it as discouraging women from participating on equal terms in the workforce. The reason for this is that the full spousal deduction, ¥760,000 ($6,550), is given when the dependent spouse makes ¥700,000 ($6,035) or less a year. When the dependent spouse (usually the wife) makes over ¥700,000, this triggers an incremental reduction, which reaches ¥380,000 ($3,275) when her income reaches ¥1,030,000 ($8,880). When her income reaches ¥1,410,000 ($12,155) and above, there is no deduction. Labor economists have shown that the spousal deduction affects many women's decisions about whether to work full-time or part-time, and about accepting low-paid work, since their marginal earnings are wiped out by the loss in spousal deductions (Shibata 1992; Shiota 2000, 170–171; *Asahi Shimbun* 2002). Various commissions on promoting gender equality have joined these critics in recommending that the spousal deduction be eliminated because of its dampening influence on women's workforce participation and wages, and recently this analysis was also taken up by the Finance Ministry (*Zaimushō*), which announced in December 2002 that it was considering eliminating the tax deduction for dependent spouses—the first time since World War II that there has been a serious discussion of raising income taxes (*Asahi Shimbun* 2002).[2]

Attacks on the spousal deduction are part of a larger debate about women's employment as a shock absorber for the ups and downs of the labor market, and about the increasing reliance on female part-time and temporary workers to avoid having to hire expensive full-time male workers during difficult economic times. For example, Sakiko Shiota argues that women's withdrawal from the labor market in the 1970s following the oil shocks enabled Japan to execute a "soft landing," with minimal impact on the core male labor force (Shiota 2000, 182). More recently, Charles Weathers argues that temporary workers have gained popularity during Japan's long recession because they can be paid less and fired more readily than regular workers, giving companies ways to cut costs and react flexibly to changing economic conditions. Temporary workers don't demand raises, since they don't want to price themselves out of a job. They rarely receive bonuses or the full package of fringe benefits, social insurance benefits, and travel allowances that regular workers get. And even though temps are due ten days' paid vacation for every six months they work, firm managers commonly pressure them into forgoing their vacation time by threatening not to give them further assignments (Weathers 2001, 214–215). Pointing to the particular difficulty women encountered finding full-time jobs during

Japan's prolonged economic slump, Richard Katz reports that the proportion of working women who work part-time rose from 32 percent to 45 percent between 1985 and 1999 (Katz 2003, 4).

But women aren't as content as they once were to accept this secondary role in the economy. Women are unable to find jobs that are commensurate with their education and qualifications, and the huge opportunity costs of quitting work to raise children and then returning to a poorly paid job after this hiatus are related to a quiet rebellion taking place in Japan.[3] Working women are delaying or forgoing marriage and children. They are extending their period of relatively carefree freedom and high consumption into their thirties by living at home with their parents rent-free; having someone else take care of them; and (when possible) taking, and trying to keep, full-time career-track jobs (Katz 2003, 4; Schoppa, 2006).

Childcare

The Child Welfare Law established a nonprofit childcare system in 1947 to care for children whose parents were ill or working. Since its inception, government support for childcare has fluctuated along with labor surpluses and shortages (Peng 2002, 31) and, in recent years, dramatically low fertility rates.

Childcare services in Japan are high quality, well regulated, and publicly subsidized. The fundamental distinction is between licensed and unlicensed centers. Licensed childcare centers (*ninka hoikuen*) must meet minimum government standards for space, play areas, kitchens, safety features, training and number of teachers, how much they charge families (depending on the family income), and prioritizing who may be admitted for care. But not all licensed centers are publicly run: about 58 percent of licensed centers are public, 42 percent are private, and in recent years the government has been encouraging a move toward more private-run centers in order to provide more flexible, user-friendly services and to save money. Costs are significantly lower in private centers, due to the impact of the public employees' union in protecting teachers' seniority and pay in public centers. Private centers are generally more flexible about offering extended hours than public ones, again because the unionized teachers in public centers are unwilling to work longer hours or to have their work days or weeks broken into irregular or short shifts. All licensed childcare centers, public and private, receive government subsidies from the national, prefectural, and local

TABLE 6.1
Total number of children enrolled in licensed childcare centers, 1991–2002

Year	Number enrolled	% of preschool children enrolled	% of children under 3 enrolled	No. of children on waiting lists for childcare centers
1991	1,622,326			
1992	1,618,657			
1993	1,604,770			
1994	1,592,698			26,114
1995	1,593,873			28,481
1996	1,610,199			32,855
1997	1,642,754	21%	13%	40,523
1998	1,691,128			39,545
1999	1,736,390	24.3%	14%	33,641
2000	1,788,302			34,153
2001	1,798,292	25%	15.6%	35,144
2002	1,879,000			25,000

SOURCES: Total enrollment data for 1991–1998 are reported in Foundation for Children's Future, *Child Welfare*, Jan. 2000. Those for 2001 are reported in *Child Welfare* No. 5, 53; those for 2002 in *Child Welfare* No. 6, 40. Waiting list data from *Child Welfare* No. 5, 56. All figures come from MHW or MHLW survey data; percentages of preschool children and children under 3 enrolled in childcare calculated from data from MHW 1998 and MHW 2000.

governments, making them more affordable for the families whose children attend, who are charged on a sliding fee basis according to their income.

My data on percentages of all pre-school-age children and children under age three who attend public childcare are not complete, but the figures in Table 6.1 for numbers enrolled show a dip in total enrollment figures from 1992 to 1994, then steady increases from 1995 to the present. The percentage figures that are available for 1997, 1999, and 2001 suggest modest but steady growth in the percentage both of children under age three and of pre-school-age children who are enrolled in licensed childcare centers. The enrollment figures for children under three are especially significant because this is one of the areas of highest unmet demand: mothers who want to return to work often find that there are no spaces available in the groups for infants under age one, which of course are the most expensive and labor-intensive childcare cohort because of the three-to-one baby-to-teacher ratio required by law. If more spaces were available, enrollment figures would surely be higher. Indeed, the high numbers of children on the waiting list for childcare spaces reflect a serious shortage of childcare for younger children, especially in cities. This has been a focus of discontent among daycare users, and of policy reform, since the mid-1990s.

TABLE 6.2
Children enrolled in licensed childcare centers by age in 1997 and 1999

Age of child	No. of children in childcare, 1997	% of children in childcare, 1997	No. of children in childcare, 1999	% of children in childcare, 1999
Less than 1 year	56,000	4.7	63,000	5.2
1- and 2-year-olds	406,000	17.1	440,000	18.5
3-year-olds	381,000	31.8	397,000	33.8
4- to 5-year-olds	800,000	26.7	836,000	35.2

SOURCE: MHW 1998, 2000.

TABLE 6.3
Children enrolled in kindergarten by age in 1997 and 1999

Age of child	No. of children in kinder-garten, 1997	% of children in kinder-garten, 1997	No. of children in kinder-garten, 1999	% of children in kinder-garten, 1999
3-year-olds	350,000	29.2	358,000	30.5
4- to 5-year-olds	1,439,000	48	1,420,000	59.7

SOURCE: MHW 1998, 2000.

Compared to the percentages of children under the age of three who attend publicly regulated and subsidized childcare in Sweden (40 percent) or France (34 percent), Japan's 16 percent seems rather low; but it is far higher than the proportion of children under the age of three who attend center-based care in Germany (2 percent) or indeed everywhere else in the world except Belgium and Scandinavia (see Gornick, Meyers, and Ross 1997, 127 for comparative data). Attendance figures suggest a childcare system that is attractive to users, and a society where putting even small children in organized childcare is becoming more socially acceptable. The problems seem to be ones of high costs, shortages of supply, and bureaucratic rigidity. Applying for childcare is time-consuming and bothersome, and once one's child is admitted to a center, communicating with teachers and taking care of personal care items (washrags, smocks, sun hats, sheets for the futon, and so on) is a daily and exacting routine.

Some scholars fold the numbers for children who attend kindergarten into the figures for children who are cared for in the childcare system (Tables 6.2 and 6.3). But in Japan, the childcare and kindergarten systems have had different functions and missions since their inceptions: the one was to protect child welfare among children who were at risk because their mothers were absent from the home, the other was to provide educational and social stimulation to pre-school-age children, differences reflected in the fact that they are administered by different ministries (Ministry of Health, Labor, and Welfare and Ministry of Education). Ordinarily childcare centers are open for eleven hours a day, and kindergartens are only open for a four-hour morning session, so few Japanese see kindergartens (*yochien*) as a viable way to provide care for their children while they work. With the declining fertility rate and decreasing demand for kindergarten, however, some kindergartens are reconsidering their mission and offering extended care to help meet the needs of mothers who work part time (*Asahi Shimbun* 2000a; Takai and Sugiue (MHLW) 2001, 19). But even with extended care options, the kindergarten day rarely covers enough hours to permit a parent to work full-time and commute back and forth to the center during the hours available.

In addition to providing childcare for pre-school-age children, Japan also provides subsidized after-school care for children in the first three years of elementary school (generally children under age 10). There were 11,800 children enrolled in after-school children's clubs in 2000, up from 8,000 in 1994 (Foundation for Children's Future 2002b, 59).

Unlicensed (*muninka*) centers and providers are not subsidized, nor are they required to meet the standards set by the national government. They vary widely in quality and cost. Families use unlicensed care for a variety of reasons, including convenience (e.g., locations close to home, flexible hours, availability of options like extended hours or weekend day care); preference for having their children cared for in smaller groups or homier settings; ability to take their children to the babysitter even when they're sick; and inability to get their children, especially infants, into licensed facilities because of long waiting lists. Table 6.4 shows data on unlicensed providers.

Unlicensed childcare centers and providers have been the biggest source of scandal and complaint about inadequate and dangerous care for babies and children. In particular, "baby hotels" are often nothing more than rooms in an apartment where a woman cares for babies and children in cramped conditions, unable to take them outdoors to play or for a walk, or to provide appropriate attention and stimulation to the children in her care. But unlicensed centers are a mixed bag: some are very high quality, including some of the centers run for profit by corporations, on-site centers provided by employers (e.g., for nurses in hospitals), and experimental ventures like centers across from train stations in urban areas. One *eki-mae* ("across from the train station") center

TABLE 6.4
Numbers of children in unlicensed forms of childcare

Form of care	No. of institutions	No. of children	Year
Baby hotels	838	21,000	2000
Unlicensed childcare centers (*muninka*)	8,856	214,000	2000
Hoiku mama (home childcare providers)	1,185 homes (*katei fukushin*)	4,622	1999
Babysitters	133 companies	23,000	2000
Family members		No data available	

SOURCES: Data for 1999 are from Fundation for Children's Future, *Child Welfare,* Jan. 2000, 25. Data for 2000 are from Takai and Sugiue (MHLW), 2001.

I visited in a suburb of Tokyo, run by Pasona Childcare International, provided an airy, spacious children's play room and was close enough to a nearby park to go out on walks and to play (Sato 1998).[4] In the mid-1990s, the central government and several municipalities supported the development of some of these private unlicensed centers, offering significant subsidies that made them more affordable for the parents who prefer their convenience. Indeed, in discussions dating back to 1997, Ministry of Health and Welfare (MHW) officials have often talked enthusiastically about the merits of encouraging more private provision of childcare services, on the grounds that more reliance on the market and the profit motive will lead to better quality, more choice, and cheaper prices for consumers. One worries that private, corporate-run centers must make a profit, and if they do not receive any public subsidies, either their fees will be high or their quality low. Yet ministry officials never acknowledged or addressed this problem in their discussions with me.

When asked how many babies and children are cared for by family members while their mothers work, MHLW officials told me that the government did not collect such data. This seems an odd omission, as one would expect that a significant proportion of children would be cared for by parents (doing shift work or working at home), aunts, uncles, grandparents, and the like. Indeed, there is evidence that working mothers in Japan rely heavily on other family members to care for their children: women who live with their parents or parents-in-law are more likely to work (and more likely to work full-time) when their children are small than women who do not (Oishi 2002; Foundation for Children's Future 2003, 57). (Of course these same women are also more likely to have to take time off to care for their elderly parents or parents-in-law once they become frail.) One might attribute this failure to keep statistics on family members caring for children to being fastidious about respecting the privacy of familial care arrangements. Or perhaps it is a vestige of the assumption that of course family members, preferably mothers, should and ordinarily do stay home to care for their children—suggesting that what interests MHLW officials are arrangements that involve childcare centers or paid caregivers, not private familial arrangements.

Childcare Leaves

Under the Labor Standards Act, women are entitled to a fourteen-week maternity leave, six weeks before the baby is born and eight afterward. They are entitled to 60 percent of pay during this leave, plus another 25 percent as an additional maternity allowance, which took effect in April 1999, and a lump sum payment that generally covers the direct costs of a normal birth (Women's Online Media 2000). The leave can be extended to ten weeks before the due date in the case of multiple births. Since the maternity leaves are well established and have not been a matter of significant change or controversy in recent years, I focus here on recent changes in, and controversies about, the childrearing leave law.

Japan passed a parental leave law in 1992 that provided a year-long job-protected leave for parents taking care of infants and mandating that they should be paid 25 percent of their normal pay; this was increased to 40 percent of usual pay in April 2000. But the law has not worked very well in practice, for reasons that reveal characteristic patterns and flaws in Japanese policy making. For example, uptake rates for the parental leave law have been low: in 1999, only 56.4 percent of female employees who were eligible to take the leave did so, and only 0.42 percent of eligible male employees. The low uptake rates are symptomatic of deeper problems. The law relies on "administrative guidance"—persuasion, essentially—rather than meaningful enforcement mechanisms, like lawsuits, that would force employers to obey the law. Nothing serious happens to a firm that refuses to grant the leave or otherwise penalizes employees who claim these benefits. Although a firm's name can be made public in a quasi "hall of shame," there are no monetary or other sanctions. Such leaves are difficult to manage in a workplace culture where one's colleagues are typically expected to pick up the slack while one is on leave. Hiring temporary replacements is viewed as difficult, both from the point of view of training those people and of having to let them go when the permanent employees return from leave. Frequent grumping and strained personal relations are directed at the leave-taker, who is (however unfairly) regarded as a "slacker" for taking time off from work. A woman who takes the leave worries that someone else will be sitting at her desk when she returns from the leave. Finally, 40 percent of wages may not be enough to support the household, forcing some workers to return to work because their income is needed (Muraki 2001).

If there are problems with women taking the leave, they are exponentially greater for men. Most men still expect women to be full-time housewives; men who aspire to take on a significant proportion of childrearing responsibilities are regarded as weird and as lacking in loyalty to the company. In a weak economy, few men would take such a risk. Since men usually make more money than women, having their salaries cut to 40 percent would represent an even greater financial burden than the same cut in women's salaries.

In order to address these problems, the MHLW announced a series of initiatives: one measure sets numerical targets of 80 percent for women and 10 percent for men for taking childrearing leave, though again there appears to be no enforcement mechanism, just the power of persuasion (Curtin 2002). Other measures that have been enacted include a prohibition on employers laying off or treating unfavorably employees who take childrearing leave; a guarantee of reduced or flexible hours for parents who are eligible for, but don't take, the childrearing leave until their child is three years old; a revision of the Labor Standards Act that allows both mothers and fathers of pre-school-age children to refuse to work more than 150 hours of overtime a year or more than 24 hours of overtime in a given month; and subsidies for companies that actively promote parenting leaves (NIPSSR 2003). These are substantial attempts to encourage corporate compliance with the childrearing leave; it remains to be seen how successful they will be.

Let us turn now to a more global, reflective consideration of these policies. The last decade has been a period of intense discussion, concern, and policy innovation with respect to policies to support working mothers and families. Deliberative councils devoted to considering the "aging society" and low fertility phenomena were appointed by the government and met and talked at length, issuing reports that laid the groundwork for adopting the "Angel Plan," the first of two five-year plans for overhauling childcare services, in 1994. (The choice of names for programs is interesting: the visuals accompanying the "Angel Plan" pamphlets and materials evoke cherubic babies, floating fairylike in the air.) The early policy approaches centered on improving the childcare

TABLE 6.5
National government spending on childcare, 1997–2001

Year	In oku ¥	In billions of dollars	In billions of Euro
1997	3,117	2.69	2.33
1998	3,369	2.90	2.52
1999	3,669	3.16	2.75
2000	3,796	3.27	2.84
2001	3,915	3.38	2.93

SOURCE: Takai and Sugiue, MHLW, 2001, 1.

system: providing more spaces in centers, improving the quality of care, fostering diversification and privatization by encouraging new providers to enter the market, and increasing spending on subsidies and pilot programs. The Angel Plan was followed in 1999 by the "New Angel Plan." In that same year an emergency supplementary budget allocated ¥2,000 oku ($1.72 billion) to build more childcare centers, cut the number of children on waiting lists, and offer more high-demand services (Kamohara 2001). Yearly childcare spending from 1997 to 2001 rose steadily from $2.7 billion to $3.4 billion (Table 6.5). To put this into comparative context, total federal spending on childcare for 2001 in the United States (with a population of 273 million compared to Japan's 120 million) was $4.36 billion (2002 budget figures from the Office of Management and Budget and the Department of Health and Human Services), though admittedly this leaves out state funding as well as programs such as Head Start.

Some problems and policies had taken on sharper focus by the late 1990s. Ministry officials reduced from ten to seven the number of income categories used for determining rates, which had the effect of shifting user fees toward flat-rate pricing. Also parents were allowed to decide what center to send their children to on the basis of their preferences and financial considerations, rather than having an official at city hall dictate this to them. Both of these shifts were framed in terms of enhancing choice and pushing providers to be more innovative and to offer better services for lower prices. Parents' needs and preferences for centers with extended hours—a necessity for a worker with a normal full-time job and a commute who would not be able to make it to a childcare center by the ordinary closing time at 6:00—led to initiatives to increase the number of centers offering this option.

Deregulation became a catchword at the Ministry of Health and Welfare's Childcare Bureau, leading to a variety of changes: relaxing rules about the minimum number of children in a licensed childcare center, relaxing rules about having a kitchen on the premises for food preparation, permitting children to start childcare during the middle of the school year instead of having to wait until April 1, and allowing private companies to run licensed centers without requiring them to acquire special *"fukushi hōjin"* status (literally, welfare legal person—similar to nonprofit organization status in the United States) (Hihara 1999). This last measure was supposed to encourage businesses, such as the baby care products companies Vanessa and Pigeon, to enter the market for providing daycare services, though as yet few such corporations have done so (Fukuda 1999, 88–102; Study Group 2000a, 59). The "Campaign for a Zero Waiting List for Day Care Centers," announced in 2002, picked up on Prime Minister Koizumi's earlier promise to eliminate waiting lists for childcare (Foundation for Children's Future 2003, 11).

The most recent MHLW initiative was christened in 2002 the "Plus One Proposal to End the Low Birthrate" (*shōshika taisaku purasuwan*), or "Plus One" for short (Curtin 2002; Foundation for Children's Future 2003, 36). Perhaps the Plus One program reflects the merger of the MHW and Ministry of Labor, because the focus is on encouraging a more family-friendly atmosphere in the workplace rather than on improving the quantity and quality of childcare. For Japan, the Plus One initiative is more ambitious than expanding and improving the childcare system, because it addresses the structure and atmosphere of the workplace. As we saw in the section on childrearing leaves, these measures include setting numerical goals for uptake rates for the childrearing leave (80 percent for women and 10 percent for men), prohibiting employers from retaliating against workers who take the leave, offering a ¥1 million ($8,620) subsidy to employers who set up proactive plans to implement the leave, permitting workers to refuse to work overtime beyond certain reasonable limits, and allowing parents of small children to work flexible and reduced hours. These policies are aimed at changing personnel practices that reflect deep-seated animosity to having mothers continue to be full-time regular workers. Such changes are important because the barriers to women's full participation in the workforce cannot be met simply by improving childcare and legislating parental leaves; they have to do with expectations about serious, committed workers, and prejudices toward workers who ask for "special" treatment in order to interrupt their work lives to have babies and attend to the needs of their children. Were these policies vigorously enforced, they could effect a sea change in the structure and environment of the workplace by making it easier to stay in one's job through one's childbearing years. The "Plus One" policies challenge workplace practices that squeeze young women with children out of good jobs. Like the proposal under consideration at the Finance Ministry to eliminate the dependent spouse tax deduction, they could begin to restructure the opportunity costs of being married and having babies.

Without a doubt, enacting laws and announcing "campaigns" and policy initiatives whereby the government puts its authority behind changes in corporate and individual behavior is a crucial move toward broad social change. But without effective implementation, which would require making sure that the laws are broadly enforced, it seems unlikely that "administrative guidance"—using governmental authority and persuasion to educate and encourage employers and others to respect workers' rights and to bring about sweeping changes in the atmosphere of the workplace—will make much headway against entrenched corporate resistance, social norms, and the individual worker's reluctance to assert rights when companies are downsizing and laying off workers.

Explaining the Process

How should we understand the policy process that produced the reforms of the last ten years in child allowance, tax, workplace, childcare, and parental leave policies? One way to begin is by considering who are the stakeholders in these policies, as well as who is invited to be part of policy deliberations. Stakeholders include parents of young children, especially mothers; young children; child and family welfare professionals; childcare teachers and their unions; national, prefectural, and city governments, which are responsible for contributing financial support for licensed childcare centers and for administering the childcare and child allowance programs; gray-market providers of childcare services, including babysitter companies and unlicensed childcare centers and providers; companies interested in starting up childcare centers for profit; construction companies that build new centers or rehab old ones; those who own, operate, and work at childcare centers and kindergartens; and employers whose employees request childrearing leave or flexible or part-time schedules, and who stand to benefit from extended-hour and more reliable arrangements for the care of their employees' children.

To what extent are these stakeholders drawn into deliberations and decision making about family policies?[5] In the olden days (pre-1993), officials in the Ministry of Health and Welfare (now MHLW) had primary responsibility for deliberating about and crafting policy proposals that were then circulated to the prime minister and his office, and to the leadership councils in the Diet. Close collaboration with the Liberal Democratic Party's Policy Research Council and the Diet members in the social policy "tribe," the *kōsei zoku*, was the norm.

Since the mid-1990s and the advent of coalition governments, how-ever, the LDP's control over the Diet and policy debates has waned, and the old "LDP era" style of ironing out disagreements with opposition parties and pressure groups to secure prompt passage has changed— though as yet the new mode of interactions between the bureaucrats and the party leaders is not clear (Etō 2000a, 26–27; Nonaka 2000, 115– 118). Nevertheless, with respect to most family-support policies, the policy-making pattern of the LDP era (the period of single-party rule from 1955 to 1993) still seems to hold.

When I asked MHW bureaucrats about how they decided whom to invite to serve on advisory councils related to the low birth rate prob-lem, and specifically why they didn't ask particular groups represent-ing parents of children in childcare or stay-at-home mothers from the Tokyo suburbs, their responses struck me as off-the-cuff and a bit lame: one explained that they couldn't invite a particular parents' group called the *hoikuen wo kangaeru oya no kai* (parents' group to think about child-care centers) to sit on a council because "they didn't represent all par-ents" (Hihara 1999)—as though any one group could do so! Of course there were rationales for choosing members of the councils to which I was not made privy; my point is that the process does not seem to wel-come unscripted and, perhaps, critical comments from affected parties during the policy incubation stage, or to include opportunities such as hearings or testimony in which advocacy groups might make argu-ments for or against particular policy approaches.

Remi Lenoir, writing about France, said that one could not imagine deliberations about family policy taking place in France without the par-ticipation of three groups: the National Union of Family Associations (UNAF), the National Union of Family Allowance Funds (UNCAF) (the autonomous manager of the funds that pay for family policies), and the National Institute of Demographic Studies (INED) (Lenoir 1991, 144). It is instructive to consider what the same list would include in Japan. Certainly it would include the Japanese equivalent of INED, the Na-tional Institute for Population and Social Security Research (NIPSSR); demographic concerns frame the entire debate about family policy in Japan. But there would be no counterpart to the National Union of Family Allowance Funds, since Japan does not have a quasi-public, privately managed financing system like France's to pay for its policies. Nor are there active family associations (like those in France) or religious groups making conservative "family values" types of arguments (like those in the United States). What is unimaginable are deliberations about family policy taking place in Japan without MHLW bureaucrats and technocrats from research institutes affiliated with the MHLW (e.g., the Foundation for Children's Future and the Red Cross Research Institute for Children's Welfare)—many of whom are themselves former MHW bureaucrats who now have research positions in think tanks that do studies and analyses that are commissioned by the Ministry. The dominant paradigm for thinking about family policy in this group is the demographic nightmare: Japan has one of the lowest fertility rates in the world; the country's economic productivity and culture will collapse if we don't do something about it; this is an emergency. Of course there are other views about low fertility: that perhaps Japan would be a pleasanter place to live with 80 million inhabitants than it is with 120 million; the huge consumption of natural resources and the lack of space in cities would improve tremendously. After all, why should the government act as though women were cows who needed priming in order to produce more offspring? Why not take women's silent rebellion—their refusal to marry and reproduce—seriously and respect their choice? But those views, for all their power and the frequency with which they are voiced in the media, apparently do not enter into the conversations about family policy taking place in the Japanese government.

What sort of voice do women and feminists have in the official governmental debates about family policies? Some scholars have argued that women's groups have in fact played an important role in shaping policy on both childcare (Peng 2002) and long-term care insurance for frail elderly people (Etō 2000b). Yet at the same time sociologist Ito Peng criticizes the Japanese state for having a thin commitment to gender equality, and critiques family policies for failing to address the stark choices young women face that lead many of them to decide not to have babies (Peng 2000, 2001). In terms of formal policy discussions, women's impact seems to have been uneven and sporadic.

Part of the reason for this is that the advisory councils are stocked with men from think tanks, government ministries, unions, and so on who are not very interested in foregrounding a distinctively female voice or sensibility about the obstacles facing women who work and raise children. Part of the reason is also that women and women's groups in Japan are themselves divided over issues of childcare and parenting leaves. For example, many individual feminists focus on issues like sexual harassment, the traffic in prostitutes, or reproductive rights (Mackie 2003), but seem bored by "housewives' issues." Other feminists, including Chizuko Ueno, Keiko Higuchi, Sakiko Shiota, and Mari Osawa, frequently speak to the reasons why women are having fewer babies and the problems that women encounter when they want to work, marry, and have children. There are similar divisions in women's groups: although a number of grassroots consumers' rights activists, almost entirely women, engage issues like childcare and long-term care for the elderly, they do not present a unified position or voice, nor do they devote themselves exclusively to issues facing working mothers. There is, in short, no unified voice to feminism or women's voices. Certainly many scholars and observers from outside Japan are interested in developing feminist analyses of Japan's employment structure (Gottfried and O'Reilly 2002) and the gendering of the welfare state (Peng 2002).

Of course talk about families and family policy does not only occur in stuffy conference rooms among members of advisory councils; there is also a lively public debate taking place in newspapers and monthly magazines, on talk shows, in chat rooms and on email lists, and over dinner tables and beer mugs. The popular culture version of Japan's demographic crisis pins the blame on young unmarried women who are still living at home, frequently referred to as "parasite singles" because they work but pay no rent and often do no work around the house (notice, however, that young men in the same situation are not called parasite singles). Young women are raked over the coals for buying expensive Louis Vuitton handbags and other fashionable items; for taking trips to Europe and nice vacations; for being ultra consumption oriented; and especially for not being interested in settling down and assuming the responsibilities of adult life, including establishing a household and raising children.

This ideological framing on the part of bureaucrats, politicians, and the media makes it sound like the women are at fault; they're being selfish, refusing to grow up, refusing to take up the constraints and sacrifices their own mothers did and engage their lives as adults with grace and style. Repeatedly hearing the low fertility crisis explained in terms of women's reasons for not marrying and women's reasons for not having babies fosters the impression or assumption that fundamentally it's all about the personal, somewhat suspect, choices that young women are making. Such a framework makes it easy to ignore the issue of structural, societal problems in the way work opportunities are structured, making the decision to drop out of the workplace and raise children extremely costly for a well-educated, ambitious woman.[6]

Japanese society has monumentalized the importance of childrearing and has made women's success as mothers a focus of extraordinary stress and preoccupation. It is not surprising that Japanese women worry about their performance as mothers, given the concern with how well children perform academically, whether they get into the right schools, and given the fact that fathers are still largely distant figures in their children's lives, leaving all that responsibility and anxiety resting on women's shoulders (Hirao, this volume). Expressions like "childrearing stress" or "childrearing neurosis" are heard frequently in Japan and capture some of the emotional resonance of decisions about having and raising babies.

The brochure covers for annual reports from MHLW with pastel cartoons of children and family snapshots evoke an image of the family as a peaceful and warm haven. These images (and program names like "Angel Plan") seem to be part of the public framing of the debate about family policy, especially the need to encourage people to start having more babies again. Yet we know that families are not all havens and peaceful, that families harbor resentments and violence, that they produce unhappy marriages and troubled children and adolescents as often as not. The pervasive coziness of the family with children as an icon in public debate about policies to support families in Japan, like the pervasive imagery of the selfish young woman tripping about in her high-fashion clothes with her designer handbag, tells us much about the ideological framing of family policies today in Japan.

Conclusions

We are left with the puzzle of why Japan's policies are not raising fertility rates. Some have suggested that modern societies have lost interest in children, and that low fertility in Japan is inevitable. It is doubtless true that low infant mortality, adequate old-age pensions, the costs of urban living, and the opportunity costs of having children have given postindustrial societies a different calculus for having children than in agrarian societies; but this kind of argument does not account for the substantial variation we observe in fertility rates across rich democracies.

A second possibility, which the Japanese government would like to believe, is that government policies are in fact on target and they just need more time to work. They have been hoping this for a long time.

Third, it may be that the supply of childcare alone is insufficient without dealing first with the deeper problem of Japan's gendered division of labor within the family. This answer seems right, but it also seems likely that the male breadwinner model that predominates in Japan does so precisely because labor market institutions reinforce it. As Estévez-Abe and Brinton have pointed out in the preceding chapters, until firms have an incentive to hire women at equal rates as men, it is unlikely that the male breadwinner model will break down on its own. What is a woman to do who earns a college degree and wants to have a good job, and not be relegated to low-paying, boring clerical or temp work for most of her working life because she stayed home for a few years to care for babies? She is caught between bosses who are not happy about finding temporary replacements for workers and resentful colleagues who make her feel shunned upon returning to work after her childrearing leave, on the one hand, and on the other hand playground debuts and kindergarten entrance exams and the 101 other crises of managing her child's upbringing. So she opts to work, takes nice vacations, and delays or forgoes the dreary trade-off. The trade-offs need to be less stark, the performance of these two roles not so fraught with anxiety or conflict.

The people whose interests and lives are most deeply affected by the parenting leave and childcare policies are not directly involved in the policy debate. The people who have the most to lose from significantly restructuring employment patterns are, and they favor the incremental changes in supply and demand of childcare services. It is easier to print glossy brochures urging Japan to become a family-friendly country than to undertake expensive and disorienting policies that would move men away from being corporate warriors toward being involved, nurturing fathers who take time off for family responsibilities, and to move women away from being supermoms toward being responsible, committed workers. Given the persistent asymmetries of power in the Japanese policy making process, women still must steer a treacherous course somewhere between the Scylla of the ideal worker and the Charybdis of the supermom. Until the labor markets change so they no longer place a large penalty on women for career interruptions, or until government policies nudge men into making those interruptions in equal proportion to women, even vastly larger amounts of money to subsidize childcare are unlikely to incline Japanese women to have more babies.

Notes

1. See Abe, 2002, p. S69, Table I for these income thresholds.
2. At the same time the Finance Ministry said it was also considering eliminating the extra dependent child tax deduction for high school and college students. The deduction paid for children up to age sixteen is ¥380,000 ($3,275), whereas parents of children between the ages of sixteen and twenty-two get a ¥630,000 tax deduction (the usual ¥380,000 + ¥250,000, equivalent to $5,430). The motivation for eliminating the extra tax deduction for these children, whose supplemental educational expenses are often quite high to pay for cram schools and college, was not clear, especially with respect to the debate about encouraging families to have more children (*Asahi Shimbun* 2002).
3. See Maruyama (1999) for a good analysis of this trade-off.
4. This particular center may have been unusually good; often train station centers are criticized for being cramped and having no place for children to play outside because of their location in the shadow of the train station, often a developed commercial area.
5. My perceptions and judgments are shaped by the kinds of information and access I have had in conducting my fieldwork, and by the kinds of studies I have read. These have been skewed toward talking with Ministry officials at the MHW and now the MHLW, with researchers at various institutes, especially the National Institute for Population and Social Security Research, and with other social welfare scholars, especially those interested in gender and issues affecting women. I am not a close student of Diet and prime ministerial decision making, nor have I had access to the *kōsei zoku* (social policy "tribe") or other policy leadership councils. With those caveats in mind, I set out below how I see the policy process working.
6. I acknowledge the impact of Diana Khor's article, "The Construction of Gender through Public Opinion Polls in Japan" (2002) on my thinking here about framing.

References

Abe, Aya K. 2002. "Effects of Child-relating Benefits in Japan." *Journal of Population and Social Security*: Social Security Study (August), found at www.ipss.go.jp/English/WebJournal.files/SocialSecurity/WebSocial Security.html.

Asahi Shimbun (evening edition). 2000a. "Kodomo kakuho ni chie shibore— yochien, hoikuen (Wringing Some Wisdom about Insuring Care for Children out of the Kindergarten Daycare System)." May 13, p. 5.

Asahi Shimbun (evening edition). 2000b. "Bebi-hoteru 'akutenken': Kōseishō akushitsu nara heisa meirei mo" (Baby Hotel Inspections: MHW will order poor quality baby hotels to close). June 30.

Asahi Shimbun. 2002. "Josei ni totte . . . wareru giron (A debate that doesn't make sense for women)." Dec. 10, p. 3.

Curtin, Sean. 2002. "The Declining Birthrate in Japan: Part One—Numerical Targets for Childcare Leave," Social Trends 17 (Nov. 18) (accessed May 13, 2003 from www.glocom.org/special_topics/social_trends/20021118_trends_s17/index.html).

Curtin, Sean. 2003. "Family Trends in 2003: Declining Birthrates, Fewer Marriages, More Divorces," Social Trends 26 (Feb. 6) (accessed on May 13, 2003 from www.glocom.org/special_topics/social_trends/20030206_trends_s26/index.html)

Curtis, Gerald L., ed. 2002. *Policymaking in Japan: Defining the Role of Politicians*. Tokyo: JCIE (Japan Center for International Exchange).

Etō Mikiko. 2000a. "Women's Empowerment and Social Policy-making in Japan: Challenges of Ordinary Housewives." Paper presented on November 21, 2000, at Lucy Cavendish College.

Etō Murase Mikiko. 2000b. "The Establishment of Long-term Care Insurance." In Otake Hideo, ed., *Power Shuffles and Policy Processes: Coalition Government in Japan in the 1990s*. New York: Japan Center for International Exchange.

Foundation for Children's Future. 2002a. *Child Welfare: Information from Japan*, No. 4 (March). Tokyo: Foundation for Children's Future (material excerpted and translated from the 2001 MHLW White Paper).

Foundation for Children's Future. 2002b. *Child Welfare: Information from Japan*, No. 5 (August). Tokyo: Foundation for Children's Future.

Foundation for Children's Future. 2003. *Child Welfare: Information from Japan*, No. 6 (March). Tokyo: Foundation for Children's Future.

Fukoin Aki (representative of the *hoikuen wo kangaeru oya no kai* [parents' group to think about childcare centers]), interview, Nov. 4, 1999.

Fukuda Moto. 1999. *Shakai hoshō no kōzō kaikaku: Kosodate shien juushigata shisutemu e no tenkan* (Social Security Reform: Revolutionizing the Childrearing Support System). Tokyo: Chuohoki Shuppan.

Gornick, Janet C., Marcia Meyers, and Katherin Ross. 1997. "Supporting the Employment of Mothers: Policy Variation Across Fourteen Welfare States." *Journal of European Social Policy* 7(1): 45–70.

Gottfried, Heidi, and Jacqueline O'Reilly. 2002. "Re-Regulating Breadwinner Models in Socially Conservative Welfare Regimes: Comparing Germany and Japan." *Social Politics* 9(1): 29–59.

Hihara Tomomi (Ministry of Health and Welfare, Child-Family Bureau, Child Care Section), interview, Nov. 15, 1999.

Hino Tetsuko. 1999. "Do government measures to address 'fewer children' satisfy women's demands?" (*Josei no youkyuu ni kotaerareruka seifu no "shoushika" taisaku*). *Monthly: Women & Movement*, November.

Honda Hajime (Director, Child-Rearing Promotion Division at the Ministry of Health, Labor and Welfare, Tokyo), interview, Jan. 18, 2001.

Horie Izumi (Public Employees Union, Hobosan union), interview, Nov. 13, 1999.

Kamohara Motomichi (Chief of the division for child allowances, Ministry of Health, Labor and Welfare, Child-Family Section, childrearing environment office), interview, Jan. 25, 2001.

Katz, Richard. 2003. "The Myth of Louis Vuitton: Too Rich for Their Own Good?" *Oriental Economist*, May, 3–4.

Khor, Diana. 2002. "The Construction of Gender through Public Opinion Polls in Japan: The 'Problem' of Women's Employment." *U.S.–Japan Women's Journal, English Language Supplement*, no. 22.

Lenoir, Remi. 1991. "Family Policy in France Since 1938." In John S. Ambler, ed., *The French Welfare State: Surviving Social and Ideological Change*. New York: New York University Press.

Mackie, Vera. 2003. *Feminism in Modern Japan*. Cambridge: Cambridge University Press.

Maruyama, Katsura. 1999. "The Cost Sharing of Child and Family Care Leave." *Review of Population and Social Policy* 8: 49.

Memorandum of the Conference of Section Managers in Charge of National Measures to Address Fewer Children, Regarding the Temporary Special Subsidies for Measures to Address Fewer Children in 1999; http://www1 .mhlw.go.jp/shingi/s9907/txt/s0722–1_18.txt, printed May 22, 2001.

MHLW (Ministry of Health, Labor, and Welfare), 2001 "New Angel Plan" handout.

MHLW, 2002: http://www.mhlw.go.jp/english/database/db-hw/populate/ pop4.html (accessed July 13, 2002).

MHW (Ministry of Health and Welfare). 1998. Kōsei Hakushō (MHW White Paper).

MHW (Ministry of Health and Welfare). 2000. Kō sei Hakushō (MHW White Paper).

Muraki Atsuko (Director of Equal Employment Policy Division at the Ministry of Health, Labor and Welfare, Tokyo), interview, Jan. 22, 2001.

NIPSSR (National Institute for Population and Social Security Research), website accessed May 2003.

Nonaka Naoto. 2000. "Characteristics of the Decision-making Structure of Coalitions." In Otake Hideo, ed., *Power Shuffles and Policy Processes: Coalition Government in Japan in the 1990s*. Tokyo: JCIE (Japan Center for International Exchange).

Oishi, Akiko S. 2002. "The Effect of Childcare Costs on Mothers' Labor Force Participation." *Journal of Population and Social Security*: Social Security

Study.   www.ipss.go.jp/English/WebJournal.files/SocialSecurity/Web SocialSecurity.html.

Osawa Mari. 1994. "Bye-bye Corporate Warriors: The Formation of a Corporate-Centered Society and Gender-Biased Social Policies in Japan." University of Tokyo Institute of Social Science Occasion Papers in Labor Problem and Social Policy, no. 18.

Osawa Mari. 1996. "Gender-Biased Social Policies in Japan and Korea." In Osawa Mari, Hara Hiroko, and Maeda Mizue, eds., *Ajia Taiheiyō chiiki no josei seisaku to joseigaku* (Women and Gender in Asia-Pacific: Policy Development and Women's Studies in Eight Countries). Tokyo: Shinyousha.

Peng, Ito. 2000. "Childcare Policies in Japan: Postwar Developments and Recent Reforms." In Thomas P. Boje and Arnlaug Leira, eds., *Gender, Welfare State and the Market: Towards a New Division of Labour*. New York: Routledge.

Peng, Ito. 2001. "Women in the Middle: Welfare State Expansion and Devolution in Japan." *Social Politics* 8: 191–196.

Peng, Ito. 2002. "Gender and Generation: Japanese Child Care and the Demographic Crisis." In Sonya Michel and Rianne Mahon, eds., *Child Care Policy at the Crossroads: Gender and Welfare State Restructuring*. New York: Routledge.

Saimura Jun (Japan Red Cross Research Institute, Social Work section head), interview, Nov. 12, 1999.

Sato Atsuko (President, Pasona Childcare International, Hikarigaoka, Tokyo), interview, Aug. 4, 1998.

Schoppa, Leonard. 2006. *Race for the Exits*. Ithaca, NY: Cornell University Press.

Schwartz, Frank J. 1998. *Advice & Consent: The Politics of Consultation in Japan*. Cambridge: Cambridge University Press.

Shibata, Aiko. 1992. "The Effects of Japanese Income Tax Provisions on Women's Labour Force Participation." In Nancy Folbre, Barbara Bergmann, Bina Agarwal, and Maria Floro, eds., *Women's Work in the World Economy*. New York: NYU Press.

Shiota, Sakiko. 2000. *Nihon no shakai seisaku to jendaa: danjo byōdō no keizai kiban* (Japan's Social Policy and Gender: Economic Basis of Gender Equality). Tokyo: Nihon Hyouronsha.

Stockwin, J. A. A. 2002. "Reshaping of Japanese Politics and the Question of Democracy," *Asia-Pacific Review* 9(1): 45–58.

Study Group on Counter-Measures to Address the Problem of Fewer Children. 2000a. "Seminar on the Present Conditions and Future Tasks of the Measures to Address the Problem of Fewer Children: Daycare Services." *Shukan Shakai Hoshou*, No. 2106, Oct. 9, p. 59.

Study Group on Counter-Measures to Address the Problem of Fewer Children. 2000b. "Seminar on the Present Conditions and Future Tasks of the Measures to Address the Problem of Fewer Children, Article 6: Economic Support." *Shukan Shakai Hoshou*, No. 2111, Nov. 13, p. 59.

Takai Yasuyuki and Sugiue Haruhiko (Ministry of Health, Labor and Welfare, Employment-Equality/Child-Family Section, Child Care Section assistant section heads), interview, Jan. 25, 2001.

Ueno, Chizuko. 1998. "The Declining Birthrate: Whose Problem?" *Review of Population and Social Policy* 7: 103–128.

Weathers, Charles. 2001. "Changing White-collar Workplaces and Female Temporary Workers in Japan." *Social Science Japan Journal* 4(2): 201–218.

Women's Online Media. 2000. "Maternity Leave in Japan," updated Sept. 30, 2000, at http://wom-jp.org/, accessed on May 18, 2003 (original sources are the Labor Standards and the Childcare Leave Act).

CHAPTER 7

The Political Economy of Daycare Centers in Japan

JUNICHIRO WADA

Introduction

Working mothers regularly vent frustrations about the inadequacies of childcare services in letters to the editor in Japanese newspapers. The issues surrounding this subject go well beyond questions of female professional advancement. For these women, the crux of the problem seems to lie in the fact that public childcare in Japan is inflexible and in short supply. In particular, disgruntled Japanese mothers cite the limited supply of daycare centers (*hoikuen*) for children under three years old. Furthermore, waiting lists are long, and selection processes are often mystifying. These women tell of consulting newspapers for tips on procuring a spot. Even when they "get in," unyielding childcare policies can fail to meet the unique needs of these women and their youngsters, including extendable care (*encho hoiku*) and care for ill children (*hyoji hoiku*). Women are often forced to augment public daycare with after-care in the private sector for these services.

Japan's low fertility rate may well be due in part to childcare woes. As Figure 7.1 indicates, Japan's total fertility rate in 1966 was already low, at 1.58. Many attribute the unusually low birthrate to the fact that 1966 was the year of *Hino-e Uma* (fiery horse). According to superstition, girls born in that year were liable to kill their husbands, so many mothers are thought to have refrained from childbirth in 1966.

But fertility rates continued to drop even further. In 1989 the Japanese total fertility rate fell to 1.57, constituting what was termed the "1.57 shock." Since then, we see slow but steady improvements in Japanese childcare policy. The national government created the so-called "Angel

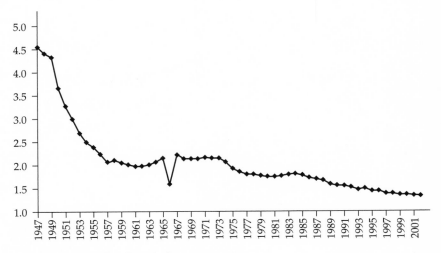

FIGURE 7.1   Fertility Rate in Japan, 1947 to 2001

Plan" in 1994 and "New Angel Plan" in 1999, reforms to expand the day-care center system. Despite recent trends of decreased investment in public works, the national government also lent support to efforts on the part of local governments to develop quasi-licensed daycare systems, such as *Yokohama-gata Hoikushitsu* (Yokohama Nursery Room) in Yoko-hama and *Ninsho Hoikusho* (Certificated Daycare Center) in metropolitan Tokyo.

This chapter argues that the 1994 election reforms helped to prompt some changes in social policy, particularly by way of reducing electoral malapportionment. A lack of daycare centers where they were really needed—in the cities—meant that substantial aggregate government subsidies of childcare could not have much positive effect on fertility. Electoral redistricting increased the political representation of Japan's urban residents and thus facilitated changes in daycare policies that have benefited the urban population. But the system is far from fixed, for slowing the redistribution to the countryside makes only margin-ally more money available for urban childcare. It is unlikely that the new daycare regime will, by itself, do much for fertility.

The Japanese Daycare System

Traditional Japanese childcare policy stems from a system of legally mandated childcare placement for children lacking care. Japanese law

TABLE 7.1
Monthly running costs of childcare by age in City B in Tokyo, 1997

	<12 months	1 year old	2 years old	3 years old	4 years old and older
Public	¥610,000	¥258,000	¥200,000	¥119,000	¥98,000
Private	¥352,000	¥169,000	¥154,000	¥91,000	¥85,000

SOURCE: Asako et al. 1999, 50.

TABLE 7.2
Exchange rate

Exchange rate	1995	1996	1997	1998	1999
$1	¥102.91	¥115.98	¥129.92	¥115.20	¥102.08

SOURCE: Bank of Japan

stipulates that children without adequate care must attend a licensed daycare center. Until 1998 parents were not allowed to specify a particular daycare center for their child, which often led to insufficient supply and inflexible services.

Conditions for the Supply of Daycare Services

Public childcare services are costly to run. Table 7.1 shows the findings of Asako and colleagues (1999), contrasting the public and private per capita costs of childcare in City B in Tokyo. (Exchange rates are shown in Table 7.2.) Running costs do not include fixed costs such as land and buildings, which are prohibitive in and around Tokyo.

Childcare costs decrease with age because older children require fewer caretakers per child. Tables 7.3 and 7.4 indicate the required and actual ratios of staff to children based on the age of the children under care. Japanese requirements for caretaker-to-child ratios might meet or exceed European or American standards, but they make it difficult to provide a sufficient supply of caretakers in the private sector, particularly in daycare centers for very young children.

Both the seniority wage system and age differences between public and private daycare providers explain the discrepancies in operating costs between licensed public and private daycare centers that appear in Table 7.1. Komamura's findings (2001) reveal that seniority wage regulations for daycare providers are more prominent in the public sector

TABLE 7.3
National requirements for licensed daycare centers, 1998

	RATIO OF CHILD MINDERS TO CHILDREN BY CHILD AGE							OTHER STAFF FOR >90 CHILDREN		
<12 months	1 year old	2 years old	3 years old	4 and 5 years old	Manager	Cook	Child minder for break	Part-time child minder for annual vacation	Doctor
3:1	6:1	6:1	20:1	30:1	0 or 1	2	Part time (3/4 time)	16 days per year for one child minder	Part time

SOURCE: Asako et al. 1999, 52.

TABLE 7.4
Actual staffing of public daycare centers, City B in Tokyo, 1998

	A CAPACITY 100		B CAPACITY 106		C CAPACITY 109		D CAPACITY 120		E CAPACITY 130	
	Capacity	M	Capacity	M	Capacity	M	Capacity	M	Capacity	M
Child minders (M) by children's age groups										
<12 mos.	—	—	6	2	9	3	—	—	9	3
1 year	15	6	15	6	15	6	12	5	13	6
2 years	18		18		18		18		18	
3 years	20	1	20	1	20	1	30	2	30	2
4 years	23	1	23	1	23	1	30	1	30	1
5 years	24	1	24	1	24	1	30	1	30	1
Manager	1		1		1		1		1	
Senior child minder	1		1		1		1		1	
Cook	3		4		4		3		4	
Child minder for break	2		2		2		2		2	
Extra child minder	2		2		2		2		2	
Nurse	—		1s		1		—		1	
Dietitian	—		1s		1s		—		1s	
Doctor	1p		1p		1p		1p		1p	

SOURCE: Asako et al. 1999, 52.

NOTE: s: short time contract; p: part time

than in the private sector. In addition, childcare providers employed by the state tend to be older than those who are privately employed. In the case of City B, the average public caretaker is 41.9 years old, whereas the average private childcare provider is only 33.2 years old. Due to wage structures in the public sector and the seniority and age of providers, the average annual income of a public daycare provider is ¥7,500,000, remarkably high for a profession that only requires two years of junior college. Asako and colleagues (1999, 27) attribute the high cost of public childcare to the presence of superfluous employees in the public sector compared to the private sector.

Price Setting of Daycare Services

In addition to the national government, prefectural governments as well as city, town, and village governments pay a large portion of the cost of the daycare centers. Usually local governments use local funds to subsidize childcare costs. In the case of City B, about 12.6 percent of these costs ultimately fall on parents.

The fees for licensed private daycare centers and licensed public daycare centers are equivalent. The fee depends on family income, and most families pay less than the maximum fee. In City B, even the highest income class pays only ¥17,100 per month for children four or five years old, ¥20,200 for children three years old, and ¥43,900 for children less than three years old. Fees for a second child are discounted by one-half, and those for a third child by three-quarters. Under this price setting system, it is not surprising that demand for childcare exceeds supply. Furthermore, it is unclear whether or not this redistributive system is efficient. As Takayama (1982) points out, it may exacerbate inequalities between professions of differing income levels.

The Rigidity of Services

The inflexibility of public childcare is central to its failures. Even among the licensed (i.e., adequately subsidized) childcare facilities, flexible services such as extendable care, night care, or interim childcare are more available in the private sector (Hayashi 1996, 162; Asako et al. 1999, 24–25). The rigid employment system for public employees has proven a barrier to providing such services. Furthermore, due to the strong presence of the public labor union, it is difficult to employ part-time caretakers.

160   Junichiro Wada

Rural Childcare

Having examined childcare in urban areas, we now turn to rural areas. Is the shortage of daycare services a nationwide problem? Evidence suggests that the problems that plague urban childcare are unique to the urban setting. In rural areas, space is more abundant. As Figure 7.2 indicates, the utilization rate of childcare (total enrolled children/total capacity) is low in rural areas.[1] According to Asako and colleagues (1999, 22), more than 70 percent of rural municipalities do not have waiting lists for licensed childcare. In fact, such municipalities are often able to use buses to serve children from outside areas.

Moreover, in rural areas, quasi-licensed daycare centers, called *hekichi hoikusho* (backcountry daycare centers), have been permitted and supported by the national government since 1961. The requirements for *hekichi hoikusho* are very loose, but these daycare centers can receive block grants irrespective of the number of children they serve. The requirements for high teacher-child ratios for regular licensed daycare centers indicated in Table 7.3 are relaxed for daycare centers in rural areas (see Figure 7.3). However, urban areas would also benefit from a looser set of regulations governing teacher-child ratios, the presence of a doctor or nurse, the size of garden space, and the like.

In 1968, the national government began to support small, licensed daycare centers called *shokibo hoikusho*, with capacities between thirty

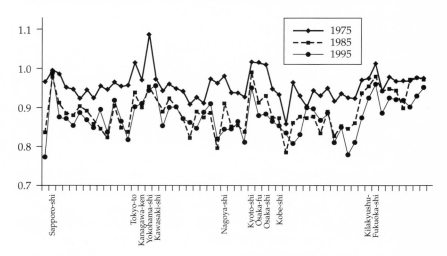

FIGURE 7.2 Rate of Filled Vacancies of Japanese Daycare Centers

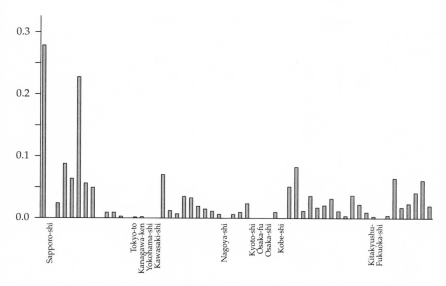

FIGURE 7.3 Capacity of Backcountry Daycare Centers, 1995

(later lowered to twenty) and sixty children. Initially, this type of day-care center was intended for urban areas, where it is difficult to add typical licensed daycare centers. But in 1971, less populated areas began to use *shokibo hoikusho,* and since then these daycare centers have been limited to rural areas. Consequently, as illustrated in Figure 7.4, the av-erage capacity of daycare centers has dropped only in rural areas.

Rural areas with few children have greatly benefited from *shokibo hoikusho.* These small daycare centers can get better per-child subsidies from the national government than their larger counterparts. In addition, on average, houses are much bigger in rural areas, and three-generation families are common. The prevalence of three-generation families is significant to our study because, as Yamashige (2001) and others have argued, the presence of a grandmother is often the determining factor in a mother's decision to work.

Lack of extended hours is also less problematic in rural childcare programs than in their urban counterparts. Typical public nurseries are open for eleven hours in Japan (Asako et al. 1999, 23). Whereas moth-ers in rural settings generally find these hours sufficient, many urban mothers face long commutes to work that extend the workday beyond eleven hours. Urban mothers employed in education and the public sector, however, are an exception. Even in urban areas, these women

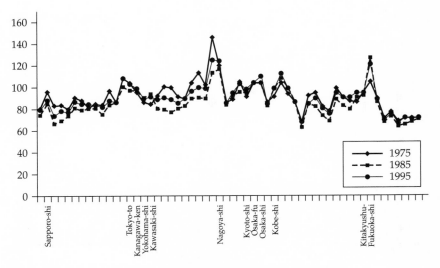

FIGURE 7.4 Average Capacity of Daycare Centers

TABLE 7.5
Reason for enrollment in the Daycare Center of City E in Osaka

Reason for enrollment		Number of children	% of children
Mother working outside			
Public employment	Teacher	43	5.4
	Nurse etc.	31	3.9
	Child minder	21	2.6
	Other	36	4.5
	Subtotal	131	16.7
Nongovernment	Teacher	5	0.6
	Nurse etc.	23	2.9
	Child minder	5	0.6
	Other	175	22.3
	Part-time	268	34.1
	Subtotal	476	60.7
Family-operated business		67	8.5
Total		674	85.9
Mother working in home			
	Piecework	10	1.2
	Family-operated business	19	2.4
Childbirth		4	0.5
Illness		14	1.7
Care		18	2.2
Other		45	5.7
Final total		784	100.0
(Motherless of fatherless family)		(127)	(16.1)

SOURCE: Asako et al. 1999, 87.

tend to work close to home and thus public childcare centers are able to meet their needs. Therefore, it is not surprising, as seen in Table 7.5, that women in the educational and public sectors are heavily represented among childcare patrons. Table 7.5 shows that 17.3 percent of children in daycare have mothers who are teachers or in other public sector employment, which looms large compared to the percentage of women in the public sector.

The Daycare System as the Equilibrium of a Game of Political Actors

How can we explain the fact that, on the one hand, Japanese childcare services are high quality and affordable, while on the other hand, they are scarce and inflexible? Why has it taken so long for working mothers—especially those on daycare waiting lists in urban areas—to gain a hearing? To address these questions, I will present a political analysis inspired by Fukuda (1999, 97–99), a former official of the Ministry of Welfare who worked to reform the public childcare system during the mid-1990s. We begin by examining the players in the political game of childcare supply.

Caretakers

The Liberal Democratic Party (LDP) is undoubtedly the strongest player in rural districts. Before electoral reform, two or three LDP representatives and one Japanese Socialist Party (JSP) representative would hold seats in a typical rural electoral district, not to mention the LDP's majorities in both houses of the Diet. But the LDP's core constituents did not view the provision of childcare as a central issue; for many, it was a cost to be avoided though some rural communities clearly benefited.

This ambiguous position is not true of the Socialists' constituencies. The Japan Trade Union Confederation (Rengo) and its largest member, the All Japan Prefectural and Municipal Workers' Union (Jichiro), include many public caretakers with vested interests in current childcare policy. This group usually insists on simply expanding childcare services, while resisting reforms necessary to do so, such as decreasing the cost or changing the employment system and increasing the revenue. Jichiro has significant political power, especially in rural areas where municipal governments and the public sector are dominant employers. The LDP may have chosen to acquiesce to caretaker demands to placate the JSP, and to keep the JSP base from expanding in reaction.

Working Mothers

Ironically, the agitations of working mothers may actually depress the supply of childcare. An insider/outsider phenomenon seems to be at work (Olson 1965). Once working mothers gain admission into daycare centers, they organize themselves as *oyanokai* or *hahanokai* (parents' groups or mothers' groups). They then collectively work to decrease daycare fees, improve the quality of care, provide more caretakers per child, and better the working conditions of daycare employees. This group is significantly more successful than the unorganized mothers on waiting lists for childcare, and these "improvements" wind up increasing the costs of childcare and hindering the expansion of childcare services. As Tables 7.3 and 7.4 show, City B has more caretakers than the national requirement, despite a waiting list there too.

Local Governments

Local governments, such as town and village assemblies, resist reform in the childcare system because the status quo benefits rural areas, particularly where the national government fully funds childcare. These areas are able to meet the demand for childcare, and thus have no need for waiting lists. Even the supply of services for children under three years old is sufficient in these areas and, in fact, the steep requirements for caretaker-to-child ratios provide much-needed employment. Rural towns and villages often illegally send children who do not technically qualify for childcare to licensed daycare centers instead of kindergartens. This practice allows local governments to collect subsidies from the national government without having to restructure their services. Thus, assessments of the need for childcare are often dubious at best.

Mayors' assemblies have not significantly changed, but cities in urban areas have made some independent modifications. In urban areas—or to be exact, ordinance-designated cities (big cities) and the cities around Tokyo and Osaka—many parents who have been waiting for licensed (adequately subsidized) daycare centers for a long time have had to turn to unlicensed daycare centers. In some cases, parents opt for unlicensed childcare because licensed daycares cannot offer extended hours. Parents pressed for more public support, but it was prohibitive to establish new licensed daycare centers in urban areas. In Yokohama City, it costs

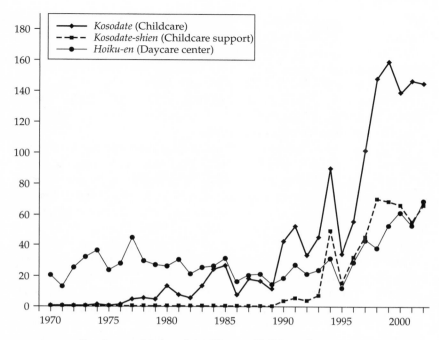

FIGURE 7.5 Conference Notes of the Diet on Childcare Issues, 1970 to 2002

¥2 billion to build a new licensed daycare center (Maeda 2002), and Jichiro objected to employing more part-time childcare workers to serve in an extended-care facility as is done in rural facilities.

The National Legislature

As Figure 7.5 indicates, government representatives seldom addressed childcare issues on their official websites before the mid-1990s. Although representatives of urban areas posed an exception to this rule, they made up a small minority in the national government, due to malapportionment. As we have seen above, childcare shortages largely plague urban areas where political power is traditionally weak.

Changes in the Current System

Following the "1.57" shock of 1989, Japanese childcare policy has undergone visible reform. The national government made the so-called "Angel Plan" in 1994 and "New Angel Plan" in 1999 in attempts to expand the childcare system. These new policies became a major emphasis of the national budget. Although it is unclear whether the expansion of childcare services alone can improve the total fertility rate, it is nevertheless clear that the national government has begun to support such policies. Innovations included *ekigata hoikushisetsu* (daycare facilities in front of train stations) established in 1994 and *bun'en* (satellite daycare centers) established in 1998. Both of these lack playgrounds, which are normally required for daycares in urban areas.

Local governments began to develop quasi-licensed daycare center systems too. *Yokohama-gata Hoikushitsu* (Yokohama Nursery Room) in Yokohama opened in 1997, and *Ninsho Hoikusho* (Certificated Daycare Center) opened in metropolitan Tokyo in 2001. Local governments also began to approve and subsidize unlicensed childcare independently of the national government, especially for children under three years old. Although the ratio of caretakers to children in such daycare centers usually meets national requirements, the facilities usually have insufficient playgrounds or lack both playgrounds and a nurse.

The national government has also begun to deregulate the childcare system. Before April 2000, only municipal governments and social welfare corporations were allowed to establish daycare centers; now business enterprises and individuals share this privilege. Both *Yokohama-gata Hoikushitsu* and *Ninsho Hoikusho* are privately owned, and Yokohama City has begun to sell its public daycare facilities to the private sector. Clearly, these developments counter the aims of Jichiro.

The "Shock"

The national government has announced its support for quasi-licensed daycare centers in urban areas. Because expanding fully licensed services to meet urban demand would be difficult, quasi-licensed childcare programs offer a viable alternative. The recent emphasis on urban childcare facilities shows that the national government has shifted its priorities. Both the new emphasis on urban childcare and the radical cut in public works benefit the urban public at the expense of rural dwellers who had disproportionately benefited from generous public childcare and government construction projects.

Although Jichiro has resisted the move toward privatization of childcare, privatization certainly cuts costs and increases the flexibility of Japanese daycare centers. On balance, deregulation should benefit urban working mothers on waiting lists for childcare, though the government still has a role in ensuring quality and safety of care.

What sparked this change in childcare policy? Some attribute changes in perception to the "1.57 shock" of 1989. But, if this were the case, why did the Japanese government wait until the mid-1990s to change policy when, as Figure 7.1 indicates, fertility rates had been falling all along? Factors beyond changes in perception associated with the drop in fertility rates must have come into play.

The dramatic shift in childcare policy indicates changes in the equilibrium of the political game. Increasing organization and political power among "outsiders" may have influenced policy, but this begs the question of why the balance has shifted in the first place. In my judgment, the 1994 electoral reform that increased the political representation of the city was the foremost agent of change. Figure 7.6 illustrates the increased political power of cities, which coincided with policy changes that clearly benefited metropolitan areas. Correcting malapportionment strengthened the political power of urban working moth-

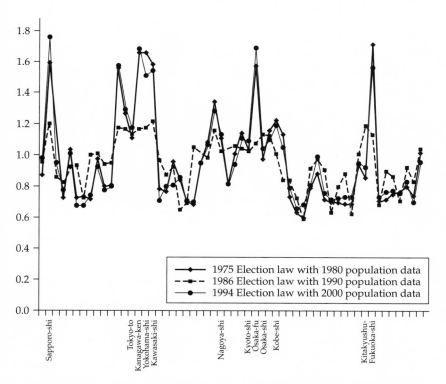

FIGURE 7.6 Population by Representation (Normalized by Total Population and Total Representation)

ers and weakened that of the public labor union. As Figure 7.5 showed, the Japanese legislature began to take up childcare issues once political parties found themselves accountable to urban voters.

Conclusion

This chapter has argued that changes in Japan's daycare policies have redistributed benefits from rural to urban areas in the last decade, since electoral rules were changed. This disaggregated picture presents a view that contrasts somewhat with Boling's emphasis (this volume) on continuity at the macro level, but it is a matter of emphasis, as many Japanese mothers in urban areas still await affordable and flexible childcare options. Furthermore, it seems unlikely that the supply of childcare is the only problem Japanese mothers face. As others in this volume have argued, improving women's ability to supply their labor can only go so far unless the demand for female labor also increases. Until the labor market becomes more accommodating to women seeking to balance family and career, and until other demands on a mother's time are alleviated, as Hirao's chapter in this volume shows, it is hard to imagine an amount of public support for childcare that will have a strongly positive effect on fertility.

Note

1. In this chapter, data for nine big cities are divided from prefectures. We consider nine big cities (Sapporo, Yokohama, Kawasaki, Nagoya, Kyoto, Osaka, Kobe, Kitakyushu, Fukuoka) and three big prefectures (Tokyo, Kanagawa [excluding Yokohama and Kawasaki], and Osaka [excluding Osaka City]) as urban areas and show their names on the figures.

References

Asako, Kazumi et al. 1999. *Hoiku Saabisu Kyokyu no Jissho Bunseki Kenkyu Hokokusho* [Report: The Empirical Analysis of the Supply of Childcare Services]. Tokyo: Onshi Zaidan Boshi Aiikukai.

Doi, T., and M. Ashiya. 1997. "Kokko Shishutukin Bunpai to Seiken Yoto no Kankei [Distribution of National Treasury Disbursement and Ruling Party]." *Nihon Keizai Kenkyu* 34.

Fujimoto, T. et al. 1983. "Yosanhaibun to Seijiyoso [Budget Allocation and Political Factor]." *Kokyo Sentaku no Kenkyu* 3.

Fukuda, Motoo. 1999. *Shakai Hosho no Kozo Kaikaku* [Structural Reform of Social Security]. Tokyo: Chuo Hoki.

Fukuda, Motoo. 2002. "Hoiku Saabisu no Kyokyu [Supply of Childcare]," in Kokuritsu Shakai hosho Jinkomonaai Kenkyusho, ed. *Shoshi Shakai no Kosodate Shien [Improving Childcare in a Low Birth Society]*. Tokyo: Tokyo University Press.

Hayashi, Y. 1996. "Contemporary Status and Problem of Childcare Business." *Kikan Syakaihosho Kenkyu* [Quarterly Journal of Social Security Research] 32(2): 158–166.

Hayashi, Nobutsugu. 2001. "Hoiku Saabisu Jigyo no Genjo to Kadai [Current situation and the Problem of Childcare]." *Kikan Shakaihosho Kenkyu* 32(2).

Hori, K. 2000. *Kokyo Jigyo no Seiji Keizaigaku* [Political Economy of Public Investment]. Tokyo: Tokai Daigaku Shuppankai.

Horiuchi, D., and J. Saito. 2003. "Reapportionment and Redistribution: Consequences of Electoral Reform in Japan," *American Journal of Political Science* 47: 669–682.

Imai, Hiroyuki. 2000. "Shoshika Doko to Kosodate Shien Seisaku [Fertility Decline and Family Policy]." Paper presented at Nihon Jinko Gakkai 52 kai Taikai [52nd Annual Meeting of the Population Association of Japan], June 2 and 3 at Waseda University.

Komamura, Kohei. 1996. "Hoiku Juyo no Keizai Bunseki [Economic Analysis of the Demand of Childcare]." *Kikan Shakai Hosho Kenkyu* 32(3).

Komamura, Kohei. 2002. "Hoiku Saabisu no Hiyo Bunseki to Jukyu no Misumacchi no Genjo [Cost Analysis of Childcare and Current Mismatch]," in Kokuritsu Shakai hosho Jinkomonaai Kenkyusho, ed. *Shoshi Shakai no Kosodate Shien [Improving Childcare in a Low Birth Society]*. Tokyo: Tokyo University Press.

Maeda, Masako. 2002. "'Kosodate Mappu' ni miru Hoiku no Genjo Bunseki [An Analysis of Childcare as Seen from a 'Childminding Map']." Working Paper, School of Pharmaceutical Sciences, Showa University, Tokyo.

Ogura, M. 1984. "Doro Jigyohi no Chiikikan Haibun no Koritsusei" [Efficiency of Allocation of the Road Constructing]. *Kikan Gendai Keizai* 8.

Olson, M. 1965. *The Logic of Collective Action*. Cambridge: Harvard University Press.

Takayama, Noriyuki. 1982. "Hoiku Saabisu no Hiyo Futan [Cost Sharing of Childcare Services]." *Keizai Kenkyu* 33.

Wada, J. 1985. "Seijikatei no Keizaigakuteki Bunseki [Economic Analysis of Political Process]." *Hermes* 36.

Wada, J. 1996. *Japanese Election System*. New York: Routledge.

Yamashige, Shinji. 2002. "Hoikusho Jujitsu Seisaku no Koka to Hiyo [Effects and Costs of Improving Daycare Centers]," in Kokuritsu Shakai hosho Jinkomonaai Kenkyusho, ed. *Shoshi Shakai no Kosodate Shien [Improving Childcare in a Low Birth Society]*. Tokyo: Tokyo University Press.

Yoshino, N., and H. Yoshida. 1988. "Kokyo Toshi no Chiho heno Haibun no Jissho Bunseki [Empirical Analysis of Allocation of the Public Investment]." *ESP* June: 42–47.

CHAPTER 8

The Privatized Education Market and Maternal Employment in Japan

KEIKO HIRAO

Introduction

Japanese mothers face a great deal of pressure to be involved intensively in their children's education. Getting into top schools is so competitive,[1] and the importance of an academic pedigree is so important for landing the best jobs, that Japanese families expend vast amounts of time and money herding their children through after-school "cram schools" (*juku*) in the private market. This burden falls most heavily on mothers in the traditional Japanese family, adding one more constraint on a woman's ability to supply her labor to the market. This task of looking after their children's education is likely to depress fertility because it exacerbates for women the difficulties of balancing family and career.

Many scholars have pointed out the prominence of private education services in Japan. Past studies that discuss Japanese education have usually dedicated some pages to the existence of such services and the functions they play (Hood 2001; Schoppa 1991; Simmons 1990; White 1987a; Wray 1999). The term *juku*, which is already listed in the *American Heritage Dictionary*, is circulated in English written and verbal communications as a word, though italicized, that requires little explanation among those who have some knowledge of Japan.

Approximately 60 percent of middle-school students and 30 percent of upper-grade elementary school children in Japan attend *juku* on regular bases (Ministry of Education 1994). The "excessive" enrollment in *juku* programs has been repeatedly criticized as dysfunctional for children's well-integrated development, and the majority of parents

(66.9 percent) share this criticism, saying that *"juku* attendance is over-heated" (Nihon PTA Zenkoku Kyogikai 1997). Nevertheless, Japanese parents, when sending their children to *juku*, acknowledge these services as necessary and useful in "helping children better understand school curriculum" (34.1 percent) and "making children more interested in study" (27.3 percent) (Ministry of Education 1994). In fact, as discussed in detail later in this chapter, empirical findings suggest that *juku* attendance is positively correlated not only with children's self-reported school performances but also with their social adaptation (Benesse Institute of Education 1998, 2002a, 2002b, 2002c; Tokyo Metropolitan Government 1999). Although the effect of *juku* attendance—and the supposedly underlying competitive learning environment—on children's physical, psychological, and social well-being has been and will continue to be a focus of public debate, the private educational services that operate outside the formal school classrooms have established themselves as an integral part of the educational system in Japan.

Traditional neoclassical economic theory identifies the household as a unit of production (home production), as well as a unit of consumption, with the prime example of a commodity "produced" by the household being children. It also specifies that: (1) the commodities produced in the household have "quantity" and "quality," just like those produced in the marketplace; (2) the inputs for this production are parents' time and market goods/services (that parents purchase with money); (3) time and money can be substituted; (4) the parental roles are shared between fathers and mothers according to the comparative advantage of their earning power; and (5) the value of one's time is assessed by the opportunity cost (Becker 1981). This argument leads us to expect that the family demand for children's education, when a large portion of human capital accumulation is privatized, raises the family need for financial resources and, thus, will give incentives for mothers to work for pay. On the other hand, family demand for children's education can be indicative of the parents' preferences for higher-quality childrearing. Holding constant the availability of financial resources, the demand for higher-quality childrearing raises the value of (mothers') time invested in bringing up the children. If the services provided within the household are less substitutable, it also raises the value of a parent's time input.

As a critique to the traditional economic and rational choice models, many scholars are paying more attention to the institutional forces that shape individual preferences. This is also true of cultural preferences that place great importance on education. In the context of the present study, institutional variation would take the form of regional differences in enrollment in higher education. It is expected that sending a child to *juku* takes on a different meaning in areas with low college enrollment rates than in areas where going to college is somewhat taken for granted.

With these environmental factors in mind, we expect that the family demand for children's education should have dual implications for maternal employment. It will raise the family need for financial resources and thus will exert a push on mothers to work for pay. On the other hand, it can be indicative of the parents' standard of quality childrearing, which raises the value of the mother's time used for home production. Which of these forces takes precedence when families choose a strategy for providing education for their children? Is maternal employment responsive to the demands on the family budget for children's extra-school education? If so, in what way? Or are household expenditures on education responsive to the extra budget that wives can provide? Do the regional differences in demand for higher education mediate the relations between *juku* enrollment and female labor-force participation? This chapter addresses these questions by using published government statistics. These statistics include the National Survey of Family Income and Expenditure, the Family Survey on Income and Expenditure, the Employment Status Survey, the Survey on Extra-school Programs, the Survey on Educational Spending, the Establishment and Enterprise Census, and other government statistics.

This chapter is organized as follows. The following section gives a general overview of how the privatized education market has developed and how families have responded to the demand for education. The third section deals with the longitudinal trends in household spending on education. The fourth section discusses regional variation in development of the private education market and its relation to the prefectural profiles of female labor participation patterns.

Extra-school Education: The Strategic Nexus Between Family and School

In 1981, when the Management and Coordination Agency started to list *juku* as an independent minor industry category in the Establishment and Enterprise Census (EEC), there were approximately 19,000 such establishments. In fifteen years, the number increased to as many as 49,500.[2]

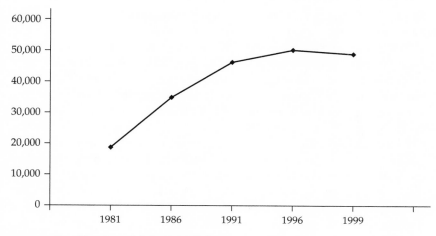

FIGURE 8.1 Number of *Juku* Establishments

SOURCE: Management and Coordination Agency, *Establishment and Enterprise Census*, various years.

The number of *juku* establishments has leveled off in the 1999 EEC, with a weeding out of some minor establishments due to the economic recession and a tightening of family budgets (Figure 8.1). However, when we take into account the average annual family spending on *juku* and tutoring services per child in each age group multiplied by the corresponding cohort size for that age group, the market size of private educational services is still estimated to be as large as $12.6 billion a year.[3] On average, Japanese households, including those without children, are spending approximately 20 percent of their education budget for services purchased outside the formal school system (Ministry of Public Management, Home Affairs, Post, and Telecommunications 2001).

The prominence of this private educational industry in Japan's educational system presents one of the keys to understanding the ways in which the family interacts with educational institutions and with the labor market in developing the human capital of future generations. Of particular interest is the impact of family dynamics of intergenerational resource transfer on children's education. Education not only extends one's scope of knowledge but also functions as a vital indicator of the economic well-being of an individual, because it has a significant influence on how social resources are shared among individuals through its ties with employment opportunities. This is particularly true in our industrialized societies where "child outcome," or more bluntly, "reproductive success" of a family, is often measured by the educational attainment of the offspring.

The family demand for children's education has dual implications for maternal employment. It will raise the family's need for financial resources and thus will exert a push on mothers to work for pay. On the other hand, it can be indicative of the parents' standard of quality childrearing, which raises the value of mothers' time used for home production.

Past studies that discuss the roles of families in the Japanese educational scene have paid special attention to mothers as an active agent in securing their children's success in school (Boocock 1991; Ellington 1992; Garfinkel 1983; Uno 1993; White 1987a, 1987b). Indeed, "families," when described as "involved in children's education," have often been used as synonyms for "mothers." This is because mothers are supposed to be the mediators of children's life at school and their life at home. The roles expected of mothers include: attending school meetings faithfully, being precisely informed about their children's school performance, and carrying out many intricate tasks to assist their children's school lives, such as making elaborate lunches (Allison 1991) and supplying items required for various school activities.[4] These "education moms" devoting the major part of their lives to their children's educational achievements have almost always been depicted as stay-at-home, full-time housewives. This is probably because many of the ethnographic studies took place in urban, white-collar communities, where female labor-force participation is relatively low (Allison 1991, 1996; Imamura 1987, 1989). But how do we account for the mothers' role as providers? According to the Special Survey of the Labor Force Survey, the number of dual-income families has equaled the number of single-income families since 1992. Although the monetary contributions of wives to the household income are still regarded as supplemental, Japanese mothers are shouldering significant roles as providers.

The Development of the Privatized Education Market in Japan

Public Policies and Privatization of Education

In June 1999, the Educational Council on Lifelong Learning at the Ministry of Education released a report entitled *Experience of Nature and Life*

Cultivates the Emotional Development of Japanese Children (Educational Council on Lifelong Learning 1999). In this report the ministry acknowledged, for the first time, that private educational enterprises, such as *juku*, are providing "rich and diverse learning opportunities" to Japanese children. The report maintains its criticism that *excessive* attendance to *juku* is harmful for children and suggests surveillance by community organizations such as parent-teacher associations to monitor the operating hours of *juku*. The report was, however, seen as epochal in the ministry's policy regarding private educational services. This is because officials have long ignored the existence of such services or have seen them as a "necessary evil" at best.

The Ministry has implemented several education reforms to remedy the excessive competition and "examination hell." The past initiatives include zoning of high school districts in major cities (to level out the academic performance among schools) and introduction of first-stage unified tests for college entrance, a Japanese equivalent of the SAT. The latest reform, which took effect in April 2002, stipulates the downsizing of the course content taught in schools by 30 percent and the closing of schools on Saturdays. The time spent in school was accordingly reduced by 70 hours per year for elementary school students and by 35 hours per year for junior high school students. The reform aims for "education free of pressure" (*yutori kyoiku*), education that will give children more latitude.[5]

Contrary to the Ministry's intention, the privatization of the education market has involved younger children in educational competition—a paradoxical nonegalitarian outcome resulting from a policy motivated by egalitarian ideals. This is partly because private schools and *juku* institutions are not bound by curriculum guidelines. In fact, many private schools openly reject the idea of pressure-free education. According to a survey by the Ministry of Education, approximately 30 percent of private schools nationwide and 50 percent in the Tokyo metropolitan area did not close their schools on Saturdays so that they can secure an adequate number of class periods (*Asahi Shimbun*, December 24, 2001). Enthusiastic parents who can afford the tuition are increasingly attracted to sending their children to such private middle schools.

Although the official statements of the Ministry of Education have ignored the existence of private services, in some cases the roles are being reversed between formal schools and private extra-school institutions. For example, the scores on standardized tests administered by large *juku* are often used by teachers to assess their students' chances of admission to successive upper schools. Some public high schools are reported to have sent their teachers to private cram schools that specialize in training teachers how to increase students' competitiveness in entrance examinations for colleges (*Asahi Shimbun*, November 23, 2001).

Juku Enrollment and Its Effect on School Performance

Compared with 25 years ago, more parents are using private instruction for their children. The rate of enrollment in *juku* has increased from 12 percent in 1976 to 24 percent in 1993 for elementary school children, and from 38 percent (1976) to 59.5 percent (1993) for middle school children (Ministry of Education 1976, 1985, 1994 (Figure 8.2). The rate of attendance has increased even among the lower grades. In 1991, 12.1 percent of first-grade children were attending *juku*, compared with 6 percent in 1985 (Ministry of Health and Welfare 1994). The nationwide trend in the late 1990s is not known, as the Ministry of Education has not conducted a survey since 1993, the results of which were published in 1994. *The Basic Survey on Children's Learning*, conducted by the Benesse Institute of Education in a rural area in the Tohoku region, a local city in Shikoku, and the Tokyo metropolitan area, suggests an overall stagnation in the

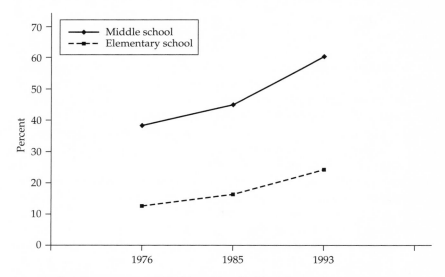

FIGURE 8.2 Percentages of Children Enrolled in *Juku*, 1976 to 1993
SOURCE: Ministry of Education, *Survey on Extra-school Education*, various years.

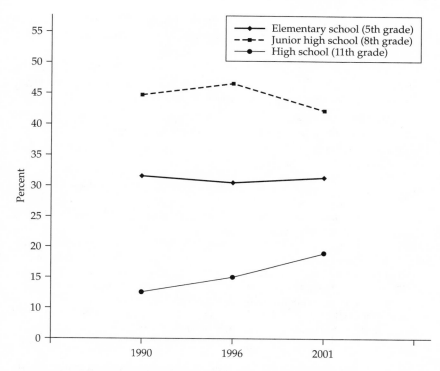

FIGURE 8.3 Percentages of Children Enrolled in *Juku*, 1990 to 2001
SOURCE: Benesse Institute of Education, *Basic Survey on Learning*, various years.

increase of enrollment rates in the 1990s (Figure 8.3). At the same time, however, the survey reports that attendance rates are on the rise in rural areas. The average enrollment rate for elementary school children in Tokyo is 45.8 percent, whereas the rate in a capital city in the Shikoku area is 34.2 percent. Even in a rural area of the Tohoku region, more than one in five elementary school children are attending *juku* (Benesse Institute of Education 2002a).

Many *juku* establishments, particularly those providing preparatory programs for entrance examination for private middle schools, treat parents' (mothers') involvement as indispensable. Some of the "progressive" establishments offer special classes for parents (usually for mothers) to teach them the key points of the materials covered in classes and also to give tips on how to supervise their children's study at home. Some *juku* institutions that boast more customized services organize tours for parents and students to visit schools to which they might consider applying. Moreover, most establishments have conferences with parents so that they can discuss the progress of their students and bring up problems to be solved.

Popular books of parental tips for children's academic success, or how-to books on selecting the right *juku*, often make a special note that parental involvement is crucial in making full use of extra-school services and that sending children to *juku* requires tremendous input on the part of parents (Kosodate Ura Netto 1996; Sugiyama 2001). Hirohito Uchiyama, who runs a major cram school, also notes the importance of the role assumed by mothers as follows:

> There are several "parental roles" that have to be assumed when making children prepare for the entrance examinations. These roles generally include: keeping in close contact with a reliable *juku* instructor, making the most effective study plans that suit their children the best, seeing to it that their children are carrying out their assignments as has been planned, and managing their daily lives. Carrying out these tasks naturally requires tremendous effort for every parent. They have to have a certain amount of time available to dedicate to their children. Filing the returned tests and packing supper to take to *juku* require their time and effort. When we compare two children, one with busy parents and the other with a stay-at-home mother with abundant time to dedicate, it is undeniably the latter who has a higher chance for admission. (Uchiyama 2002, 64)

If *juku* requires extra involvement, is making full use of it a luxury affordable only for the wealthy stay-at-home mothers, who are rich in financial resources and time resources as well? A question is raised as to whether purchasing the extra-school services functions as a substitute for parents' time input. This question can be answered only when we can control actual parental behavior, such as supervising children's homework.

The Tokyo portion of the *Basic Survey on Children's Learning* (Benesse Institute of Education 2002a) reports that mothers who are highly involved in their children's education (the group they identified as "education mothers") are more likely to stay at home or work at home. They do not, however, report whether these education mothers are more likely to use extra-school services for their children. That is, the relations among (1) parenting style (how much they are involved in children's education), (2) household income (the affordability of financial resources), (3) mother's work status, and (4) *juku* attendance of children are yet unknown. The question still remains open, as the individual-level data that address these issues are not publicly available. The analyses presented in the following sections of this chapter are thus limited in scope in that they address only the financial aspect of the education market.

How Families Spend on Education

Japan ranks as one of the lowest among the Organization for Economic Cooperation and Development (OECD) countries in public spending on schools by national and local governments, when measured in terms of its proportion to the gross domestic product. Total public spending on education in Japan is only 3.53 percent of the GDP, whereas public spending in France accounts for 5.88 percent, and that in the United States accounts for 4.82 percent (Figure 8.4). The share of Japanese public spending is particularly low at postsecondary levels. Approximately 74 percent of Japanese colleges are privately operated (Ministry of Education 2000b), whereas in the United States only 20 percent of colleges are private (Yano 1993). Although the Japanese governments grant subsidies to private schools, the tuitions for private schools are notably more expensive than those of public schools. In other words, a substantial portion of the children's schooling cost in Japan is already privatized.

Figure 8.5 plots the average share of educational expenses over the total consumptive expenses for workers' households (excluding those

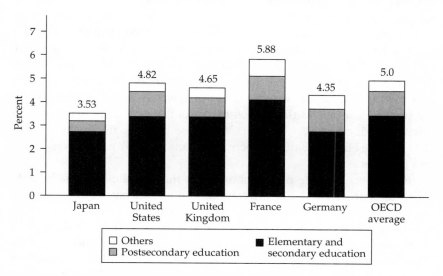

FIGURE 8.4 Public Spending on Education as a Proportion of GDP
SOURCE: Ministry of Education, Culture, Sports, Science, and Technology, 2002b.

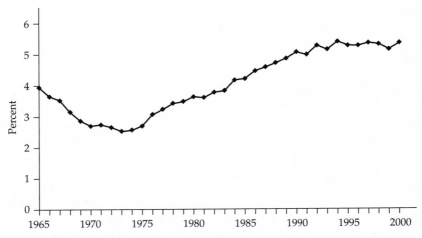

FIGURE 8.5 Share of Educational Expenses over the Total Consumptive Expenses for Workers' Households, 1965 to 2000
   SOURCE: Management and Coordination Agency, *Family Income and Expenditure Survey*, 1965–2000

in agriculture, self-employed, and single-person households), reported in the Family Income and Expenditure Survey from 1965 to 2000. It should be noted that these figures are seriously underestimated, because they aggregate all workers' households, including those without children. Nevertheless, it gives an overview of the longitudinal trends in the share of educational expenses over the last thirty-five years, which can be roughly divided into three periods. The first period (1960s to mid-1970s) experienced a decline in the share of education expenses; the second period (late 1970s to mid-1990s) witnessed an increase in the share; the last period (late 1990s to present) shows a flattening of the share of educational expenses. Over these periods, the average number of household members decreased constantly from 4.3 persons to 3.2 persons.

Private schools are much more costly than public schools. Parents who send their child to a private middle school pay ¥1,223,125 total, whereas parents who send their child to a public middle school pay ¥404,169 per year. Likewise, the total educational cost for a child in a private high school is ¥1,010,125, whereas that of a child in a public high school is ¥515,605 (1998). The parents of children attending private schools pay about 20 percent of the total cost for extra-school education.

Where *Juku* Prospers: Prefecture-Level *Juku* Attendance and Patterns of Female Labor Force Participation

Is maternal employment responsive to the family demand for education? A rephrased version of this question would state: do families with two incomes show different patterns of consumer behavior from those with single incomes when purchasing educational services? As mentioned previously, none of the published data gives adequate information to answer the first question, but the Family Income and Expenditure Survey (Management and Coordination Agency/Ministry of Public Management, Home Affairs, Post, and Telecommunications) offers partial evidence for answering the second question. Likewise, the Survey on Extra-school Programs (Ministry of Education), when collated with other statistics at prefecture levels, allows us to assess, though at an aggregate level, the relation between usage of extra-school services and patterns of female labor force participation.

Table 8.1 presents average annual expenditures on education by employment status of wives reported in the 2002 Family Income and Expenditure Survey. On average, Japanese workers' households (excluding those in agriculture) spend ¥212,016 a year, or 5.3 percent of the total consumptive expenses, on education, of which 22 percent goes to extra-school education.[6] Families with a single income spend about the same, whereas those with working wives spend ¥284,184, or about 30 percent more than the amount spent by single-income families. When families with one child are compared, single-income families spend ¥146,448 a year on education, whereas those with working wives spend ¥249,216, 70 percent more than the budget spent by a single-income family. The difference is smaller for those with two children; single-income families with two children spend ¥350,844 on education, while those with working wives spend ¥420,624, 20 percent more than the amount spent by single-income households. It is impossible to estimate the effect of the additional child on household expenditures on education, as the report does not allow us to control the age of the first child or the age of the head of the household. It is speculated that families with one child and families with two children are in different life stages.

When these figures are calculated as a proportion of total consumptive expenditures, families with two incomes are allocating larger proportions of the family budget to educational expenses. Single-income families with one child are spending 4 percent of the family budget on education, whereas dual-income families with one child are spending

TABLE 8.1
Average annual expenditures on education by workers' households

	Average for all	SINGLE-EARNER FAMILIES			DUAL-EARNER FAMILIES		
			NUMBER OF CHILDREN			NUMBER OF CHILDREN	
		Average	One	Two	Average	One	Two
Education cost	¥212,016	¥214,548	¥146,448	¥350,844	¥284,184	¥249,216	¥420,624
Tuition	¥159,360	¥157,908	¥115,908	¥257,460	¥211,272	¥207,360	¥302,424
School supplies	¥5,292	¥5,160	¥3,048	¥8,280	¥7,164	¥6,384	¥10,680
Extra-schooling cost	¥47,352	¥51,480	¥27,504	¥85,092	¥65,748	¥35,460	¥107,532
Consumptive expenditure	¥4,020,504	¥3,871,008	¥3,656,688	¥3,948,336	¥4,254,516	¥4,218,528	¥4,324,776
Education cost as % of total consumptive expenditure	5.3%	5.5%	4.0%	8.9%	6.7%	5.9%	9.7%
Extra-schooling cost as % of educational expenditure	22.3%	24.0%	18.8%	24.3%	23.1%	14.2%	25.6%

SOURCE: Ministry of Public Management, Home Affairs, Post, and Telecommunications. *Family Income and Expenditure Survey.* 2002.

5.9 percent of total expenses on education. The difference is smaller between single-income families with two children and dual-income families with two children: 8.9 percent for single-income families and 9.7 percent for dual-income families. The total consumptive expenditure for dual-income families is approximately 10 percent higher than that for single-income families. However, the educational expenses among dual-income families are 32 percent higher than the expenses among families with nonworking wives. As the employment status of wives and their work histories are unknown, the causal order between household expenditure on children's education and wives' employment decisions is unknown. However, at least we can tentatively observe a pattern in which dual-income families are generally spending more for their children's education, both in real terms and proportionately to the overall family budget.

There is substantial regional variation in the higher education enrollment rates. Tokyo ranks at the top of the scale (60.5 percent), and Iwate Prefecture ranks at the bottom (29.3 percent) (Ministry of Education 2000c). Generally, prefectures with high enrollments in universities and junior colleges are found in the Kanto, Chubu, and Kansai areas, or

TABLE 8.2
Pearson correlation matrix of market size of juku, *college enrollment rate, and* juku *attendance*
(n = 47)

	Market size of *juku*	College enrollment rate	*Juku* attendance (upper elementary)	*Juku* attendance (middle school)
Market size of *juku*	1			
College enrollment rate	0.601***	1		
Juku *attendance (upper elementary)*	0.689***	0.702***	1	
Juku *attendance (middle school)*	0.659***	0.588***	0.815***	1

*$p < 0.05$ **$p < 0.01$ ***$p < 0.001$ (two-tail test)

along the Pacific Coast, where we can find Tokyo and ten out of fourteen major cities, as designated by government ordinance. Likewise, *juku* attendance varies from 8.8 percent to 58.2 percent for upper-elementary school children, and from 26.5 percent to 81.2 percent for middle school students (Ministry of Education 1994). The differences in the sizes of the extra-school education market at prefecture levels, as measured by the ratio of persons engaged in the *juku* industry (both full-time and part-time) to the population above fifteen years of age, generally show a similar pattern. As Table 8.2 shows, higher supplies of extra-school services are found in the areas with greater demands for higher education, and these are the prefectures with more parents sending their children to extra-school institutions.

Do the regional differences in enrollment for extra-school services reflect the socioeconomic profiles and female labor force participation of the regions?

Specifically, do the areas with high enrollment in *juku* show different patterns of female labor force participation?

In order to differentiate prefectures with more demand for education from those with less demand, the 47 prefectures are divided into two groups by the enrollment rates in higher education, with the dividing line being the national average. Sixteen prefectures are accordingly identified as prefectures with high enrollment rates in universities and junior colleges (HE), and 31 prefectures as the ones with low enrollment rates in higher education (LE). Table 8.3 presents the national average and group means for selected variables. Note that the group means do not sum up to the national average, as the prefecture-level data aggregate variations within each prefecture. Female work status is defined as follows: Housewives are identified as women (above fifteen years of

TABLE 8.3
Descriptive statistics on prefecture profiles

| | National average | GROUP MEANS BY ENROLLMENT IN HIGHER EDUCATION | | | | |
| | | BELOW NATIONAL AVERAGE (LE) ($n = 31$) | | ABOVE NATIONAL AVERAGE (HE) ($n = 16$) | | |
		Mean	s.d.	Mean	s.d.	Prob.
Demographic profiles						
Population size (in 1,000s)		2,207	1,566	3,571	3,510	
Under 15 years old (%)		16.8%	0.01	15.8%	0.012	**
Dual-earner household ratio	30.7%	35.4%	0.05	33.2%	0.07	
Ratio of urban population	77.9%	69.6%	12.18	67.6%	12.63	
Education market						
Juku attendance (upper elementary)	32.1%	25.8%	9.4	36.9%	10.2	
Juku attendance (middle school)	59.4%	53.5%	14.8	61.0%	10.1	
Number of *Juku* workers per 1,000 population	2.4	1.8	0.7	2.4	0.6	**
Proportion of students at private schools (middle school)	5.9%	3.1%	0.00	6.47%	0.00	**
Proportion of students at private schools (high school)	30.4%	24.2%	0.07	28.0%	0.12	
Female ($\geq$ 15 years old) labor force participation						
Full-time	39.6%	42.7%	0.05	40.3%	0.06	
Part-time	19.2%	18.4%	0.02	19.36%	0.02	
Housewife	41.2%	38.9%	0.04	40.31%	0.05	
Industrial/economic profiles						
Primary industry worker ratio (ages 15–64)	6.0%	10.5%	3.85	5.2%	3.32	***
Tertiary industry worker ratio (ages 15–64)	61.8%	58.8%	5.32	60.5%	5.13	
Disposable monthly income of workers' households in nonagriculture sectors	¥482,174	¥479,375	9,154	¥512,275	12,742	*
Male monthly wages (in ¥1,000)	334.0	¥295.0	23.31	¥331.0	24.3	***
Female monthly wages (in ¥1,000)	209.6	¥189.0	14.27	¥210.0	17.3	***
Gender wage gap	0.643	0.643	0.020	0.636	0.02	

SOURCES: Management and Coordination Agency, *Population Census*, 1990; Management and Coordination Agency, *Social Life Stastistics Index*, 1995; Ministry of Education, *Survey on Extra-school Education*, 1994; Management and Coordination Agency, *Establishment and Enterprises Census*, 1998; Management and Coordination Agency, *Employment Status Survey*, 1997; Ministry of Health, Labor, and Welfare, *Basic Survey on Wage Structure*, 1996.

*$p < 0.05$ **$p < 0.01$ ***$p < 0.001$

age) whose primary status is "doing housework and not working for pay." Part-time workers are identified as women who are "primarily doing housework but also working for pay." Similarly, full-time workers are identified as those who report their status as "primarily working for pay." The ratio of each category is taken over the sum of population in these trichotomized categories.[7]

Although the ratio of the urban population[8] does not show statistical differences, HE prefectures generally have "urban" characteristics, including: a lower ratio of workers in primary industry; a lower proportion of minors in the population; higher disposable income per household; high wage rates for men and women; higher *juku* attendance, particularly at younger ages; and a relatively developed privatized education market, both in terms of the proportion of students in private middle schools and the size of the extra-school education industry. On the other hand, indicators for female labor force participation and gender wage gap do not differ between HE and LE prefectures.

Figure 8.6 plots the proportions of the female population in each category of the employment status versus *juku* attendance rates for two different age groups of children: upper-elementary school and junior high school students. The ellipses of 95 percent concentration are constructed for HE (black dots, solid line) and LE (white dots, broken line) prefectures. These plots show how these two indicators are related to each other within the two groups of prefectures: those with high demand for education and those with less demand for education. Although the small number of observation points does not allow us to run statistical tests, these plots indicate the patterns in which *juku* attendance and female labor force participation are associated with each other. The patterns can be summarized as follows.

First, in both LE prefectures and HE prefectures, *juku* attendance is inversely related with the ratio of full-time workers among women. The negative relation is stronger in HE prefectures, especially for *juku* attendance of older children. Second, in LE prefectures, *juku* attendance for both age groups of children is positively related with the proportion of part-time workers. For HE prefectures, however, the positive relation can be observed only for *juku* attendance of older children. Third, in LE prefectures, *juku* attendance is not related with the proportion of nonworking females, but in HE prefectures these two indicators are positively related.

The family demand for extra income for children's education is not the sole determinant of female labor force participation decisions, of

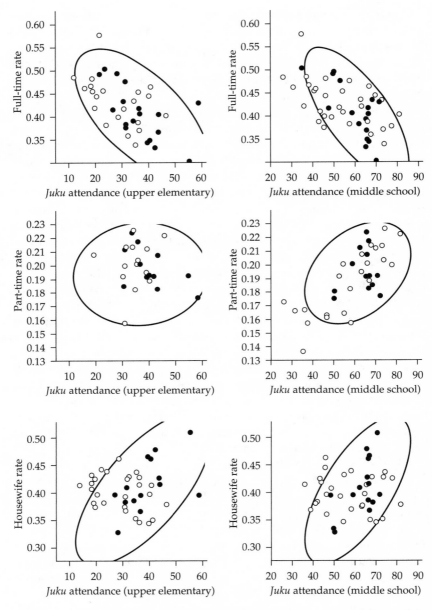

FIGURE 8.6 *Juku* Attendance and Proportion of Female Population in Each Employment Status

course. It is very plausible that the differences in female labor force participation patterns are due to the differences in the employment opportunities for female workers, as other chapters in this book argue. Also, differences in household composition, particularly the proportion of extended families, were not fully addressed in this analysis. A related possibility is that mothers who send their children to *juku* are not necessarily the same persons reflected in the data, because the data on female labor force indicators include women without children. Also omitted is the heterogeneity of the workforce. It is true that "full-time workers," for example, consist of people with different occupations and income, from those working in white-collar professional jobs to blue-collar workers in factories, which are not equally distributed among prefectures. Equally important are the regional differences in the availability of public childcare (Maeda 2002). Employment decisions may have been determined prior to decisions about investments in children's education. There are numerous factors that need to be controlled but do not appear in the prefecture profiles discussed in this chapter.

Notwithstanding the fact that many of the important factors traditionally considered as determinants of female labor force participation are omitted from the prefecture-level analyses, the findings suggest a tentative answer to the question addressed in this chapter. As far as the rate of *juku* attendance and female labor force participation are concerned, the pattern is strikingly consistent: they are *inversely* related, particularly in the areas with high demand for college education. The education burden depresses female labor force participation.

Conclusions

In this chapter I have conceptualized the private education market as an institution that connects the family and the school in the course of developing human capital of children. As we have seen, the privatized educational industry has developed into an integral part of the Japanese education system, and children's school performance and consequent educational attainment have become increasingly dependent on the services that parents purchase outside the formal school system.

The share of educational expenses in the family budget has risen steadily during the past forty years. This was not only because of the increase in the college enrollment rate, but also because of the increasingly privatized nature of the educational input. On average, 20 percent of a family budget for children's education goes to *juku* and tutoring services. The economic recession in the late 1990s has squeezed family spending, but its effect was not constant across socioeconomic groups. The "cooling down" of *juku* attendance was observed only among less-wealthy families. Those who can afford it are still investing consider-able amounts for their children's education.

Is maternal employment responsive to the demand for financial resources for children's education? A regional analysis showed that in areas with higher college enrollment, prefecture-level *juku* atten-dance and female labor supply are *inversely* related. That is, among prefectures with more demand for higher education, the more parents send their children to *juku*, the less likely women are to be in the labor force.

Although data limitations prevent me from making stronger infer-ences, I can speculate that services provided by *juku* do not simply function as substitutes for the time mothers put in for their children; rather, the purchasing of these services mirrors the parents' standard of quality childrearing, which raises the value of a mother's time used for home production. In other words, for wives who can afford to stay at home, family demand for children's "quality" seems to impose a deter-rent effect on maternal employment.

The most prevalent coping strategy for the work-and-family conflict for Japanese families has been for women to leave the labor market during the parenting years and come back later, mostly as low-wage part-time workers, when the children are grown (Iwai and Manabe 2000; Obuchi 1995a, 1995b). This so-called M-shaped participation pat-tern has been very persistent in spite of the legislative changes that aim for a gender-equal, family-friendly society (Hirao 1999, 2001a; Nagase 1999; Tanaka 1998). In fact, the lifetime work participation pattern of female graduates of four-year colleges looks like a "giraffe" (instead of being M-shaped) with a long and high "neck" standing out from a smoothly arching "back" that doesn't form a second peak (Ministry of Labor 2000, Hirao 1998). When nonworking housewives are asked whether they wish to work for pay, the majority answer affirmatively. The potential labor supply is equally high for educated women who are staying at home, but those who actually decide to work are overrepre-sented by women with lower educational backgrounds (Japan Institute of Labor 1993, 1997a, 1997b, 1998).

In 1996 the Japan Institute of Labor conducted a survey among 1500 women ages twenty to forty-four on their work attitude and their labor force participation behavior. The survey did not include informa-tion on parenting behavior, but the results seem to be in accordance with the hypothesis that the demand for "quality childrearing," including the educational attainment of children, is deterring the labor supply of highly educated mothers. Among those who left their jobs either upon marriage or childbirth, 78.9 percent of college graduates said, "it was impossible to maintain work while doing housework and childcare."

As many scholars have noted, the standard of childrearing is remarkably high in Japan (Hirao 2001b; Yu 2001). When the context of "good parenting" requires heavier involvement for a more extended period of time, those who internalize these parenting norms would feel more conflict in balancing work and family responsibilities. Moreover, those who have higher education are more likely to channel their resources into home production (quality childcare) rather than into paid employment.

All of this means that we ought to expect a further decline in fertility, because the high cost of raising children is a major reason for why married couples decline to have as many children as they might wish to have (Institute for Research on Household Economics 1998; National Institute of Population and Social Security Research 1999). Given that this cost falls disproportionately on the shoulders of women in terms of their time commitment, women are choosing to have fewer children. Among Japanese women, it is the highly educated women with high opportunity costs who are most likely to face the discrete alternatives between being childless and staying at home with children.

Notes

1. With the shrinking size of the school-age cohort, the overall competition for college entrance has been somewhat relaxed. Nevertheless, admission to top-tier universities is still very competitive and even requires earlier planning, as many such schools are introducing diverse admission tracks so that they can recruit the best and the brightest.

2. The size of establishments, measured by the number of employees, ranges from "less than five" to "more than 300."

3. The estimate is obtained by multiplying (a) the average annual *juku* spending per child in each age group (Ministry of Education 2000a) by (b) the corresponding cohort size reported in the 2000 Population Census (Management and Coordination Agency 2000). The estimate is based on the average spending for children attending public schools and thus is underestimated. The exchange rate: 120 yen to a dollar.

4. Although recent studies found an increasing importance of paternal roles in children's education (Hirota 1999; Kobari 2001), they are still regarded as secondary to the roles played by mothers.

5. Corresponding to the criticism that downsizing of the curriculum content would lead to a decline in the academic competitiveness of the students, the Ministry of Education (MEXT) indicated that the guideline should be interpreted as the minimum standard of what should be taught at schools. Also, the MEXT partially revised the guideline in the year 2004. The inconsistencies of the MEXT over the guidelines have invited confusion among schoolteachers who are actually engaged in teaching.

6. This figure is, again, underestimated, as the Family Income and Expenditure Survey aggregates households without children. Supplemental Education includes costs for *juku*, tutoring services, and corresponding services. Costs for nonacademic activities, such as piano lessons or sports activities, are listed in a different category.

7. The conventional method of measuring these indicators is to take the proportion of the workforce in each category of work status over the total productive population. This method yields biased results, particularly when calculating the percentage of housewives, as the non-workforce includes people going to school. In other words, the housewife percentage will be underestimated for prefectures with large student populations. Likewise, the conventional method is sensitive to the unemployment rate, as the unemployed population, by definition, is counted as part of the workforce because the persons surveyed have the "intention" to engage in productive activities. This analysis, therefore, excludes students and the unemployed from the denominator.

8. It is measured by the proportion of people living in cities with populations over 50,000.

References

Abe, Masahiro. 2001. "Josei no rodo kyokyu to sedai koka (Cohort effect in female labor supply)." Pp. 21–43 in *Daisotsu josei no hatarakikata* (The labor patterns of college educated women), edited by Akira Wakisaka and Yasunobu Tomita. Tokyo: Japan Institute of Labor.

Allison, Anne. 1991. "Japanese Mothers and Obentos: The lunch-box as ideological state apparatus." *Anthropological Quarterly* 64:195–208.

———. 1996. "Producing Mothers." Pp. 135–155 in *Re-Imaging Japanese Women*, edited by Anne Imamura. Berkeley: University of California Press.

Aramaki, Sohei. 2000. "Kyoiku kikai no kakusa ha shukusho shitaka: kyoiku kankyo no henka to shusshin kaisokan kakusa (Have the education opportunities equalized?)." Pp. 15–35 in *Niho no kaiso shisutemu 3: sengo shakai no kyoiku shakai* (The stratification system in Japan 3: Educational society in the post-war Japan), edited by Hiroyuki Kondo. Tokyo: Tokyo University Press.

Becker, Gary S. 1981. *A Treatise on the Family.* Cambridge, MA: Harvard University Press.

Benesse Institute of Education. 1998. *Dai ni kai gakushu kihon chosa hokokusho: shogakusei ban* (The second basic survey on learning: Elementary school children). Okayama: Benesse.

———. 2002a. *Dai san kai gakushu kihon chosa hokokusho: shogakusei ban* (The third basic survey on learning: Elementary school children). Okayama: Benesse.

———. 2002b. *Dai san kai gakushu kihon chosa hokokusho: chugakusei ban* (The third basic survey on learning: Middle school children). Okayama: Benesse.

———. 2002c. *Dai san kai gakushu kihon chosa hokokusho: kokosei ban* (The third basic survey on learning: High school children). Okayama: Benesse.

Benjamin, Gail R., and Estelle James. 1988. *Public Policy and Private Education in Japan*. University Park: Pennsylvania State University Press.

Boocock, Sarane Spence. 1991. "The Japanese Preschool System." Pp. 97–126 in *Windows on Japanese Education*, edited by Edward R. Beauchamp. New York: Greenwood Press.

Brinton, Mary C. 1988. "The Social-Institutional Bases of Gender Stratification: Japan as an Illustrative Case." *American Journal of Sociology* 94:300–334.

———. 1993. *Women and the Economic Miracle: Gender and Work in Postwar Japan*. Berkeley: University of California Press.

Brown, Phillip. 1990. "The 'Third Wave': Education and the Ideology of Parentocracy." *British Journal of Sociology of Education* 11:65–85.

Chuo Koron (Ed.). 2001. *Ronso churyu hokai* (Controversy: The demise of the middle-class). Tokyo: Chuo Koron.

Coleman, James S. 1988. "Social Capital in the Creation of Human Capital." *American Journal of Sociology*, Supplement 94: S95–S120.

———. 1990. *Foundations of Social Theory*. Cambridge, MA: Harvard University of Press.

———. 1993. "The Rational Reconstruction of Society." *American Sociological Review* 58:1–15.

Economic Planning Agency. 1996. *Kokumin seikatsu senkodo chosa* (Survey on national life styles and preferences). Tokyo: Government Printing Office.

Educational Council on Lifelong Learning, Ministry of Education. 1999. *Seikatsu taiken, shizen taiken ga nihon no kodomo no kokoro wo hagukumu* (Experience of nature and life cultivates the emotional development of Japanese children). Tokyo: Ministry of Education.

Ellington, Lucien. 1992. *Education in the Japanese Life-Cycle*. Lewiston, NY: E. Mellen Press.

Garfinkel, Perry. 1983. "The Best 'Jewish Mother' in the World." *Psychology Today* 17:56–60.

Hirao, Keiko. 1998. "Who Returns to the Labor Market? Hazard Analyses on the Rate of Return after Marriage and Childbirth." Paper presented at the Annual Meetings of Japan Sociological Association, Kwansai Gakuin University.

————. 1999. "Josei no shoki kyaria keiseiki ni okeru rodo shijyo heno tei-chakusei: gakureki to kazoku ibento wo megutte (The effect of higher education on the rate of labor-force exit for married Japanese women)." *Nihon Rodo Kenkyu Zasshi* (Monthly Journal of the Japan Institute of Labor) 471:29–41.

————. 2001a. "Mothers as the Best Teachers: Japanese Motherhood and Early Childhood Education." Pp. 180–203 in *Women's Working Lives in East Asia*, edited by Mary C. Brinton. Stanford: Stanford University Press.

————. 2001b. "The Effect of Higher Education on the Rate of Labor-Force Exit for Married Japanese Women." *International Journal of Comparative Sociology* 42:413–433.

Hirota, Teruyuki. 1999. *Nihonjin no shituke ha suitai shitaka* (Has the Japanese discipline declined? The future of educational families). Tokyo: Kodansha.

Hood, Christopher. 2001. *Japanese Education Reform.* New York: Routledge.

Imamura, Ann. 1987. *Urban Japanese Housewives: At Home and in the Commune.* Honolulu: University of Hawaii Press.

————. 1989. "Interdependence of Family and Education: Reactions of Foreign Wives of Japanese to the School System." Pp. 16–27 in *Japanese Schooling*, edited by James J. Shields Jr.. University Park: Pennsylvania State University Press.

Inoue, Osamu. 2001. *Shiritsu chuko ikkanko shika nai!* (There is nothing but private middle schools!). Tokyo: Takarajimasha.

Institute for Research on Household Economics. 1998. *Shohiseikatsu ni kansuru paneru chosa* (Japanese Panel Study of Consumers). Tokyo: Government Printing Office.

International Labor Office. 1995. *Yearbook of Labour Statistics.* Geneva: International Labour Office.

Iwai, Hachiro, and Rinko Manabe. 2000. "M ji gata shugyo patan no teichakuto sono imi (Stability of M-shape participation and its implications)." Pp. 67–92 in *Nihon no kaiso shisutemu 4: jenda, shijo, kazoku* (The stratification system in Japan 4: Gender, market and family), edited by Kazuo Seiyama. Tokyo: Tokyo University Press.

Japan Institute of Labor. 1993. *Joshi saishushoku no jittaini kansuru kenkyu* (Research on women's reentry behavior to the labor force). Tokyo: Japan Institute of Labor.

————. 1997a. *Josei no shokugyou kyaria ishiki to shugyo kodo ni kansuru kenkyu* (Female occupation, career attitude, and patterns of labor-force participation). Tokyo: Japan Institute of Labor.

————. 1997b. *Kogakureki josei no rodoryokuritsu no kitei youin ni kansuru kenkyu* (Determinants of labor supply of highly educated women). Tokyo: Japan Institute of Labor.

————. 1998. *Kogakureki shufu no shugyo ishiki to seikatsu jittai* (Work attitudes and life of college educated housewives). Tokyo: Japan Institute of Labor.

Kanbara, Fumiko. 2001. " 'Kyoiku suru kazoku' no kazoku mondai (Family issues of 'educative family ideals')." *Japanese Journal of Family Sociology* 12 : 197–207.

Kariya, Takehiko. 2001. *Kaisoka nippon to kyoiku kiki* (Social stratification in Japan and education crises). Tokyo: Yushindo Kobunsha.

Kataoka, Emi. 1998. "Kyoiku tassei ni okeru meritokuraci no kozo to kazoku no kyoiku senryaku (Meritocracy and cultural reproduction in Japan: Cultural capital investment in extra-school education and school success)." Pp. 1–16 in *Kyoiku to sedaikan ido* (Education and social mobility), *1995 SSM Research Series, volume 12*, edited by Kazuo Seiyama and Sachiko Imada. Tokyo: 1995 Social Stratification and Mobility Survey Research Group.

Kawaguchi, Akira. 1997. "Danjokan chinginkakusa no keizai riron (Economic theories on gender wage gap)." Pp. 207–241 in *Koyokanko no henka to josei rodo* (Changes in employment practice and female labor force), edited by Hiroyuki Chuma and Terukazu Suruga. Tokyo: Tokyo University Press.

Kimura, Kunihiro. 2000. "Rodo shijyo no kozo to yuhaigujosei no ishiki (The structure of labor market and the attitudes of married women)." Pp. 177–192 in *Nihon no kaiso sisutemu 4: genda, shijo, kazoku* (The stratification system in Japan 4: Gender, market and the family), edited by Kazuo Seiyama. Tokyo: Tokyo University Press.

Kobari, Makoto. 2001. "Shogakko jyuken no jyunbikyoiku to yoji no hattatu (The relation between the entrance selection of national or private elementary schools and development of young children)." *Nyuyoji kyoikugaku kenkyu* 10 : 1–9.

Kodama, Ryoko. 2001. "Kyoiku kaikaku to kazoku (Education reforms and the family)". *Japanese Journal of Family Sociology* 12 : 185–196.

Kondo, Hiroyuki. 2000. "Kaiso kenkyu to kyoiku shakai no iso (Phases in social stratification and educational society)." Pp. 3–13 in *Niho no kaiso shisutemu 3: sengo shakai no kyoiku shakai* (The stratification system in Japan 3: Educational society in the post-war Japan), edited by Hiroyuki Kondo. Tokyo: Tokyo University Press.

Kosodate Ura Netto. 1996. *Mayowanai chugaku juken* (How to support and survive your children taking entrance examination for junior high school). Tokyo: Jyoho Senta Shuppan Kyoku.

Lynn, Richard. 1988. *Educational Achievement in Japan: Lessons for the West.* Basingstoke, UK: Macmillan.

Maeda, Masako. 2002. " 'Zenkoku kosodate mappu' ni miru hoiku no genjo (The analyses on childcare availability)." Pp. 193–214 in *Shoshishakai no kosodate shien* (Childcare support in an aging society), edited by National Institute of Population and Social Security Research. Tokyo: Tokyo University Press.

Management and Coordination Agency. 1965–2000. Family Income and Expenditure Survey. Tokyo: Nihon Tokei Kyokai.

————. 1997. *Shugyo kozo kihon chosa* (Employment status survey). Tokyo: Nihon Tokei Kyokai.

————. 1998. *Jigyosho kigyo tokei* (Establishment and enterprise census). Tokyo: Nihon Tokei Kyokai.

————. 2000. *Kokusei chosa* (Population census). Tokyo: Government Printing Office.

————. 2001. *Rodoryoku chosa* (Labor force survey). Tokyo: Nihon Tokei Kyokai.

Ministry of Education. 1976. *Gakushu juku to ni kansuru jittaichosa hokokusho* (Survey on extra-school Education). Tokyo: Ministry of Education.

————. 1977. *Gakushu juku to ni kansuru jittaichosa hokokush* (Survey on extra-school education). Tokyo: Ministry of Education.

————. 1985. *Gakushu juku to ni kansuru jittaichosa hokokusho* (Survey on extra-school education). Tokyo: Ministry of Education.

————. 1994. *Gakushu juku to ni kansuru jittaichosa hokokusho* (Survey on extra-school education). Tokyo: Ministry of Education.

————. 2000a. *Heisei 10 nendo kodomo no gakushu hi chosa hokokusho* (1998 Survey on educational spending). Tokyo: Government Printing Office.

————. 2000b. *Gakko kihon chousa* (The basic school statistics). Tokyo: Government Printing Office.

————. 2000c. *Gakko kihon chousa* (The basic school statistics). Tokyo: Government Printing Office.

Ministry of Education, Culture, Sports, Science, and Technology. 2002a. *Kodomo no gakushuhi chosa* (Survey on educational spending). Tokyo: Ministry of Education, Culture, Sports, Science, and Technology.

————. 2002b. *Kyoiku shihyo no kokusai hikaku* (International comparison on education indicators). Tokyo: Ministry of Education, Culture, Sports, Science, and Technology.

Ministry of Health and Welfare (Ed.). 1994. *Kosei hakusho* (White paper on health and welfare). Tokyo: Gyosei.

Ministry of Labor (Ed.). 2000. *Josei rodo hakusho* (White paper on female labor). Tokyo: Zaidan hojin 21 seiki shokugyo zaidan.

Ministry of Public Management, Home Affairs, Post, and Telecommunications. 2001. *Kakei chosa nenpo* (Annual report on the family income and expenditure survey). Tokyo: Ministry of Public Management, Home Affairs, Post, and Telecommunications.

Nagase, Nobuko. 1999. "Shoshika no yoin: shugyo kankyo ka kachikan no henka ka (Work and childbearing choice of married women in Japan: The effect of labor practices)." *Journal of Population Problems* 55:1–18.

Nakamura, Takayasu. 2000. "Kogakurekishiko no susei: sedai no henka ni chumoku shite (The trends for academic credentialism: Cohort analyses)." Pp. 151–173 in *Nihon no kaiso sistemu 3: sengo nihon no kyoiku shakai* (The stratification system in Japan 3: Educational society in post-war Japan), edited by Hiroyuki Kondo. Tokyo: Tokyo University Press.

Nakanishi, Yuko. 2000. "Gakko ranku to shakai ido (School ranks and social mobility)." Pp. 37–56 in *Niho no kaiso shisutemu 3: sengo shakai no kyoiku shakai* (The stratification system in Japan 3: Educational society in the post-war Japan), edited by Hiroyuki Kondo. Tokyo: Tokyo University Press.

Nakata, Yoshifumi. 1997. "Nihon ni okeru danjo chingin kakusa no yoin bunseki (Determinants of gender wage gap in Japan)." Pp. 173–205 in *Koyo kanko no henka to josei rodo* (Changes in employment practice and female labor), edited by Hiroyuki Chuma and Terukazu Suruga. Tokyo: Tokyo University Press.

National Institute of Population and Social Security Research (Ed.). 1999. *Dai 11 kai shussho doko kihon chosa dai ni hokokusho: kekkon to shussan ni kansuru zenkoku chosa* (The eleventh japanese national fertility survey in 1997, Volume II: Attitudes toward marriage and the family among the married Japanese couples). Tokyo: National Institute of Population and Social Security Research.

Nihon PTA Zenkoku Kyogikai. 1997. *Gakushujuku ni kansuru anketo chosa hokokusho* (Survey report on juku). Tokyo: Nihon PTA Zenkoku Kyogikai.

Obuchi, Hiroshi. 1995a. "Josei rodo no shomondai (Issues in female labor)." Pp. 1–11 in *Josei no raifusaikuru to shugyo kodo*, edited by Hiroshi Obuchi. Tokyo: Government Printing Office.

———. 1995b. "Josei no raifu saikuru to M ji gata shugyo (Women's life cycle and M-shape participation pattern)." Pp. 13–35 in *Josei no raifusaikuru to shugyo kodo*, edited by Hiroshi Obuchi. Tokyo: Government Printing Office.

Osawa, Machiko, and Haruko Suzuki. 2000. "Josei no kekkon, shussan oyobi jintekishihon no keiseini kansuru paneru deta bunseki (Panel analyses on women's marital and fertility behavior and human capital formation)." *Kakeikeizai kenkyu* 48:45–53.

Sawayama, Mikako. 1990. "Kyoiku kazoku no seiritsu (The formation of education family)." Pp. 108–131 in *<kyoiku> Tanjo to shuen* (The birth and death of "education"), edited by Henshu Iinkai. Tokyo: Fujiwara shoten.

Schoppa, Leonard J. 1991. *Education Reform in Japan: A Case of Immobilist Politics*. New York: Routledge.

Seiyama, Kazuo. 1998. "Trends of Educational Attainment and Labor Force Participation among Japanese Women." In *Josei no kyaria kozo to sono henka* (Changing career structures of women) *(The 1995 SSM Research Series, volume 12)*, edited by Kazuo Seiyama and Sachiko Imada. Tokyo: 1995 Social Stratification and Mobility Survey Research Group.

Shigekawa, Junko. 1997. "Tumanoshugyokeitaibetsu, kinmukeitai, shokushubetsu kakei kozo hikaku (Comparison of household expenditure by the work status of wives)." *Kikan Kakei Keizai Kenkyu* 35:24–36.

Simmons, Cyril. 1990. *Growing Up and Going to School in Japan: Tradition and Trends*. Philadelphia: Open University Press.

Singleton, John. 1989. "Gambaru: A Japanese Cultural Theory of Learning." Pp. 9–15 in *Japanese Schooling*, edited by James J. Shields Jr. University Park: Pennsylvania State University Press.

Stevenson, Harold W. 1992. "Learning from Asian Schools." *Scientific American*, 70–76.

Stevenson, Harold, Hiroshi Azuma, and Kenji Hakuta (Eds.). 1986. *Child Development and Education in Japan*. New York: W. H. Freeman.

Stevenson, Harold W., and James W. Stigler. 1992. *The Learning Gap: Why Our Schools Are Failing and What We Can Learn from Japanese and Chinese Education*. New York: Summit Books.

Sugiyama, Yumiko. 2001. *Machigai darake no juku erabi* (The wrong ways to chose the right *Juku*). Tokyo: WAVE Shuppan.

Takada, Yoko. 2000. "Kodomo no kyoiku heno kitai to oyako kankei (Educational aspirations and parent-child relations)." Pp. 169–191 in *Kyoiku ki no kosodate to oyako kankei* (Childrearing in school age and parent-child relations), edited by Fumiko Kanbara and Yoko Takada. Kyoto: Minerva Shobo.

Takeuchi, Hiroshi. 1999. "Benkyo ganbarizumu no kozo to hokorobi (The structure and demise of effort-based study habit)." *Kikan Kakeikeizai Kenkyu* 44:12–18.

Tanaka, Shigeto. 1998. "Kogakurekika to seibetsu bungyo: josei no furu-taimu keizoku shugyo ni taisuru gakko kyoiku no koka (Higher education and the sexual division of labor: The schooling effect on women's continuous full-time continuous employment)." In *Josei no kyaria kozo to sono henka* (Changing career structures of women) *(The 1995 SSM Research Series, volume 12)*, edited by Kazuo Seiiyama and Sachiko Imada. Tokyo: Tokyo University Press.

Tanaka, Takafumi. 2001. "Kyoikuhi futan no genjo to kikai fubyodo (Cost of education and inequality in education opportunity)." *Japanese Journal of Family Sociology* 12:175–183.

Tokyo Metropolitan Government, Bureau of Citizens and Cultural Affairs. 1999. *Survey Report on Children's Lives and Values in the Metropolitan Area*. Tokyo: Tokyo Metropolitan Government, Bureau of Citizens and Cultural Affairs.

Uchiyama, Hirohito. 2002. *Yumei chugaku jyuken gokaku saseru hahaoya no himitsu* (Secrets for mothers to raise children's chance of admission to a famous junior high school). Tokyo: Esu ji enu.

United Nations Development Programme. 2000. *Human Development Report*. New York: United Nations Development Programme.

Uno, Kathleen S. 1993. "The Death of 'Good Wife, Wise Mother'?" In *Postwar Japan as History*, edited by Andrew Gordon. Berkeley: University of California Press.

Wakisaka, Akira, and Yasunobu Tomita (Eds.). 2001. *Daisotsu josei no hata-*

rakikata (The labor patterns of college educated women). Tokyo: Japan Institute of Labor.

Watanabe, Hideki. 1995. "Kyoiku suru oya kara kyoiku wo tehai suru oya he (From educative parents to parents who recruit education)." *Jido shinri* August, 74–80.

———. 1999. "Henyo suru shakai ni okeru kazoku no kadai (Family issues in changing society)." Pp. 119–135 in *Henyo suru kazoku to kodomo* (Children and changing families), edited by Hideki Watanabe. Tokyo: Kyoiku Shuppan.

White, Merry. 1987a. *The Japanese Educational Challenge: A Commitment to Children.* New York: Free Press.

———. 1987b. "The virtue of Japanese mothers: Cultural definitions of women's lives." *Daedalus* 116:149–163.

Wray, Harry. 1999. *Japanese and American Education: Attitudes and Practices.* Westport, CT: Bergin & Garvey.

Yano, Masakazu. 1993. "Wagakuni no kyoikuhi to kakei no genjo (The household expenditure and educational cost in Japan)." *Chosa kiho* 26:1–17.

Yu, Wei-hsin. 2001. "Family Demands, Gender Attitudes, and Married Women's Labor Force Participation: Comparing Japan and Taiwan." Pp. 70–95 in *Women's Working Lives in East Asia*, edited by Mary C. Brinton. Stanford: Stanford University Press.

PART FOUR

Conclusions and Prescriptions

CHAPTER 9

Conclusion

FRANCES MCCALL ROSENBLUTH

Introduction

To summarize the overarching theme of this book, Japan's low fertility is overdetermined, because Japanese women are stuck between a rock (an inhospitable labor market) and a hard place (the government's reluctance to subsidize family work). Japanese women face difficulties that are different in degree, but not in kind, to those faced by women in other rich democracies. Variation in the severity of these constraints, we find, corresponds to variation in the ability of women to advance in a man's world, and seems, by extension, to affect women's decisions about whether, when, and how many children to have. We are not making a normative appeal that women ought to try to balance family and career; only that women should not be more burdened than men in making their choice.

In the remainder of this chapter, I summarize the principal arguments that chapter authors have made in the preceding parts of the book. I then discuss the policy implications, particularly as they relate to Japan, of a commitment to freeing women of the constraints that make it difficult for them to combine family responsibilities with career success. To change women's reluctance to try to mix motherhood with employment, so apparent now in Japan, how might the government use policy measures to ease the constraints? Even if we agree that this is a worthy question—and some dismiss the use of government policy out of hand—the hard work of sorting out the implications of different policy choices has only begun.

Summary of the Book

The authors of the foregoing chapters, from the perspectives of their various disciplines, have laid out pieces of a big jigsaw puzzle that in composite depict Japanese women as unwelcome in the core labor force and burdened with heavy family responsibilities. To the possible rebuttal that this is no more than a derogatory characterization of a traditional family, we point to Japan's low and falling birth rates. Japanese women are rejecting their role in the traditional family because specialization in family work leaves them vulnerable to mistreatment in the event of marital discord and poverty in the event of a breakup. This, of course, was always true; what is different between agrarian and postindustrial Japan is that, in today's economy, women can at least hypothetically earn economic independence as long as they do not break their careers to have children.

Shirahase provided a statistical overview of women's work, income, and fertility in Japan. Japan's urbanization and the attending shift to a large firm economy are highly correlated with the downward trending birthrate, both because of the need to commute away from home and because of the particular nature of the labor markets that developed in Japan. The steep decline in fertility with the rise of women's own source of income points to a large penalty for career interruption in Japan, as with the German example sketched out in Chapter 1. The more ambitious a woman is about career success, the more hesitant she is likely to be about taking time away from work to rear children. If it were just a matter of taking a few months here or there for maternity leave, government subsidies for parental leave and childcare might help substantially to ease the burden. But when combined with internal labor markets where long hours at the office are required to compete successfully, family responsibilities and work mix less well.

In Part Two of the book, Estévez-Abe, Brinton, and Kenjoh explain what it is about Japanese labor markets that makes career success particularly difficult for mothers. Estévez-Abe introduces the "welfare state paradox": labor-protection schemes such as Europe's various wage and job guarantees, or Japan's lifetime employment system, have the ironic and unintended consequence of hurting women. This is because labor protections encourage the acquisition of firm- or industry-specific skills over the course of a career, which increases the costs to employers of midcareer departures. Estévez-Abe argues that in Japan's firm-centered employment system, in which employees are hired for life in exchange for investing in firm-specific skills, employers bear a substantial cost if workers leave the firm, either temporarily or permanently, during their productive years. They therefore prefer to hire men, and even in the face of Japan's Equal Opportunity Employment Law of 1985 that disallows gender discrimination, they find ways to keep women out of the core workforce. The implications are grim: as long as the workplace is not conducive to female advancement, the money the government spends on childcare may do very little to help women stay in the workforce throughout their life cycles.

Brinton explores one segment of the economy, the clerical sector, where employment differences between Japan and the United States are particularly stark. The clerical sector drew in U.S. women in large numbers following World War II, driving up female labor force participation rates and contributing to a growing social acceptance of mothers in the workforce. The demand for female labor and female educational attainment reinforced each other, as families began investing more in the education of their daughters as they saw the possibilities for a return on their investment. By contrast, clerical jobs in Japan have remained largely male, in large part because the lifetime employment system requires firms to make full use of the personnel to whom they have committed for life. Japanese women have therefore lacked the draw of the clerical sector to serve as an engine for changing social norms and educational investment decisions.

Kenjoh, in comparing across several countries the attachment of women to the labor market after the birth of their children, makes the interesting suggestion that the availability of high-quality part-time work seems to have helped Dutch women keep working after childbirth. By implication, the absence of comparably high-paying part-time jobs in Japan gives women a starker set of options, and women might be happy to have more children if doing so did not entail such a potentially large loss of economic independence. Kenjoh is emphatically not advocating the marginalization of women into insecure and low-paying part-time work, which already exists in Japan. The second "hump" of the M-shaped curve, in fact, largely consists of those sorts of jobs, again because the commitment to lifetime workers through the ups and downs of business cycles requires a flexible portion of the workforce to which the company is not committed for life. Kenjoh's suggestion, instead, is to induce companies to shift more or less the entire workforce to a voluntary continuum between part and full time with equal employment security but prorated benefits. Scholarly opinion is divided on how well this scheme meets the needs of laborers, with some expressing concern that employers are using it to shift business cycle adjustment costs onto the labor force (Becker 2001). But given the substantial, if hidden, costs that women bear in being shut out of the core labor force in many welfare states, the possibilities of the Dutch system are intriguing, particularly if men can be incentivized to share with their partners the family and earning responsibilities in more equal measure.

Part Three of the book turns to constraints on Japanese women's supply of their work to the labor markets, and what the government is doing to ease those constraints. Boling recounts the long string of measures to enhance maternity leave and to subsidize childcare in hopes of boosting the birthrate, but given what we know about how hard it is for women to achieve career success, it comes as little surprise to learn that the measures have had little success to date. More recent government pronouncements recognize that women need help both with childcare and with labor market access to feel that having children will not derail their careers (Japanese Ministry of Health, Labor, and Welfare, 2005). But proposals to deal with problems in the labor market lack concreteness, and firms are reluctant to give up the real culprit, lifetime employment, given how well it has served them in past decades.

Wada finds childcare provision in Japan both rigid and inadequate, particularly for urban dwellers. He argues that the 1994 electoral reforms, which at least partially reduced the overcounting of rural voters, shifted the government's priorities toward meeting the childcare needs of urban voters. That seems plausible, though it is hard to imagine that the move to privatize childcare services might not be motivated by the desire of the Liberal Democratic Party (LDP) to weaken public sector labor unions of which the public child minders are a part. The LDP's main opposition party, the Democratic Party of Japan (DPJ), counts unions as one of its core constituencies, and the LDP can indirectly hurt the DPJ's mobilizational capacity by reducing unionization rates. We have seen the LDP use this strategy in the 1980s against the old Socialist Party of Japan, with the privatization of the national railway system and telecommunications services. In any case, the redistribution of government childcare subsidies from rural to urban centers and the increasingly flexible rules governing childcare facilities are unlikely to be sufficient without also making it possible for women, or anyone else, to succeed in the labor force without working forty to fifty hours a week. The internal labor markets of Japan, which seem to have served the Japanese economy so well during the high growth years, are showing their price tag in the form of disgruntled women and low fertility.

Hirao's chapter might be called the straw that broke the camel's back. If it is not enough for Japanese women to struggle with insufficient child-care facilities in the face of inflexible labor markets, they also bear disproportionate responsibility for an extremely time-consuming form of education all the way through high school. Instead of being a substitute for after-school care, cram schools require mothers to take on a whole new set of responsibilities in researching the schools, learning what they need to about the curriculum, making sure their children are keeping up with the material, and keeping them nourished and supplied as they study. Although paying for all of this is a burden that might conceivably induce families to pursue two careers, Hirao finds that the time constraints seem to trump the financial ones and, on balance, pull women out of the workforce.

The problem Hirao identifies is also rooted in Japan's labor markets, for the stakes associated with getting into a top school are raised by the fact that labor markets are so immobile. It is important for ambitious students to get a good job at the outset because it is hard to switch firms and move up later in life. Getting into a good school is more about signaling intelligence to a prospective employer than about learning skills.

Possibilities for Change

Now that we know how difficult and deeply rooted the problem of balancing career and family is for Japanese women, we see that the Japanese government has a monumental task ahead if it wants to induce higher fertility. Women need to feel that family and career are reconcilable goals. The situation is a classic Catch-22: as long as firms hire workers for life, an employer bears higher costs when hiring someone who is likely to interrupt her career for family work; but as long as women face employment discrimination, the cultural norms, educational investment choices, and household division of labor supporting the male breadwinner model are unlikely to be challenged. Women feel trapped in an unsought role and escape by being childless. More women are delaying marriage, with an unprecedented 27 percent of Japanese women aged thirty to thirty-four remaining unmarried, rather than marry the typical male who "expects the wife to cheerfully surrender her job, or juggle a career with keeping house and raising the kids" (*Mainichi Daily News*, November 26, 2004).

How might a society go about evening the employment playing field between the genders? At the outset, we reject what we consider two extreme positions: that equity should be established without regard to economic efficiency; and at the other extreme, that economic efficiency should be maximized without regard to its distributional consequences. Efficiency is important because the size of the pie determines what is available to distribute, but we should not assume that winners in a more efficient system will pay off the losers. If we take seriously the effect of asymmetric exit options on spousal bargaining power, a gendered division of labor that maximizes family income can leave the wife in a weak position within the family.

In sizing up Japanese women's challenges, looking both at variation within Japan and in comparison with other countries, the most formidable seems to be the nature of Japanese labor markets. Government provision of childcare, while chary by Scandinavian standards, is generous compared to that of the United States and other liberal market economies where many women subcontract part of their family work to other women out of their own and family income. Because of the tendency of large and medium-sized Japanese firms to hire a core set of workers for life, to promote them by seniority, and to invest in their skills, the cost to employers of hiring for these core positions women who are likely to interrupt their careers is very high. Not surprisingly, they assiduously avoid doing so, and the equal employment legislation of the last two decades has only made a small dent in this disinclination. As anthropologist Glenda Roberts reports, Japanese corporations do not encourage male employees to get involved with childrearing, only reluctantly allow workers to attend government-sponsored seminars on childrearing, and routinely expect employees to log overtime hours (Roberts 2002, 68, 87). For Japanese women, the "Three Sacred Treasures" of Japan's labor institutions may as well be signs saying "Women Need Not Apply!" posted prominently on the doors of corporate Japan.[1]

To be sure, many Japanese, including women, are employed outside of the large firm sector. And as Sawako Shirahase pointed out in her statistical survey, women outside the large firm sector seem to have a somewhat easier time balancing family and career. But the large firms stand at the pinnacle of the Japanese economy, and present options for the greatest job security. And even many smaller firms, particularly the subcontractors for the large firms, put a premium on firm-specific skills and, therefore, on long tenure in office. Knowing that motherhood means being locked out of this world, many Japanese women are delaying childbirth and having fewer children to limit the damage to their careers.

It is hard to imagine how generously the government would have to subsidize childcare to even out the playing field between men and women given these labor market conditions. For one thing, the government would have to provide a great deal more childcare for infants than it currently does to allow women to limit the length of their career interruption and, hence, the cost to employers of hiring women. Once back at work, competing in internal labor markets means having to stay at the office at least as long as the others, hanging out with the boss after hours, and being available for overtime whenever necessary. Add to that a long commute for people living in big cities, and that adds up to a twelve- to fourteen-hour day, five or more days a week. Childcare facilities would need to have early drop-off and very late pickup options on a flexible basis. Then again, a mother working these kinds of hours might wonder why she had a baby in the first place. These are the feelings of guilt and self-doubt with which a man with a stay-at-home wife need never grapple. They also reinforce the norm that "mothers should stay home."

In short, increasing government subsidies for childcare without changing the labor market institutions is likely to be a poor investment. Countries with high female labor force participation rates and high fertility—Scandinavia and the liberal market economies— achieved this by giving women easy access to jobs. In the Scandinavian case, women are disproportionately in the large public sector. Many of these public sector jobs, as Margarita Estévez-Abe pointed out, are general skills jobs for which the cost of career interruption is quite low. And even when they are in skilled government positions, such as doctors or lawyers, their status as government employees entitles them to an employment contract that is to some degree unhinged from the cost to the employer. Swedish women do in fact interrupt their careers for quite a long time without penalty—typically eighteen months for childcare leave when their baby is first born, and then reduced working hours until their youngest child is eight years old.

By contrast, in liberal market economies, the fluidity of the labor markets rather than government largesse provides women with access to work and advancement. Because employers factor into their employment decisions a certain amount of mobility for both men and women, women who are likely to take time out for childrearing pose a smaller relative cost to the liberal market employer than to an employer in the specific-skills economies of Europe or Japan. Even within liberal market economies, there are varying degrees of skill specificity and skill obsolescence across sectors and firms, and that is reflected in different levels of a "mommy penalty" (Anderson, Binder, and Krause 2002). For an investment banker or corporate attorney, for example, who invests heavily in client information and goodwill, breaking a career for child-rearing is likely to be more costly than for someone who can fairly easily take up a cashier or bookkeeping job with another firm. So even in liberal market economies, there is something of a negative relationship between the woman's income and fertility. But compared to economies where employers expect long tenure in office and invest in their workers accordingly, liberal market economies present women with a relatively open door.

In the following section, I consider prospects for changes in Japanese labor market institutions.

Demand for Female Labor

We have seen that Japan is a typical specific-skills economy, at least in its large firm sector, in that companies hire generalists with the expectation of lifetime employment and on-the-job training. Women are particularly disadvantaged in this type of labor market because the cost of career interruptions due to family work is large for both employer and employee. Employers are likely to respond by not hiring women for these core positions or by paying them less. Women, for their part, are less likely to invest in the kind of education that makes them most attractive to these employers because they don't expect to get a return on their educational investment.

We once thought the best hope for Japanese women gaining access to labor markets was a tight labor market, which would force employers to break with their practice of keeping women off to one side (Brinton 1989). When there is an excess demand for labor, excluding women from consideration for hiring and promotion becomes more inefficient, and is unstable among competitive firms. But the prolonged economic doldrums since 1991 have relegated that possibility too far off in the future to provide much reason for cheer. The same is true of hope in foreign employers: in a slack labor market, there are so many underemployed men with experience and training that foreign companies looking for the best possible hires are likely to tap into that labor pool before hiring young women right out of college. As Joyce Gelb (2004) and others have noted, antidiscrimination laws have not eliminated the corporate disinclination to hire women into upwardly mobile positions. Surveying the employment scene, women may be discouraged from investing in the kind of education that potentially gets them managerial-track jobs, and instead use their education to enhance their opportunities in the marriage market. One reason sociologists have found less connection than expected between women's education and female labor force participation in Japan is that many women use education as an expensive signaling device or decoration to attract "good" husbands.

There are deductive reasons to think, however, that the internal labor markets of big firms in Japan that have been so hard for women to penetrate will begin to break up. New electoral rules since 1994 are gradually transforming Japan's political landscape, and even the LDP, which once was in a position to give business and agriculture most of what they wanted, must now appeal to large swaths of voters in each district. The 1996 financial "Big Bang" that began breaking up financial cartels is arguably one example of the regulatory effects of this political upheaval, and the ripple effects are still moving through the labor and product markets (Rosenbluth and Schaap, 2000). The effects of more competitive financial markets include the inability of main banks to stay with customers through all vagaries of the business cycle, try as they might. As banks become more bottom-line oriented, they price loans more closely to market, forcing corporations in turn to make tighter judgments about the value of contracting lifetime commitments with new employees of yet unknown quality and potential.

The politics of regulation under the new electoral rules are making Japanese product markets more competitive as well. Unlike under the old rules when politicians could use campaign contributions to cobble together 18–20 percent of the vote in a district to ensure a seat, politicians now have to win a plurality of votes in a district and risk losing if they lose policy flexibility by "selling" entry barriers to firms or industries. In this environment, firms need to be more nimble, rely less on long-term relationships with suppliers and customers, and promote employees who demonstrate competence in competitive markets. Old-boy networks and being "one of the guys" lose some of their economic value when the prospect of bankruptcy looms larger. Of course change in electoral rules was itself a response to underlying demographic and sectoral shifts, as politicians reconsidered their ability to stay in office in a country with richer, more mobile voters who are less likely to be proprietors of small businesses (Pempel 1998).

Chances are we are still seeing just glimmers of what is to come in Japan, and many firms are still trying to protect their reputations as long-term employers. After all, this labor institution "worked" for many years and, should the labor market become tight once again, the reputation could once again become valuable. But some observers miss seeing how substantial are the changes in the underlying political system; it is not just a matter of weathering years of a bad economy. The political game that governs the price of policy favors is not what it once was. Parties are being forced to remake themselves into parties of the voter, the consumer, the taxpayer. Politicians who continue to try to play by the old rules can expect to be weeded out over time, and their corporate constituents have to adapt to more competitive markets.

That is the good part of the scenario of a new political equilibrium. On the negative side, we can expect, in the short run, higher unemployment as bankruptcies increase in response to more competition. In the long run, a wider wage distribution will emerge as labor markets function more fluidly. Intragender wage inequality will widen, and some women will be able to subcontract part of their family work because there will be other women who are willing to work for less. A gap will begin to emerge in the resources available to children, and childhood poverty will grow. To the extent that the Japanese labor market starts to look more like that of the United States, pessimists about the American scene such as Janet Gornick and Marcia Meyers tell a tale of caution, even dismay (2003).

Whether we should be optimistic or pessimistic about the impending changes in Japan's labor markets for gender equality hinges in large part on whether one expects that fluid labor markets will in fact allow women to advance in roughly equal proportions to men, or whether one expects that discrimination will persist and women will be stuck doing low-skill service jobs for low pay. On the optimistic side, we identified structural, as opposed to enduringly cultural, reasons for why employers should have preferred men in Japan all of these postwar years. Once those labor structures start to deteriorate, we expect the norms to begin to change as well, and we expect the efficiency advantages to promoting competent women to begin to take hold.

But we also note that many of the higher-skills jobs in the emerging information-intensive service industries have components of specific skills (client contacts) or fast obsolescence (the latest computer technology). Even if we believe, as Helen Fisher (1999) does, that women have natural abilities in team-based production that give them an advantage in the high-tech service sector, discontinuous careers on account of childbirth should continue to take their toll in wages and promotions. In England, for example, where there are now slightly more female than male doctors and trial lawyers, women tend to specialize in the less time-intensive, and therefore less remunerative, parts of those professions (*Economist* 2005, 55).

Government Policy

We have just considered a scenario of labor market change, quite independent of government policy measures. What can the Japanese government do to capture what is good about a more fluid labor market, while mitigating its negative consequences? We can start by eliminating what is politically infeasible. Japan is unlikely to adopt a Scandinavian approach to gender issues, which is rooted in strong left/labor power. The prominence of single-member districts in Japan's new electoral rules makes increasingly small the possibility of a social democratic party worthy of the name. As in other single-member district systems, Japan's major political parties are likely to hew close to the political center.

For the same reason—the centrism built into Japanese politics from the new electoral rules—Japan is also unlikely to resemble the coordinated market economies of non-Scandinavian Europe. Centrist parties will not foster a strong labor union movement and, as a result, labor will not be in a strong bargaining position vis-à-vis employers to get economy-wide wage compression, job security, and generous unemployment compensation. Decentralized deals between employers and employees by sector or firm will lead to a wide range of wages and employment deals, minus the widespread lifetime employment contracts that were possible in the cartel era of post–World War II Japan.

Without centralized wage bargaining, it is hard to imagine how labor can get the kinds of hour-reduction guarantees that European governments enforce (Gornick and Meyers 2003). How nice if both men and women could reduce their hours, but in a decentralized labor market, the competition among workers for jobs and promotions probably puts those kinds of arrangements institutionally out of reach.

There are, however, other measures that even governments of liberal market economies can implement if they are so motivated by the electorate. First, the government can incentivize fathers to take paternity leave by requiring firms to pay a take-it-or-leave-it sum for fathers alone. Adding paternity leave has the benefit of giving children more parental time, while also evening out the cost to employers of hiring men and women. Motivating parents to share more equally in the care of children reduces "statistical discrimination" because employers begin to have more equal expectations about the probability and length of the career interruptions of men and women. Note that the effects on fertility are ambiguous, since men who internalize more of the costs of childrearing may want fewer of them even as women feel freer to have more! But then again, this book is not concerned about fertility per se.

Second, the Japanese government can manipulate tax rates to reduce incentives to work very long hours. We may get back into a chicken-and-egg loop here if centrist governments are less likely to adopt strongly progressive taxation. But if public debate can incorporate considerations of the costs to children of long working hours of both parents, voters may be more willing to tie their hands in this way. Markets are unlikely to manage this kind of collective commitment because unions are weak. But the voting public can use political authority to bind itself statutorily.

It is hard to say what the likelihood is of the Japanese public voting in this strongly progressive way. On the one hand, the political center in single-member district systems tends to be to the right of the population's center, because voter turnout tends to be systematically lower at the lower end of the income scale than at the upper end (Bartels 2002). On the other hand, as women move into the working world in larger numbers, they may be more likely to vote on the left (Wolfers 2001; Inglehart and Norris 2001). We see this trend in all rich democracies, and the reason is probably that working women place greater value than housewives do on the partial socialization of family work because it allows them to pursue their outside options (Iversen and Rosenbluth 2006). The voting gap is pronounced even in the United States—with about a 5 percent gap between men and women on the left-right scale—despite the large income spread that allows well-off women to bypass government services and subcontract family work to other women in the marketplace. If a gender voting gap emerges in Japan, it could help to push political parties to consider ways to facilitate the family-work balancing act. But the pushing would not come without significant pushing back from social conservatives. In 2004, a special LDP committee on constitutional revision denounced the 1947 constitution's "women's rights" clauses for nurturing "egoism in postwar Japan, leading to the collapse of family and community" (Brooke 2005).[2]

Conclusions

We close with an irony. If, as Esping-Andersen (1990) says, the welfare states of Europe helped to "decommodify" labor by softening the link between work and livelihood, we are arguing that "commodifying" women's labor is central to improving gender equality. Some detractors of the Scandinavian model scoff at the sight of "women getting paid to take care of each other's children." It would be more efficient, they say, to pay women an allowance for every child and let them decide whether to use it to care for the children at home themselves or to put the children in public childcare. By subsidizing childcare so heavily, they argue, the government skews the incentives of people to give up their children to outside care because that is the only way of capturing this public policy benefit.

Even if it were true that Scandinavian women were all employed in childcare services, which they are not, this efficiency argument misses something crucial. A division of labor in which women stay at home while men go out and earn income leaves women in a vulnerable position. As she forgoes work experience, her expected income in the event of marital breakdown deteriorates while his continues to grow. Because she has a larger stake than he does in keeping the marriage going, she is in a weak bargaining position. Research shows, for example, that female labor force participation is a good predictor of the proportion of housework other than childcare that the husband and wife undertake (Iversen and Rosenbluth 2006).

Many women will choose to stay at home with the children for non-pecuniary reasons. There seems little doubt from the empirical evidence that children benefit from time with their parents, and we applaud anyone who wants to take parenting seriously. Our concern is rather to put the spotlight on the distributional consequences of the traditional gendered division of labor. It is time to let men in on more of the joys of parenting, and to give women more access to the labor market.

Notes

1. The "Three Sacred Treasures," a mirror, sword, and jewel said to be handed down from the gods to the imperial family, correspond in the literature on Japanese labor market institutions to lifetime employment, seniority advancement, and enterprise unionism.

2. Beata Sirota, a twenty-two-year-old woman in the U.S. occupation government section, was the primary author of the two clauses of the Constitution of Japan that together stipulate gender equality more explicitly than the American constitution does for American women. Article 14: (1) All of the people are equal under the law and there shall be no discrimination in political, economic, or social relations because of race, creed, sex, social status, or family origin. (2) Peers and peerage shall not be recognized. (3) No privilege shall accompany any award of honor, decoration, or any distinction, nor shall any such award be valid beyond the lifetime of the individual who now holds or hereafter may receive it. Article 24: (1) Marriage shall be based only on the mutual consent of both sexes and it shall be maintained through mutual cooperation with the equal rights of husband and wife as a basis. (2) With regard to choice of spouse, property rights, inheritance, choice of domicile, divorce, and other matters pertaining to marriage and the family, laws shall be enacted from the standpoint of individual dignity and the essential equality of the sexes.

References

Anderson, Deborah, Melissa Binder, and Kate Krause. 2002. "Women, Children, and the Labor Market," *AEA Papers and Proceedings* 92/2: 354–358.

Bartels, Larry. 2002. "Economic Inequality and Political Representation," paper presented at the Annual Meeting of the American Political Science Association, Boston.

Becker, Uwe. 2001. "A 'Dutch Model': Employment Growth by Corporatist Consensus and Wage Restraint? A Critical Account of the Idyllic View," *New Political Economy* 6/1: 19–43.

Brinton, Mary. 1989. "Gender Stratification in Contemporary Urban Japan," *American Sociological Review* 54: 549–564.

Brinton, Mary. 1993. *Women and the Japanese Miracle*. Berkeley: University of California Press.

Brooke, James. 2005. "Fighting to Protect Her Gift to Japanese Women," *New York Times*, May 28.

Economist. June 4, 2005, 55.

Esping-Andersen, Gøsta. 1990. *The Three Worlds of Welfare Capitalism*. Cambridge: Polity.

Fisher, Helen. 1999. *The First Sex: The Natural Talents of Women and How They Are Changing the World*. New York: Ballantine.

Gelb, Joyce. 2004. *Gender Policies in Japan and the U.S.: Comparing Women's Rights and Policies*. New York: MacMillan Palgrave.

Gornick, Janet, and Marcia Meyers. 2003. *Families That Work: Policies for Reconciling Parenthood and Employment*. New York: Russell Sage Foundation.

Inglehart, Ronald, and Pippa Norris. 2001. "Cultural Obstacles to Equal Representation," *Journal of Democracy* 12/3: 126–140.

Iversen, Torben, and Frances Rosenbluth. 2006. "The Political Economy of Gender: Explaining Cross-National Variation in the Household Distribution of Labor, Divorce, and the Gender Preference Gap," *American Journal of Political Science* 50/1: 1–19.

Japanese Ministry of Health, Labor, and Welfare. 2005. "Outline of the Third Longitudinal Survey of Babies in the 21st Century." Tokyo: Japanese Ministry of Health, Labor, and Welfare.

Pempel, T. J. 1998. *Regime Shift: Comparative Dynamics of the Japanese Political Economy.* Ithaca, NY: Cornell University Press.

Roberts, Glenda. 2002. "Pinning Hopes on Angels: Reflections from an Aging Japan's Urban Landscape," in Roger Goodman, ed., *Family and Social Policy in Japan: Anthropological Approaches.* Cambridge, U.K., and New York: Cambridge University Press.

Rosenbluth, Frances, and Ross Schaap. 2000. "The Domestic Politics of Financial Globalization," paper presented at American Political Science Association Meetings in Washington, DC, September 2000. Yale University, University of California-Los Angeles.

Rosenbluth, Frances, and Ross Schaap. 2002. "The Domestic Politics of Banking Regulation," *International Organization* 57/2: 307–336.

Thornton, Arland, ed. 2001. *The Well-Being of Children and Families.* Ann Arbor: University of Michigan Press.

Wolfers, Justin. 2001. "Comments on Edlund and Pande: Why Have Women Become Left-wing: The Political Gender Gap and the Decline in Marriage," paper presented at Wallis Conference on Political Economy, Rochester University.

Index

investment risks, 72
Italy, 44

Japanese culture: background, 5–7, 25*n*2;
effect of economic and political systems on, 6; women's roles within, 6–7
Japanese Panel Survey of Consumers
(JPSC), 125*n*1
Japanese Socialist Party (JSP), 163
Japanese Survey on Social Status and Mobility (SSM), 99
Japan Trade Union Confederation
(Rengo), 163
juku ("cram schools"): attendance, *183*;
classes for parents, 177; college enrollment rate, *183*; enrollment in, 176–177,
176, *177*; market size, *183*; number of,
172, *173*, 189*n*2; prominence of, 170–173.
See also childcare; childcare services

keiretsu firms, 10, 26*n*8
kindergarten, *137*
Komeito, 132
kōsei zoku (social policy "tribe"), 150*n*5

labor market (Japan): compared with
other countries, 37; effect of government regulations on, 11–14, 23; effect of
industrialization, 14; inaccessibility to
women, 9–11, 14–15, 23, 112; participation by age group, *40*; in rural areas, 13;
statistics, 39–40, 54; women's participation in, 13–14, 37, 38–39, *66*, *78*. *See also*
working patterns of mothers
labor market (outside of Japan), married
women in, 87–93
Labor Standards Act, 140
large firm sector, 13
Liberal Democratic Party (LDP), 11, 132,
163, 204
liberal market economies (LMEs), 16–18
liberal welfare states, 83*n*1
living arrangements, 126*n*7
long-term employment contracts, 10, 23,
202–203
Luxembourg Income Survey data (LIS),
44

Management and Coordination Agency,
172

Marxism, 26*n*6
maternity leave, 74
Ministry of Education (MEXT), 190*n*5
Ministry of International Trade and Industry (MITI), 11
M-shaped participation pattern, 13, 39, 54,
97, 112, 122, 188, 204
multigenerational households, 44

National Office Management Association,
94
National Survey of Family Income and
Expenditure, 172
National Survey of Family in Japan
(NSFJ), 40
National Survey of Living Conditions
(Kokumin Seikatsu Kiso Chosa), 44, 49
National Survey of Welfare and Attitudes
(2000), 55*n*1
Netherlands, 113–127, *113*, *114*, 203
New Zealand, 76, 81
Ninsho Hoikusho (Certificated Daycare
Center), 156
Norway, 81

occupational categories, 78
occupational segregation: cross-national
variations in, 79–81, 108*n*12; gender
skill gap effects, 78
"1.57 shock," 37, 155, 165, 166–168
opportunity costs, 7–8
optimization, 7
Organisatie voor Strategisch Arbeidsmarktonderzoek (OSA), 125*n*1
Organization for Economic Cooperation
and Development (OECD), 179

parental leave, 40, 74, 112, 125*n*5, 140
Parental Leave Act (1995), 40
part-time employment, 10, 23, 49, 113–127,
203
paternity leave, 15, 211
"Plus One," 143–144
politicians, 12
population by representation, *167*
prefecture profiles, *184*
private schools. *See* education; *juku*
("cram schools")
public policies, 11–14, 24–25, 112, 211–212.